B m
$15
#5234

W9-BSR-930

The Politics of Business in California, 1890–1920

Mansel G. Blackford

The Politics of Business
in California, 1890–1920

Ohio State University Press: Columbus

A portion of Chapter 4, "The Movement for Scientific Forestry," was previously published in *Business and Economic History,* 2d ser., vol. 4, ed. Paul Uselding, and is reprinted here by permission. Portions of Chapter 5 appeared as "Businessmen and the Regulation of Railroads and Public Utilities in California During the Progressive Era" in *Business History Review* 44 (Autumn, 1970): 307–19, and is reprinted here by permission. Chapter 6 was previously published as "Banking and Bank Legislation in California, 1890–1915" in *Business History Review* 47 (Winter, 1973): 482–507, and is reprinted here by permission.

Copyright © 1977 by the Ohio State University Press
All rights reserved
Manufactured in the United States of America

Library of Congress Cataloging in Publication Data

Blackford, Mansel G   1944–

  The politics of business in California, 1890–1920.

  Bibliography, p.
  Includes index.
  1. California—Economic conditions.   2. California—Industries—History.   I. Title.
HC107.C2B55   330.9'794'04   76-27319
ISBN 0-8142-0259-4

To Victoria

Contents

Preface   ix

Acknowledgments   xiii

1. California's Changing Economy   3

2. Agriculture: Growers Against Consumers   13

3. The Oil Industry   40

4. The Lumber Industry and Scientific Forestry   60

5. Railroad and Public Utility Regulation   78

6. Banking and Bank Legislation   96

7. Investment Banking and the Blue-sky Law   117

8. The Insurance Industry   128

9. Big Business and Tax Reform   146

10. The Politics of Business   161

Appendix   173

Abbreviations   173

Notes   177

Bibliography   205

Index   217

Preface

In recent years historians have been reevaluating late nineteenth- and early twentieth-century American history. Led by the synthetic efforts of Samuel Hays and Robert Wiebe, they have recast much of the thinking on the nature of American society, culture, politics, and business during this period.[1] Their studies stress the problems Americans faced in coming to grips with the rapid industrialization of their nation and suggest that much of the American experience between the Civil War and the First World War can best be understood as an attempt to reorder American life in the wake of social and economic disruption.[2] Historians have come to view the response of Americans to the disruption of their lives in terms of the growing organization of American society. This interpretation, which has become known as the ''organizational synthesis,'' emphasizes the spread of bureaucratic organizations and the growth of professions, together with a heightened awareness of the need for order and efficiency, as the themes best explaining the course of American development in this period. As a corollary, many scholars adopting this approach have abandoned political discontinuities, and especially the dichotomy between reform and reaction, as the key to the recent history of the United States. Rather, their interpretation stresses more the continuity of the response of Americans to the modernization of their nation.[3]

In the following study I examine the findings of the organizational synthesis interpretation by analyzing how Californians, and particularly various groups of California businessmen, reacted to the forces of economic change that were transforming their state between roughly 1890 and 1920. I deal with what were three of California's most important basic productive industries—agriculture, oil, and lumber—and three of its most significant supportive businesses—banking, investment banking, and insurance. In addition, I examine two major issues that cut across industry lines and that involved a wide variety of businessmen: state regulation of railroads and public utilities and tax reform movements. My account reveals that businessmen tried to solve their difficulties through a complex combination of private and public actions that, taken together, compose what I have labeled the "politics of business." In the private realm, businessmen restructured their firms and industries as they sought to control their changing economic environment while trying to achieve or maintain competitive advantages over each other. In the sphere of public politics, businessmen sought the same goals. Through state or, on occasion, national legislation they hoped to both channel and limit the impact of the forces of change while also often using the altered economic situation to obtain competitive advantages.

Historians have long been engaged in chronicling how businessmen restructured their firms and industries as they tried to cope with changes occurring in their business environment, but much remains to be done in this field.[4] Business historians have prepared numerous company histories and studies of single industries; and, somewhat less frequently, historians like Alfred Chandler, Jr., have compared the experiences of businessmen in different companies and industries as a basis for generalization.[5] These studies have proven to be intrinsically valuable and useful as building blocks for further research; but, because most of them have focused too closely upon the internal business decisions of management and the changing structures of business firms, they have missed much of the significance of the social and political environments within which businessmen operate. More efforts need to be made in connecting the private, internal-management business decisions with the public, external environments surrounding businesses.[6]

A growing number of historians have been trying to unravel the connections between the difficulties businessmen encountered as a result of the modernization of the American economy and their involvement in politics. Gabriel Kolko's analysis of the relationship between business and the Progressive movement broke new ground in this respect.[7] Other studies, particularly those of Robert Wiebe, indicate, however, that Kolko's interpretation is simplistic and that patterns of business political engagement were considerably more complex than Kolko's work suggests.[8] The question of the extent to which businessmen influenced legislation and state regulation of their industries during the Progressive Era certainly requires closer inspection. And, in examining this subject historians can, perhaps, help political scientists and sociologists reach some conclusions on the more general question of the extent to which modern American government has been pluralistic or elitist in nature.[9]

By investigating how businessmen in one specific locale, the state of California, responded to economic modernization, I hope to strike a balance between specialization and generalization. My study should add to our still incomplete knowledge of the economic and political development of California. Although not a detailed analysis of all aspects of the Progressive movement in the Golden State, my work should also supplement, and in places modify, the interpretations of the movement put forward by George Mowry and Spencer Olin, Jr.[10] Their works deal, of course, with much more than the business legislation of this period, but my findings suggest that, at least in this realm of study, their conclusions need to be reexamined. I hope, too, that my research will help explain in more depth the interaction between groups of businessmen and state officials in the formulation of economic policy and legislation in California, a task ably begun by the historian Gerald Nash.[11] I believe my work has implications for the study of recent American history in general. In the broadest terms, this investigation should heighten our understanding of the ways businessmen and others sought to control and take advantage of their changing economic environment through an intricate combination of private and public actions. More specifically, I hope my study will provide some insight into the workings of the American political system, and especially the question of whether it has been elitist or pluralistic in recent times.

Acknowledgments

Many people have helped me develop this study, and I would like to take this opportunity to thank them for their aid. The suggestions and guidance of Richard Abrams who directed my work on this subject as a dissertation were of great value. I also want to extend my appreciation to Walton Bean and Richard Sutch for reading and commenting upon the text of this study as a dissertation. In addition, several historians have read all or part of my work to recommend ways in which it might be revised and improved for publication. For this service I am particularly grateful to Otis Pease, K. Austin Kerr, Mary Young, and the two readers for this press.

Others also deserve my thanks. The librarians of the Bancroft Library at the University of California at Berkeley and the librarians of the various business libraries in San Francisco, particularly those at the Bank of California and the business branch of the San Francisco Public Library, proved especially helpful in aiding me in my search for sources. I also want to thank the officers of the California Bankers Association for allowing me access to their archives. Finally, I am indebted to my wife, for her constant encouragement and typing skills made it possible for this manuscript to see the light of day.

I am, of course, solely responsible for any errors of fact or interpretation that may remain.

The Politics of Business in California, 1890–1920

1

California's Changing Economy

Addressing a meeting of his colleagues in 1904, one of California's leading insurance men observed that although his "business was constantly changing," at the present time "the changes are revolving with such velocity that some of us are made dizzy by the mere contemplation of them."[1] Businessmen throughout California frequently voiced similar sentiments, for, even more than most other areas of the nation, California's economy experienced fundamental alterations in the late nineteenth and early twentieth centuries.[2] Industries previously only in their formative stages emerged as the leading sectors of California's economy, and the various segments of the state's economy became both increasingly differentiated and interdependent. Accompanying these developments were regional shifts in the Golden State's commerce, finance, and manufacturing.

Economic Development

As was true throughout the United States, railroads were the key to economic development in California, for they linked the different sections of the state and provided Californians with access to markets in the East and Midwest.[3] The completion of transcontinental connections by the Union Pacific and Central Pacific in 1869 heralded a bright future for California. Seven years later the Southern Pacific drove its rails south through the San Joaquin Valley and in 1883 finished its line to New Orleans. Shortly afterward, the Atchison Topeka and Santa Fe entered Los Angeles from Texas, and in 1898 it extended its operations to the San Joaquin Valley. Farther north, the Southern Pacific constructed branches through the Sacramento Valley in the 1880s and 1890s, and the Western Pacific invaded the region in the early twentieth century with a line from Salt Lake City to Oakland. By 1910, California possessed four direct transcontinental connections and a web of feeder lines that reached every part of the state except the northwest corner around Eureka and Humboldt Bay.[4] The spread of this railroad network spurred the development of big business in California. The opening of new markets and the advent of irrigation brought intensive agriculture to California, and fruits and vegetables soon displaced wheat as the state's leading crop. In the San Joaquin Valley and Southern California the development of the oil industry added another new element to California's economic growth. Farther north, along the coast above San Francisco and in the Sierra Nevadas, redwood and pine lumbering operations emerged as major enterprises for the first time.

When Frank Norris described large-scale wheat ranching as the principal activity of California farmers in his novel *The Octopus* in 1901, his observations had already become outdated, for the production of wheat was yielding to diversified fruit growing as the chief occupation of the state's agriculturalists. In 1890, California ranked second among the nation's wheat-growing states with an output of over 40 million bushels, but in succeeding years production dropped drastically. The fall in production so alarmed the San Francisco merchants who handled the wheat trade that in 1905 they obtained funding from the state legislature for a study by agronomists at the University of California to suggest ways to reverse the trend. The report's recommendations helped little. Soil exhaustion, increased competition with grain from Russia and Argentina, and the completion of railroad links between California and the rest of the nation, which made the growing of perishable crops for eastern markets possible, all contributed to the demise of the bonanza wheat ranches. By 1916, Californians were growing only about 4 million bushels annually.[5]

The rise of fruit growing was as dramatic as the decline in wheat production. In the first decade of the twentieth century the value of California's fruits and nuts jumped from $28,809,830 to $48,917,655 to overtake the value of the state's wheat crop.[6] Farmers expended so much effort on fruit that about one-half of the livestock and wheat consumed in California came from out of state.[7] Acknowledging this shift in production patterns, the California Bureau of Labor Statistics stopped relating seasonal unemployment to the annual cycle of hay and wheat growing and began connecting it with the vagaries of fruit and vegetable crops.[8]

California had been the home of citrus and deciduous fruits since mission days, but only in the 1880s and 1890s did large-scale production become economically feasible. Scientific advances by growers and governmental officials in combating diseases, improving stocks, and perfecting soil-sampling methods prepared the way. The work of the state board of viticulture in fighting phylloxera, a blight that attacked grape vines, and the efforts of the state horticultural commissioner in eliminating the cotton-cushiony scale that ravaged orange groves proved especially valuable.[9] Irrigation facilitated the spread of the orange culture south to the Tehachapi and the growth of intensive agriculture in the San Joaquin and Sacramento valleys. As early as 1891, irrigators in Kern County had constructed ditches capable of floating boats of several hundred tons, and hydroelectric projects began supplying power for pumps seven years later. By 1902, California had nearly 2 million acres under irrigation, one-quarter of the nation's total, and, within three years more, irrigated farms accounted for one-third of the value of California's agricultural production.[10]

If scientific research by state officials and the adoption of irrigation spurred the output of fruit and vegetables, it was the coming of the railroad that insured their dominance over wheat. As a nonperishable, wheat could endure lengthy sea voyages to Liverpool and other distribution points and did not require rail connections, but fruits and vegetables, if they were to reach other than local markets, needed the speedy service that railroads alone could provide.[11] California quickly became the nation's fruit bowl. The development of ventilator and refrigerator cars and the discovery of ways to pre-cool fruit before shipment opened national markets for perishable commodities. In 1886, growers sent their first entire trainload of oranges east, and within five years Californians were dispatching 18,693 carloads of fruits and nuts to out-of-state destinations.[12] By 1906, the shipments had risen to 81,976 carloads, and they continued to climb in succeeding years.[13] In 1916, over 400 carloads left California each day at the peak of the shipping season, and the state horticultural commissioner estimated that California's farmers were sending over 90 percent of their fruit beyond the state's boundaries.[14]

Lumbering, though it too existed in California before the American conquest, became a big business only in later years. When California attained statehood, redwood mills were running at Santa Cruz, Redwood City, Mill Valley, and Bodega Bay, and in the following decade lumbermen began operations farther north in Mendocino, Humboldt, and Del Norte counties. The mills had a hard time handling the large redwood logs (lumbermen sometimes used black powder to split them into convenient sizes), and their capacity was small. The first mill in Humboldt County turned out only 600 board feet per day. With the introduction of new techniques in the 1860s and 1870s, however, production mounted. Between 1861 and 1880 17 redwood mills, each with a daily output exceeding 30,000 board feet, went into business to supply the expanding San Francisco market. In the Sierra Nevadas lumbermen got their start cutting pine to meet the needs of miners for timbering and flumes. When mining declined, its loss was offset by the demands of fruit growers for lumber used in making boxes and by the needs of builders in the state's expanding cities. In 1855, California possessed 80 sawmills. Twenty-five years later the number had grown to about 250, and their combined yearly output totalled over 300 million board feet. Yet, despite these increases California ranked only fifteenth among the nation's timber-producing states in 1890. Eastern forests and the Great Lakes region still supplied most of the lumber requirements of the United States.[15]

National markets played a significant role in the development of California's lumber industry in succeeding years. Eastern firms, hoping to serve the national market, began operations in California, and companies already there began looking beyond their state's boundaries for customers. In 1889, the Excelsior Redwood Company became the first lumber firm to break into eastern markets. Despite high railroad rates, redwood operators exported about one-sixth of their lumber by 1900, and they sold nearly half of this amount on the eastern seaboard. Twenty years later one-quarter of the state's redwood went to purchasers east of the Rocky Mountains. As the cut of Great Lakes timber dwindled, pine men braved competition from Pacific Northwest to ship ever greater amounts of their output to eastern buyers.[16] Pushed out by the depletion of most of the virgin timber in the Great Lakes states and attracted by the possibility of profits farther west, a number of lumber firms migrated to California.

As early as 1883, a Buffalo syndicate purchased 60,000 acres of redwood land in Humboldt County, and later in the decade a group of Michigan and Wisconsin businessmen organized the Usal Lumber Company with a large mill in Mendocino County. Not until the turn of the century, however, did this migration assume the shape of a mass movement. The amount of capital invested in California's lumber industry doubled between 1899 and 1904, as eastern lumbermen moved into both the pine and redwood forests. The lumber output of the Pacific Coast states surpassed that of the Great Lakes region in the first decade of the twentieth century, and by 1920 California stood fifth among the lumber-producing states of the nation.[17]

Californians had long known about the presence of oil in their state, but, as in lumbering, the production of petroleum became a major industry only in the late nineteenth century. Access to national markets proved less important in the exploitation of oil than in that of other of California's natural resources. Prohibitive railroad rates and the lack of pipeline connections prevented Californians from sending their petroleum east. California oil found few outlets beyond the West Coast, and only rarely did Californians import petroleum from eastern fields.[18] Indians had used asphaltum in the Spanish and Mexican periods, and in 1853 the first state geologist listed it as one of California's commonest minerals. The success of E. L. Drake's oil well in Pennsylvania stimulated drilling in other regions, and California experienced its first oil boom in the 1860s. However, petroleum hunters discovered few paying properties, and the boom collapsed by the end of the decade. As late as 1890, California was producing only 307,360 barrels annually. Technological problems hindered development. California's geologic structure differed from formations encountered in eastern fields, and the failure to understand the differences thwarted the search for oil. When they did find petroleum, oil men found it difficult to penetrate California's jumbled rock formations by drilling methods devised in the East. During the 1860s they extracted more petroleum by digging wells with picks and shovels or by tunneling into hillsides than by drilling wells. The first producing well in the San Joaquin Valley was dug by hand and reached a depth of only ten feet. The chemical properties of California oil presented a still more serious obstacle, for they made it nearly impossible to use the crude as a base for high-grade kerosene. Since petroleum had not yet demonstrated its value as a fuel, this impediment severely limited the market for California oil.[19]

In the late 1890s and early 1900s California oil men solved their problems, and production soared. As their knowledge of the state's geology increased, oil seekers looking for new fields placed less reliance on surface indications, like oil seepages, and concentrated more on the underlying structural formations. As a result, they were more successful in finding new oil pools and wasted less time and money on dry holes. The introduction of rotary drilling allowed them to probe previously inaccessible areas. Progress in refining enabled Californians to use more of their crude for kerosene, but of greater importance was the growth in demand for crude as a fuel for locomotives, ships, and factories on the West Coast. At the annual convention of the California Miners' Association in 1900, the organization's president noted that it was whispered "that you oil men expect before long that your industry will outstrip that of gold mining." His premonitions proved correct. Within less than a decade the value of California's yearly output of petroleum had nearly doubled that of gold, and the oil men had broken away from the California Miners' Association to set up their own organization. By 1914, California led the nation with a production of over 100 million barrels of crude.[20]

As was the case in agriculture and lumbering (and, to a lesser degree, in the oil business), the financial institutions that developed to serve California's basic productive industries became more and more closely tied to the national economy. As the depressions of the 1870s and 1890s and the panic of 1907 demonstrated, California bankers grew increasingly susceptible to country-wide influences. The depression California suffered from in the 1870s had its origins in mainly local rather than national causes. When the Bank of California closed its doors in 1875, it did so largely because of its president's disastrous involvement in the financing of Nevada's Comstock Lode. National events affected California bankers much more directly in later periods. In both 1893 and 1907 the state's banks were caught with large deposits of specie in New York and Chicago, and the refusal of eastern bankers to release these funds led to the closing of many California banks.[21] Like bankers, insurance men felt the effects of national occurrences. The findings of the New York investigation into life insurance in 1905 altered insurance practices in California. Similarly, the decisions of the country's leading insurance firms, which did most of the life and fire business in California, sometimes influenced the state's economy as a whole. The desire of major insurance companies to increase their investments in California's industries added a fillip to the development of the Golden State in the opening years of the twentieth century.

Just as California's emergent businesses became linked with the nation as a whole, so the different regions and industries within the state grew increasingly interdependent, until no businessman could escape the consequences of the actions of his fellows. The spread of rail network within California proved essential, for instance, in the development of the oil industry. Before the construction of pipeline systems, railroads carried crude from the fields to refineries and markets in the San Francisco Bay area and Los Angeles. The railroads, in turn, converted their locomotives to burn crude and quickly became the best customers of the oil companies. Few relationships were so mutually beneficial. By stripping mountain watersheds of their cover lumbermen adversely influenced stream flow and injured the fortunes of agriculturalists dependent on irrigation. Similarly, conflicts arose between farmers who needed water for irrigation and hydroelectric companies trying to supply the power requirements of the state's burgeoning urban population.

Regional Shifts in the Economy

Regional shifts in California's economy accompanied the development of new business. Nowhere was this clearer than in the numerous battles waged between towns and cities for control over their localities, and particularly in the contest between San Francisco, Los Angeles, and Oakland for hegemony over the entire state. The integration of California's economy brought merchants and businessmen from throughout the state into competition with each other and threatened to disrupt an already unstable economic situation.

In 1878, the historian John Hittell could accurately describe San Francisco as "the metropolis" of the Far West.[22] Yet, by the close of the 1890s the residents of Seattle and Portland had shattered the dominion San Franciscans had once maintained over the Pacific Coast, and within another decade Los Angeles and Oakland were challenging San Francisco within California. These cities ended San Francisco's control over trade with the state's interior valleys, foreign commerce, and manufacturing.

The contest for the interior of California centered upon the San Joaquin Valley. The conversion from wheat ranching to smaller farms growing fruits, nuts, and vegetables heightened the valley's importance as a market for goods and a supplier of agricultural products. The discovery of oil in its southern reaches also attracted the eyes of businessmen. The commercial conquest of the valley depended upon the railroad. Whomever the rates favored had an often insurmountable advantage over its adversaries, and the battle for the valley revolved around the attempts of merchants to obtain favorable rates and block the similar efforts of their opponents.

The struggle for control of the valley, which had been developing since the 1880s, intensified after 1906. The merchants of Los Angeles took advantage of the confusion following the San Francisco earthquake and fire to penetrate north of Bakersfield into "substantially the entire Valley."[23] Officials of the Southern Pacific Railroad favored this increase in Los

Angeles's trade and set rates that discriminated against San Franciscans. By sending traffic east via Los Angeles and New Orleans they avoided sharing profits with the Union Pacific that controlled the northern route east of Ogden, Utah.[24] San Francisco businessmen soon spotted this threat to their livelihood and in early 1908 set up a traffic bureau to "resist attempted encroachments" upon their trade territories.[25] The Traffic Bureau petitioned the state railroad commission to restructure freight rates into and out of the valley, but because of the strong opposition of Los Angeles businessmen its efforts proved fruitless. The commission upheld rates favoring Los Angeles. Moreover, arguing that increased traffic justified lower rates, its members reduced class rates and most commodity rates from Los Angeles northward.[26] The rich plum of the San Joaquin Valley slipped from the grasp of San Franciscans, and much of its trade moved to market along new routes.

Challenges to San Francisco's supremacy in foreign commerce accompanied the narrowing of the city's inland hinterland. By 1911, court decisions and legislative actions had broken the grip the Southern Pacific Railroad once held over the waterfronts of Oakland and Los Angeles.[27] The tidelands were declared state property; all that remained was to transfer title from the state to the cities. Meanwhile, San Francisco's rivals had already begun to carve out deepwater ports. Los Angeles had started the construction of an outer breakwater at San Pedro, and Oakland already handled about 30 percent of the freight tonnage passing through the Golden Gate.[28]

Any problem involving San Francisco's waterfront was complicated, because the State Board of Harbor Commissioners appointed by the governor controlled its port. Furthermore, bond issues for the improvement of the harbor had to win approval from the state legislature and then gain a majority in a statewide referendum. When San Francisco had been California's only major port, this system worked fairly well, but, as other ports rose in prominence, San Franciscans complained that state regulation worked to their disadvantage. As the population of other areas increased more rapidly than that of their own city, San Franciscans feared they might lose control of the board and worried that the board would take actions injurious to their city's economic growth. Moreover, San Franciscans recognized that, as time went on, they would have less and less control over the passage of bond issues for the development of their port and feared that unfavorable statewide votes on future bond flotations might imperil their city's commercial greatness.[29]

The contest for California's ocean traffic exploded in the 1911 legislative session. When representatives from Los Angeles and Oakland introduced a bill transferring the state-held waterfronts to their cities, the business organizations and legislators of San Francisco rallied as a unit in opposition. San Franciscans believed that, should this measure pass, Oakland and Los Angeles would be able to establish port charges lower than their own. Because their city's harbor fees were set by the state board, which used them as a source of revenue, San Franciscans felt they would be unable to meet the competition of other ports. San Francisco businessmen also expressed fear of the growing power that the rest of the state had over bond issues needed for the development of their harbor facilities.[30]

The resolution of the political conflict foreshadowed San Francisco's loss of economic power. The tidelands controversy was finally settled, not in the legislative halls, but in a private meeting between representatives of the Los Angeles Chamber of Commerce and the business organizations of San Francisco. San Franciscans agreed to withdraw their opposition to the transfer in return for pledges of support on future harbor bond issues and for backing San Francisco as the site for a world's fair in 1915. Several days after the conference the San Francisco merchant bodies wired their city's delegation at Sacramento to vote for the tidelands measure, and it passed without dissent.[31] This compromise worried many San Franciscans, and with good reason. Within little more than a decade Los Angeles handled more freight tonnage than their port, and Oakland was close behind.[32]

While failing to retain command of their state's ocean traffic, San Franciscans also faced increasingly stiff competition from Oakland and Los Angeles as industrial centers. The earthquake and fire of 1906 slowed San Francisco's industrial advance. The value of its manufactured products rose only from $107,024,000 to $133,041,000 in the first decade of the twentieth century. Some firms moved to Oakland and Los Angeles, and relatively few new ones located in San Francisco. The value of goods manufactured in Los Angeles climbed from $15,134,000 to $68,586,000 and the corresponding figures for Oakland were $5,368,000 and $22,343,000.[33] To halt this trend San Francisco business and civic groups fostered a drive for ''home patronage of home industry'' and tried to lower costs of production by breaking labor unions in their city.[34] However, despite their efforts, Los Angeles moved ahead in the 1920s as a center for oil refineries, rubber plants, and motion pictures; and by 1930, the value of these and other productions surpassed that of San Francisco's manufacturers.[35]

Population movements reflected the modifications in California's economy. After rising only 22 percent in the 1890s (the lowest rate of growth in the state's history), California's population soared from 1,485,053 to 2,377,549 in the first decade of the twentieth century. This increase was distributed unevenly, for most of the newcomers settled in Southern California or the Central Valley. The population of Los Angeles rose 212 percent, to 319,198, a figure rivaling that of San Francisco's 416,912 inhabitants. In 1903, the California State Board of Trade commented upon the "pronounced and strikingly noticeable movement into the Sacramento and San Joaquin Valley" as small fruit and vegetable farms replaced the bonanza wheat ranches. Between 1900 and 1910 the population of the San Joaquin Valley doubled, and that of the Sacramento Valley also increased, though at a slower pace. Even in the Bay Area, San Francisco no longer remained the only major locus of population. As an industrial and shipping center Oakland grew from a large town of 66,960 to a city of 150,174, and Berkeley tripled its population to 40,434.[36]

In the late nineteenth and early twentieth centuries, then, California's economy underwent basic alterations. As new industries arose and patterns of trade and commerce changed, businessmen wondered what they could expect next. The coming of the railroad, more than any other single element, upset conditions in the Golden State. Many Californians asked, with Henry George, "What is the railroad to do for us, this railroad we have looked for, hoped for, prayed for so long?"[37] The answer to this question, and the more general one of how to cope with the changing economy of their state and nation, was not readily apparent to California businessmen. Yet they did realize, if sometimes only partially and incorrectly, that the growing complexity of their economic situation required alterations in their business methods; and, like businessmen throughout the United States, they relied upon a wide range of strategies to solve their problems. Many tried to insulate their firms from market fluctuations by vertical and horizontal integration. On the industry-wide level, businessmen sought to stabilize economic conditions and rationalize business practices through the formation of trade associations and various types of agreements between their companies. Few of these efforts, however, proved completely successful. Unable to resolve their problems by voluntary means, businessmen frequently turned to the state legislature for aid. So often, in fact, that at many points the story of how they met their difficulties becomes an analysis of their maneuverings in Sacramento.

2

Agriculture: Growers Against Consumers

California's farmers, like other of the state's businessmen, found both grave problems and glittering opportunities in the shifting structure of their state's economy during the late nineteenth and early twentieth centuries. Most pressing was the need to tap national markets for their new products. From the beginning of the 1880s the specter of overproduction spurred the establishment of national marketing arrangements, for the cultivation of fruits and vegetables outstripped the consumption needs of Californians. At the same time, the construction of a railroad network connecting California with the other sections of the nation opened the pleasing prospect of highly profitable outlets for their produce in the urban centers of the Midwest and eastern seaboard. To penetrate these new markets and boost their profits, California's agriculturalists led the nation's farmers in adopting novel marketing techniques.

The Cooperative Marketing Movement

Fruit and vegetable growers in California first sought to solve their problems and seize the advantages of producing for the national market through the establishment of cooperative marketing associations. The organization of cooperative marketing bodies would, they hoped, allow them to rationalize their shipments to eastern points, limit competition within their ranks, and raise the prices they received for their goods.

Beyond these general goals, California's farmers often anticipated that they could lower their specific costs of production and distribution by organizing. They desired, in particular, to win concessions on railroad rates from the Central Pacific and Southern Pacific lines, while also obtaining better and speedier service.

Even before the Civil War a few American farmers set up cooperative marketing associations to dispose of their produce at a profit. In the late nineteenth century, the number of these organizations rose, and many became affiliated with larger regional bodies like the Grange and Farmers Alliances, some of which participated in general political and social reform movements. In the early years of the twentieth century, farmers began organizing more single-mindedly to market specific crops, and in 1907, the United States Department of Agriculture could report that over one thousand selling associations existed throughout the nation. Though most of these bodies dealt with dairy products and cereal crops, cooperatives also handled fruit in Florida, Colorado, Washington, and Oregon as well as in California.[1]

Californians took an active part in the cooperative marketing campaign, but their cooperative movement differed significantly from the drive in other parts of the nation. Most importantly, Californians recognized earlier than other farmers the need to concentrate their attention on economic grievances. Though not eschewing politics (the Populist party in California drew much of its strength from farmers), they always, even in the 1890s, focused their energies upon forming efficient national marketing systems. The nature of their crops—the transformation of the bonanza wheat ranches into highly capitalized farms using irrigation to raise specialized types of produce—meant that California's fruit and vegetable growers had to be more businesslike in their approach to farming than agriculturalists elsewhere.

As tough-minded businessmen, California's farmers took their cue from industrialists in using collective action to cope with their difficulties. Farmers viewed the rise of labor unions and large corporations as portents of the future and as models of organization they should follow. Thus, Governor James Gillette, speaking before the California Fruit Growers Association in 1909, evoked prolonged applause when he urged farmers to emulate the steps lumber barons, railroad executives, and the owners of copper mines were taking to control the markets for their goods.[2] Yet, although admitting that market control was their main objective, farmers also pointed out the benefits accruing to the rest of society from their organizations. They claimed that their cooperatives, by improving the system of distribution, would eliminate waste and lower the costs of products to consumers. As A. L. Wisker of the Loma Rica Nurseries explained, "a trust is simply cooperation gone wrong."[3] Expanding their arguments, some growers urged that all of society be organized along cooperative lines. Many endorsed the sentiments of William Glass, a prominent grape grower and past president of the Fresno Chamber of Commerce, when, in a paper presented before the California Fruit Growers Association in 1920, he called for the sale of "all products, agricultural, horticultural, industrial production, by cooperative marketing."[4]

Citrus fruit growers began the drive for organization. By the middle of the 1870s they were raising more oranges and lemons than could be consumed in California and faced the threat of overproduction and low prices. Moreover, as arrangements then existed, the grower bore most of the risks but received little of the profit from the sale of his fruit. He had only two options by which to dispose of his crop. If he consigned it for sale by an eastern commission firm, he was apt to suffer high losses caused by spoilage and rough handling en route to market. Alternately, if he decided to sell his fruit on the tree directly to an eastern buyer, he often encountered combinations among the purchasers and frequently received such artificially low prices that he failed to cover his costs of operations. Whichever method they chose, growers had to contend with the danger of glutted markets. Lacking any central body to direct their shipments, they sent their fruit east in a haphazard fashion, and, as a result, most markets experienced periods of feast and famine, a situation leading to uncontrollable price fluctuations.[5]

Citrus growers first tried to organize with the formation of the Orange Growers Protective Union in 1885. Established after a year of particularly bad losses, the union aimed at instituting a new system of distribution that would, its proponents hoped, deliver the growers from the "deadly embrace" of eastern buyers and consignment men. However, concerted attacks by the middlemen, who deeply resented this challenge to their profits and control over the citrus industry, killed this venture. Buyers and consignment agents formed associations that competed with the union and refused to handle its fruit except at prohibitive charges. Deprived of outlets, the union collapsed. A period of financial anarchy that became known in the citrus fruit trade as "the red ink years" followed the organization's demise. Speculative buying, market gluts, and chronic price swings threatened the very survival of the growers. Continuing their quest for security and profits, citrus fruit men again turned to collective marketing. In 1895, they set up the Southern California Fruit Exchange, and within eight years this body was handling nearly half of the state's oranges. The exchange brought temporary prosperity to its members, but in 1903 it disastrously overreached itself by combining with eastern shipping interests as the California Fruit Agency. Within a year this unnatural alliance of dealers and growers fell apart in mutual acrimony.[6]

Following this dissolution, the growers revamped the old Southern California Fruit Growers Exchange. Soon renamed the California Fruit Growers Exchange, this organization began operations in late 1904. Learning from their past experiences, the growers sought through this exchange to control all phases of the fruit business for California's entire orange and lemon crops. Only in this way could, its advocates thought, growers regulate prices and assure themselves of profit. As the exchange's manager noted in 1911, "in the early days of the industry, when output was small," it was easy to get "enough money for California oranges under the old methods to satisfy the grower and at the same time to give the shippers a very large remuneration for their services." But, he continued, "when the output began to increase rapidly" cooperative marketing became necessary to avoid market gluts and guarantee the grower a proper share of the profits.[7]

The California Fruit Growers Exchange possessed three levels of organization, each of which served a different function. The individual growers formed local associations that were responsible for picking, grading, and packing the fruit. Members agreed to sell their entire output through these bodies. The associations pooled the fruit of their members according to grade and time picked and prorated the returns from sales among those in each particular pool. The local associations delegated the handling of actual sales to district exchanges. Based upon information furnished by a central body, district officers routed the shipments to market, sending cars only to those destinations which they thought could absorb more fruit. Local associations maintained the individuality of their fruit on paper throughout these transactions. Pooling never took place between local organizations, and the receipts of a local association came solely from the price obtained for its fruit. The capstone holding together these various groups was the central exchange that coordinated the work of all the district exchanges by sending them daily reports on fruit markets throughout the nation. In addition to this service the central body supported selling agents in hundreds of cities to supervise the final disposal of its members' fruit and insure receipt of the highest possible prices. The central exchange also set uniform quality standards for fruit packed by the local associations and advertised the exchange's products nationally under the "Sunkist" label.[8]

Within a decade the California Fruit Growers Exchange had organized most of California's citrus fruit industry. By 1917, it contained over 8,000 growers affiliated in 117 local associations and 17 district exchanges, which marketed about two-thirds of the state's oranges and lemons. The exchange dampened price fluctuations but could not completely end them. Some growers remained outside its ranks, and their uncoordinated shipments, combined with those of the Florida growers (who in 1915 produced about 40 percent of the nation's orange crop), made occasional gluts unavoidable.[9] Although it failed to gain absolute market control, the exchange did secure larger profits for its members, mainly by reducing the costs involved in packing, shipping, and selling their fruit. By purchasing timberlands and operating lumber mills the exchange lowered the cost of lumber used in fabricating boxes. Concerted actions brought freight rate reductions and rebates from the Southern Pacific and Santa Fe railroads, and growers working through the exchange found it easier to settle damage claims with the lines. Before the establishment of the California Fruit Growers Exchange, shippers and commission men had charged from 7 to 10 percent to handle a grower's crop, but by 1915 the exchange had decreased the total cost of distribution, marketing, and advertising to about 2½ percent of the delivered value of the fruit. The manager of the exchange could, with considerable justification, claim in 1914 that his organization was "not only less expensive," but also "more comprehensive than any other crop marketing service yet developed."[10]

The deciduous fruit men labored under many of the same hardships as the citrus fruit growers. Soaring production made access to new markets a necessity.[11] Yet, an inefficient system of distribution caused frequent market gluts and wide price swings. Even when growers guessed correctly and sent their cars to the right destinations, middlemen and shippers skimmed off much of the profit. Nor could the growers, as individuals, win much in the way of concessions from the railroads, and, even more than the citrus fruit growers, they required special handling and fast transportation to avoid damage to their products. In addition to these problems the deciduous fruit producers faced a difficulty unknown to the orange and lemon growers. Their crops were much more diversified. Apricots, peaches, apples, cherries, plums, and pears were among the deciduous fruits raised in California (grapes were also usually treated as a deciduous fruit). To find a common ground among the growers of such varied fruits proved nearly impossible, for each type of crop had its own special problems in cultivation, packing, shipping, and marketing.

Deciduous fruit growers responded to their dilemmas by forming two types of cooperative marketing associations. Like the citrus fruit men, they tried to organize the entire range of production in a single association, but neither the degree of market control nor the savings gained by the citrus growers proved obtainable for deciduous fruit producers by this method. At the same time that they were experimenting with industry-wide bodies, the deciduous growers set up marketing associations to deal with single, specific crops.

Deciduous fruit men made the first substantial effort to organize their industry with the establishment of the California Fruit Union in 1885. Set up as a corporation whose stock was owned solely by growers, the union, though concerned with railroad rates and service, sought mainly to control the distribution of fruit sent to urban centers in the East. Shipments through this body rose from 60 million pounds in 1886 to 160 million pounds seven years later, but its share of the out-of-state business dropped from 44 to 33 percent in the same period. Several reasons account for the decline and final demise of the California Fruit Union. The onset of the general business depression hurt the growers, but more responsible for the failure of the union were two actions of its directors. In 1887, contrary to the organization's original constitution, they admitted nonproducers engaged in the buying and selling of fruit to stock ownership, and this arrangement split the union into bickering sections. The other mistake was to sign long-term contracts to deliver all of the union's fruit to one eastern buyer. This decision was soon costing growers profits they could have earned from competitive bidding.[12]

The disbanding of the California Fruit Union left the deciduous growers in disarray for over a decade. Random shipments followed by market gluts made it impossible to benefit much even from the short crop of 1894, and railroad rates remained onerous and service slow. The forced return to consignment sales at closed auctions further aggravated the other difficulties. In early 1895, the growers sought to end their chronic problems by joining together in the California Fruit Growers' and Shippers' Association. The association's members moved quickly to rationalize the distribution of out-of-state fruit shipments. As one prominent fruit man explained, growers had for the past season "been groping around in the dark," and were "constantly sending fruit to markets already overcrowded with California products." To improve their condition the growers set up a bureau of information to provide themselves with data on deciduous fruit shipments throughout the nation. A committee on transportation secured promises of five-day ventilator car service to Chicago from the freight manager of the Southern Pacific, and other members worked to remove abuses from auction sales. However, this association did not try to sell any fruit itself, and most growers looked upon it simply as a stopgap that they would abandon as soon as an organization with marketing powers could be established.[13]

After several more years of sporadic progress the growers succeeded in forming a statewide marketing association. At a meeting held in Sacramento in 1899 fruit growers voiced particularly strong complaints about shipping charges and poor market conditions. A conference held in Fresno a year later took actions to end these problems. A committee set up at this meeting issued a call for a convention to organize a marketing cooperative, and in 1901 the deciduous fruit growers formed the California Fresh Fruit Exchange.[14]

A federated type of organization, the exchange (retitled the California Fruit Exchange in 1903) closely followed the lines of the Southern California Fruit Growers Exchange. Local packing associations sold their fruit through a central body that routed shipments to their destinations on the basis of all available market information. Salaried agents in most of the major and many of the secondary eastern cities assured exchange members of good prices for their fruit. The association worked to end consignment sales and shifted some of the risk of transit losses to the buyers. To hold a place for California produce on eastern markets, it also maintained uniform grades for its members' fruit and established easily recognized brand names.[15]

The California Fruit Exchange was soon dealing in both cured and fresh deciduous fruits and rapidly expanded its activities. The 14 local associations affiliated with it in 1909 grew in number to 63 only fifteen years later, and the volume of its business rose from the shipment of only 201 cars in 1901 to 6,281 in 1921. Yet, the exchange failed to gain market control. Even in 1921 it handled less than one-quarter of any deciduous fruit crop. Many growers preferred marketing cooperatives like the California Peach Growers Association, which because they dealt in only one specific fruit were felt to be more attuned to the individual grower's needs. The competition of fruit from other parts of the nation—apples from the Northwest and peaches from Georgia—also made control impossible. The exchange did, however, achieve some success in raising the profits of the growers. It maintained a standing committee on transportation that successfully petitioned for rate reductions and faster service from the transcontinental railroads, and, again like the citrus growers, the deciduous fruit men entered into the cooperative production and purchasing of supplies to further reduce their costs. The exchange cut the expense of handling fruit to only 2½ percent of its retail value.[16]

Many deciduous fruit growers joined cooperative marketing associations selling only one type of fruit, for by specializing in one particular crop, they believed they had a better chance of mastering market vagaries. Some single product cooperatives existed as early as the 1880s, but the extension of plantings in the early twentieth century led to the creation of many new ones.[17] The actions of the California Peach Growers Association typified the work of these bodies. The shipment of wormy peaches to Chicago and New York in 1909 had led many buyers to reject California brands during the following seasons. At the same time the expanding production of peaches throughout the nation heightened the competition for markets. In 1915, to obtain higher prices for their fruit and to increase their sales in the Midwest and East, peach growers formed the California Peach Growers Association. Within four years it was marketing three-quarters of California's dried peaches, and by establishing uniform grades of fruit, well-known trademarks, and an efficient marketing apparatus, it reopened eastern markets to California peaches. The actions of the cooperative, combined with wartime demands, boosted the prices paid members for their crops from three cents per pound in 1914 to eighteen cents per pound four years later and, as one state official noted, "placed peach growing and marketing on a profitable and secure basis."[18]

Farmers requiring national markets for other types of produce followed the lead of the fruit men. By 1919, Californians had founded cooperative marketing organizations for berries, rice, almonds, walnuts, lima beans, string beans, cantaloupes, and tomatoes.[19] Like the fruit growers, the farmers raising these products hoped to expand their markets, regularize prices, and increase their profits. The manager of the California Almond Growers Exchange spoke for most other agriculturalists when he declared that "what we want is some method of marketing that will make the market for almonds as steady and stable as the market for flour or sugar."[20] Those cooperatives which controlled a large percentage of the California output and which had an advantage of some sort over other regions in the United

States raising the same crops usually reported increased prices and profits for their members. The founder of the Sebastopol Berry Growers, which shipped its fruit to Salt Lake City, Seattle, Portland, and Spokane, claimed that the gains made by cooperative selling came "just in time to prevent half of us having our wives leave us in disgust."[21] The California Almond Growers Exchange was probably most successful. Formed in 1910, when some farmers were grubbing up their trees to plant more profitable crops, it had within two seasons doubled the price paid growers for their nuts. Organized as a federation of local associations, it was by 1919 selling 85 percent of California's almonds.[22]

By 1920, cooperatives marketed well over half of California's agricultural output, but, with a few exceptions like the association of almond growers, none of these bodies obtained anything approaching absolute control over their markets. They usually had to compete with farmers from other sections of the nation. Florida orange growers, Georgia peach growers, and apple growers in Washington prevented Californians from gaining monopolistic positions in their markets. Moreover, even in California some growers remained outside the cooperatives. Hoping to reap short-term profits, they ignored the efforts of the cooperatives to stabilize market conditions. As a result, price fluctuations, while dampened, continued for most California crops.

Although unsuccessful in achieving market control, the cooperatives did help increase the profits of California's farmers. The prices paid for the state's agricultural products rose in the early twentieth century. These increases cannot, however, be attributed solely to cooperative selling organizations, for the years between 1895 and 1915 were ones of generally rising prices for farm goods throughout the United States. The index of agricultural prices nearly doubled during this period. Nonetheless, the cooperatives in California and elsewhere were at least partly responsible for these increases.[23] Marketing associations also widened profit margins by lowering the expenses farmers incurred in packing, shipping, and selling their goods. Finally, the cooperatives aided farmers in opening new markets by the establishment of uniform methods of grading produce and extensive name-brand advertising.

The Agricultural Standardization Movement

California's farmers sought many of the same goals through the agricultural standardization movement that they had pursued through cooperative marketing associations. By defining quality standards for their produce and by setting uniform packing rules, they sought to keep immature and damaged goods off the eastern markets. An improvement in the quality of products sold in the East would, most believed, establish a favorable reputation for their produce and thus increase the out-of-state consumption of it. Concerned only with expanding eastern purchases of their state's agricultural output, preferably at higher prices, the standardization campaign was formulated to benefit California's farmers. In no sense was it designed to aid consumers. Indeed, its aim of raising food prices contradicted the best interests of consumers. Moreover, none of the regulations devised to improve the quality of produce applied to sales in California, and the state's markets soon became dumping grounds for inferior fruit and vegetables.

Though considerations of economic gain motivated the majority of those involved in the standardization movement, some viewed the campaign in a broader perspective. Impressed with what they interpreted as the modern efficiency of their nation's manufacturing industries, they longed to reshape California agriculture along contemporary business lines. Thus, one proponent of standardization, addressing the California Fruit Growers Convention in 1914, asserted that "an analysis of the manufacturing or the mercantile business or a study of the wholesaler and the retailer will show that standardization and system are the watchwords of success," and berated the state's farmers for having fallen behind other groups of businessmen in these respects.[24] Still others valued the standardization movement as part of a much larger attempt to mold all aspects of American life into more rational forms. John Irish, a fruit grower active in the standardization campaign from its inception, praised it for having "affect[ed] the mental character of the entire state." The drive "has standardized the men" and had thus, he concluded, given California women "a better standard of men than their unfortunate mothers had a chance of marrying."[25]

Begun by state officials and deciduous fruit growers working together, the standardization movement soon spread to citrus fruits and other products. The earliest attempts to control packing conditions and to set uniform grades were undertaken on a purely voluntary basis, but, when it became apparent that the desired results could not be obtained in this fashion, the growers, with the close cooperation of state officials, resorted to the passage of state legislation embodying their wishes.

Marketing problems plagued deciduous fruit growers in the opening decade of the twentieth century. Many growers, eager for the premium prices received for the first fruit of the season and hoping to avoid late summer and fall market gluts, included immature and damaged fruit in their early shipments to the East. This practice reached a climax in 1909. So much fruit was of inferior quality in that year that, according to State Horticultural Commissioner J. A. Jeffrey, "hundreds of carloads were rejected outright" in the eastern cities, and "in one province [of Canada] our fruit was refused admittance altogether."[26] Placer County alone, Jeffrey estimated, sent out 300 carloads of immature or spoiled peaches.[27]

European importers and American consuls stationed overseas also complained about the poor quality of the California deciduous fruit pack. They warned that unless growers improved their packing methods and standardized their grades of fruit, they would lose their European markets. Importers in Nantes, France, reported that "all fruits arriving in cases, such as prunes and apricots, evaporated peaches, pears, apples are badly packed" and asserted that "it is rare that a case of fruit arrives from the United States without some part of the immediate cover missing." A consul at Dusseldorf, Germany, noted that "shipments of goods of very inferior quality are becoming of frequent occurrence" and that they were "a cause of annoyance, embarrassment, and loss to importers." He urged that low grade fruit "which is apt to spoil the whole business in a country like Germany" be eliminated from the trade.[28]

The possibility of losing their domestic and foreign outlets at a time of rising production goaded the fruit growers to work with the staff of the state horticultural commissioner to standardize their crops. In December, 1909, the California Fruit Growers Association passed a resolution calling for the "standardizing of all deciduous fruit packs prepared for interstate shipment." In response to the pleas of growers Jeffrey held twenty-seven conferences throughout the state to standardize California's deciduous fruit, and by the opening of the 1910 season counties raising one-third of the output had adopted standardization rules. Under Jeffrey's supervision the growers set up bodies to standardize their crops on the local and county basis. The key to success, most believed, lay in getting shippers and growers to sign contracts not to handle any poor quality or incorrectly packed fruit. In most instances a board of directors composed of growers and shippers laid out regulations for all members in an association. Inspectors, paid by membership dues, examined the packing sheds of those belonging to the association, and fines or expulsion were the usual penalties for violations. Each organization maintained its own brand names, and membership was voluntary.[29]

From these local efforts, the growers, again in cooperation with the horticultural commissioner, moved on to establish statewide bodies. After several false starts, a convention of fruit men set up the California Deciduous Fruit Protective League in late 1911. Though it also sought to devise a better distribution system for eastern sales and to gain rate reductions from the transcontinental railroads, the main purpose of the league was to encourage standardization. Upon the request of its founders, J. A. Jeffrey resigned from his position as state horticultural commissioner to become its manager. The California Cured Fruit Exchange, which dealt only in dried fruits, worked toward the same ends. Set up as a direct result of the chronic complaints from foreign importers about the poor quality of California fruit, this body established standards for local associations trying to organize the dried deciduous fruit business. By the 1913 season the exchange had 12 of the largest packing houses in Northern California affiliated with it.[30]

Within a few years these organizations had begun to improve the market for California fruit. At the close of the 1910 season a Lodi County grape grower claimed that the benefits of the movement were ''already apparent'' and urged that the campaign be intensified. The manager of the California Fruit Distributors remarked in the same year that ''the result of this work had been plainly apparent throughout the season'' and noted that purchasers were ''well pleased and rejections much less frequent than in past years.'' Horticultural Commissioner Jeffrey found the same results. Placer County, which produced the most deciduous fruit of any county in California, suffered, he reported, no rejections in 1910, chiefly because it possessed an active standardization association. American consuls and fruit growers traveling in Europe announced significant meliorations in the foreign markets for California deciduous fruits, and they attributed this change to the standardization campaign, particularly the work of the Cured Fruit Exchange.[31]

Heartened by these favorable reports, the growers expanded the standardization movement, but they soon realized that voluntary efforts alone would not succeed. Some growers, desiring the quick profits resulting from sales early in the season, continued to disregard the long-run benefits of securing wider markets for their fruit and shipped immature specimens east. Others, unwilling to accept temporary losses on damaged crops, also ignored long-term possibilities and deluged their markets with inferior produce. These actions aroused the suspicions of eastern buyers and made it difficult for even the highest grade of fruit to find purchasers at a good price. Searching for a legal basis with which to enforce their standards, those belonging to voluntary associations turned to the passage of state legislation. Only legislation, they reasoned, could lay down compulsory statewide standards.[32] Californians took legislative steps against a background of similar actions in other parts of the nation. In 1903, Washingtonians set standards for their state's pear and apple crops, and eight years later the Florida legislature enacted measures specifying maturity standards for all oranges destined for out-of-state markets. The federal government entered the picture in 1913 with laws establishing requirements for the packaging of fruit sent abroad.[33]

Within this context of national agitation, Assemblyman L. B. Cary of Fresno introduced a bill in the 1913 legislature to create a commission empowered to set standards for all fruits, nuts, and vegetables raised in California. The grape growers from Cary's district lent strong support to this measure, and many deciduous fruit men in the San Joaquin and Sacramento valleys also backed it. As the chairman of the Placer County Growers and Shippers Association explained, the measure would "give permanency to the rules of standardization, protect the industry, and relieve those who are voluntarily endeavoring to perfect our standards." Some growers, however, fought Cary's proposal. Although admitting the need for government participation in the standardization movement, they claimed the bill tried to do too much too quickly. They especially objected to the inclusion of fruit and vegetables sold within California under its terms, for Los Angeles, San Francisco and other cities throughout the state had long been dumping grounds for goods unable to meet export standards. Lacking statewide grower support, Cary's proposition passed the assembly but died on file in the senate.[34]

During the next two years work on regulatory measures continued. Members of the California Fruit Growers Association resolved at their meeting in late 1913 that "it is the sense of this convention that we should have a statewide standardized pack of all fruit for interstate shipment" and appointed a special committee to draft legislation for the standardization of the table grape pack.[35] At a conference called by the state horticultural commissioner in 1914 fruit growers and packers agreed to press for standardization laws at the next session of the state legislature. A bill drawn up by H. E. Butler of the Penryn Fruit Packing Association, F. B.

McKevitt, a prominent grower and head of the California Fruit Distributors, and State Senator C. B. Mills of Sacramento received the meeting's backing. It set uniform standards of maturity, quality, and packing for all of California's out-of-state deciduous fruit shipments except apples. Containers were to bear labels describing where and by whom the fruit was packed, and fines penalized any deviations from the standards proclaimed. Only uncrated fruit sold in bulk was exempt from the terms of this bill. More limited in scope than Cary's proposal of 1913, this measure regulated only out-of-state shipments and did not apply at all to vegetables or citrus fruits. Apple growers prepared a special bill for their crop. Unlike the more general deciduous fruit bill, it did not make standardization compulsory, but instead provided the growers with stamps they could afix to their crates of apples, if they met the standards established by the state. The growers were to pay inspectors to examine their fruit, and state certification would, in turn, the growers hoped, improve its status on the eastern markets.[36]

Supported by the growers as "a message to the East that it will get the highest grade of fruit from California," both measures won quick approval from the legislature in 1915 and went into effect the following year.[37] State officers chosen by civil service examinations worked under the guidance of the state horticultural commissioner to inspect the fruit as it was crated in the packing sheds. By 1918, the horticultural commissioner could report that the laws had proven "very satisfactory" in improving the market for California fruit.[38] Most growers agreed with him. The Watsonville Apple Distributors, an association that marketed 600,000 boxes under the terms of the Apple Standardization Act, received ten cents more per box in 1916 than those growers and shippers who decided not to place their packs under state supervision, and the association's president praised the act as being "most beneficial to all interests."[39] F. J. Mason, another fruit grower and packer, noting that "there are less rejections, less complaint, and a greater demand at satisfactory prices," labeled the deciduous fruit standardization act "a wonderful success."[40] Nearly all deciduous fruit men soon came to see the value of state legislation. In November 1915, the California Fruit Growers Association passed resolutions endorsing the two standardization laws, and in succeeding years its members labored ardently for their enforcement and expansion.[41]

Citrus growers moved to standardize their crops for the same reasons as the deciduous fruit men. They faced increasingly stiff competition from Florida orange and lemon growers. At the same time production in California was exploding; in the decade after 1904 the acreage planted in oranges and lemons more than doubled.[42] These developments alarmed Californians. They feared the rivalry of the Florida growers, and came to believe that only by offering a pack of uniformly high quality could they secure national markets for their expanding production. Their main problem was to eliminate immature and frost-damaged fruit from their out-of-state shipments. Although inferior fruit might bring temporarily high prices at the opening of each season, it often ruined the markets for the better grades that came later. Few consumers would, after once biting into a sour orange, soon purchase another. Yet, for a long time growers did little to alter this situation, for none were individually willing to forgo the high profits often received for early carloads of fruit. As in the deciduous industry, standardization was finally accomplished only by collective action and the passage of state legislation.

Growers made some efforts to standardize their shipments as early as 1911, but not until the results of a severe freeze two years later shocked them out of their complacency did they achieve much progress. In 1911, the United States Department of Agriculture published a report that detailed handling methods that would reduce losses from decay, and its authors urged the growers to ''be sure your pack is uniform and true to grade.''[43] State Horticultural Commissioner Jeffrey also exhorted orange and lemon growers to improve the quality of their crops, and the California Fruit Growers Exchange established uniform grades for all oranges packed under its Sunkist label.[44] However, much of California's citrus fruit continued to go ungraded and without examination for maturity or disease. In 1913, a particularly hard frost damaged over half of the state's Valencia orange crop. Many growers, hoping to salvage something from this disaster, hastily shipped their injured fruit to the eastern markets. Though not all followed this practice (the California Fruit Growers Exchange refused to handle blemished oranges), enough bad fruit reached the East to ruin the reputation of California's oranges. The Chicago Board of Health condemned the damaged oranges as unfit for human consumption and prohibited their sale within the city's boundaries.[45] The manager of the California Fruit Growers Exchange complained in 1914 that ''as a result of the unprecedented frost'' California ''lost its commanding position in the leading markets of the country, especially in the East.''[46]

Hurt by the rejection of their crops, the growers worked with state and federal officials to devise tests to separate sound from damaged fruit. Fruit men in Riverside quickly discovered a simple way to differentiate frost-damaged from unfrosted oranges. In 1914, scientists in the United States Department of Agriculture, after several years of experimentation, found a method to test the maturity of oranges. They decided that an orange was edible if its ratio of soluble solids to acid was not less than eight to one.[47]

The growers and packers experienced trouble in putting these tests into operation. The California Fruit Growers Exchange adopted the eight-to-one standard for oranges in 1915 and extended its standardization efforts to lemons in the next few years.[48] Some local bodies not associated with the exchange also screened their packs for maturity and frost damage, and the Fresno County Board of Supervisors passed an ordinance requiring use of the eight-to-one rule for all oranges grown within its jurisdiction.[49] However, these actions failed to end the shipment of inferior fruit to eastern markets. As the manager of the California Fruit Growers Exchange lamented, some growers and shippers "who are unmindful of the interests of the industry as a whole" continued to market "fruit which may be orange in color but falls below the 8 to 1 quality standards."[50]

Thwarted in their voluntary attempt, the larger citrus growers and packers turned to state legislation. In late 1914, the manager of the California Fruit Growers Exchange called upon the federal and state governments to prevent interstate commerce in frost-damaged oranges.[51] Responding to his wishes and those of other fruit men, the 1915 session of the state legislature enacted a law, modeled upon a measure passed in Florida four years before, forbidding out-of-state shipments of frost-damaged oranges.[52] Claiming that only statewide controls would permit Californians to compete successfully with Florida growers, the manager of the California Fruit Growers Exchange also pressed for government regulation of maturity standards. Again the solons acceded to the growers' desires and in 1917 enacted a bill applying the eight-to-one standard to all oranges sent out of California.[53] Although they did not immediately eliminate all inferior California fruit from the eastern markets, these measures won the praise of the state's leading growers and helped them improve the national standing of their citrus fruit.

California farmers selling a wide variety of produce in out-of-state markets emulated the fruit growers. In 1913, Washington, Oregon, and Idaho quarantined California potatoes, because they suffered from fungus infections and infestations of tuber moths. Californians looked to the state horticultural commissioner for guidance and, under his supervision, established quality standards for all of the state's crop. Within a few seasons California potatoes were again finding buyers throughout the West.[54] Olive growers also standardized their output. Standardization would, one grower explained, "increase the demand for California olives as effectively as the demand has been increased by a like method for California raisins and citrus fruits." Working with state agricultural officials, the olive men established maturity tests for their crops and in 1917 secured passage for state legislation incorporating these standards.[55] By this time many other farmers had joined the standardization drive. Vegetable growers and, at one point, even alfalfa farmers tried to expand their sales by imposing uniform quality standards throughout California.[56]

Like the establishment of cooperative marketing associations, the standardization campaign benefited California's farmers. Again, it is hard to tell exactly how much, for it is difficult to separate the effects of this movement from the general price rise most American agricultural products experienced in the first two decades of the twentieth century. There is no doubt, however, that California's fruit growers and farmers attributed their prosperity to the standardization movement and cooperative marketing.

The Consumers' Revolt

Consumers throughout California agreed with the farmers' analysis of the situation, but, rather than praising the cooperative marketing and standardization campaigns, they denounced the movements for increasing the cost of food. Consumers also recognized that farmers were shipping their choicest produce out of state and blamed the cooperative marketing and standardization drives for the poor quality of produce available in California markets. By 1913, consumers were organizing to fight for lower food prices and a higher quality of produce. Food shortages caused by the First World War exacerbated the conflict between farmers and consumers. After 1914 food prices jumped in all parts of the nation, and the outcries of aggrieved consumers forced the federal government to move in the direction of managing the prices of selected items of food.[57] The cost of food rose dramatically in California as well.[58] However, few agriculturalists or consumers in California correctly assessed the impact of the First World War, and struggles between these groups continued to revolve around the role cooperative marketing and agricultural standardization played in hiking food prices.

Historians have generally applauded the efforts of farmers to increase the prices of their products.[59] This tendency has been pronounced in writings in California history. California historians have treated growers and the state officials who sought to aid the agriculturalists as heroes battling on behalf of a downtrodden people.[60] Yet, as the conflict between farmers and consumers in the Golden State demonstrated, consumers also had needs and desires that required consideration.

Consumers angry about food quality and prices founded public markets in Los Angeles, Sacramento, Oakland, and seven other California cities as early as 1913. Part of a nationwide movement, the drive to set up municipal markets aimed at reducing expenses by bringing farmers into direct contact with consumers.[61] At these marts farmers sold their produce to consumers without going through middlemen. By dispensing with the services of commission agents, advocates of these "free" markets hoped to lower the cost of food without diminishing returns to the farmers. They also believed that by cutting the time required for handling they could secure higher quality produce, for they expected that farmers within a twenty- or thirty-mile radius of each market would bring in their fruits or vegetables and sell them to city dwellers on the spot.[62]

From their separate efforts the proponents of municipal markets turned to the state legislature to extend their sphere of action. In 1915, Assemblyman H. E. McPherson sponsored a measure providing for the establishment of model commission markets in one of California's major urban centers. If this experiment proved successful, the state would later set up others. The director of the state markets would, under the terms of this proposal, accept fruits and vegetables on consignment from farmers for immediate sale to consumers. Those favoring the measure argued that by cutting out the middlemen the proposal would benefit consumers without hurting the growers. The measure's backers insured the approval of farmers by including a provision calling upon the state government to gather and disseminate eastern market information among California's agriculturalists. Supporters of the bill also claimed that, besides aiding both farmers and consumers, the commission market act would further the conservation of California's natural resources. They pointed out that tons of edible fish were used as fertilizer every year and that bushels of apples rotted on the ground each fall because of prohibitive handling charges assessed by the private commission houses. By eliminating the need for farmers and fishermen to work through such houses, McPherson's proposal would, they concluded, end the wastage of food.[63]

The commission market act encountered little opposition in Sacramento. The measure passed the assembly by a vote of forty-four to one, and Senator William Brown of Los Angeles shepherded it through the upper house by nearly as large a margin. Although the commission market act would soon become the hottest item in California politics, it attracted relatively little attention at the time of its passage. Carrying an appropriation of only $25,000, it was ignored by most politicians. Governor Hiram Johnson was puzzled about the meaning of the act and asked members of a state commission then working on a rural credits measure to advise him on how best to implement it. After waiting a full six months, Johnson appointed Harris Weinstock, the chairman of the rural credits commission, as market director.

Weinstock had long been interested in the problems of California's farmers. Though himself a Sacramento merchant, Weinstock believed that his state's economic progress depended upon rural prosperity. Beginning in 1885, he frequently participated in the state fruit growers' conventions and assisted in the organization of many of California's early cooperative marketing bodies. In 1908, Weinstock retired from active business life a wealthy man to devote the rest of his life to political reform. He concerned himself mainly with civic improvements and the reform of a local government. Yet, he also retained his earlier concern in improving the lot of agriculturalists, for he continued to push for cooperative marketing and, in 1913, served as a delegate of the American Commission on Agricultural Credit and Cooperation. Not surprisingly, Weinstock's appointment as market director won the hearty approval of the state's farmers, and members of the California Fruit Growers Association passed a resolution endorsing Johnson's choice of Weinstock at their convention in November, 1915.[64]

The confidence of the agriculturalists was well placed, for Weinstock, ignoring both the letter and spirit of the commission market act, neglected the state's consumers and labored, instead, to secure prosperity for the farmers. He sought to open new markets for their products and, upon taking office, visited eastern cities to survey the demand for California fruits and vegetables. In addition, Weinstock wrote South American importers on behalf of fruit growers and tried to interest Governor Johnson in financing a shipping line to carry fresh fruit to England.[65] All of these efforts convinced Weinstock that only by setting up a better system of distribution could Californians exploit the potential national and international markets for the goods. Accordingly, he helped establish nine cooperative marketing associations during his first year in office.[66] Weinstock also tried to set up state bureaus to rationalize the distribution of California's shipment of fruit to eastern markets. Under his plan state officers would provide daily market information to fruit men by which they would route their carloads east. The growers, in turn, were to furnish the state officials any data, including their sales figures, that they possessed about market conditions.[67]

However, the leading citrus and deciduous fruit organizations refused to participate in this scheme, and it never materialized. After considerable vacillation, the members of the California Fruit Growers Exchange decided to abstain, because they believed the value of the confidential information they would have to provide would not be balanced by any comparable gains.[68] Those belonging to the California Fruit Exchange also rejected Weinstock's entreaties. The association had just enjoyed several prosperous years, and its members agreed to join only if they would be assured of even greater profits in the future. When no promises meeting their specifications were forthcoming, they decided not to cooperate with the market director.[69]

Although solicitous about the needs of California's farmers, Weinstock did little to help the state's consumers. He set up no commission markets. Condemning those who believed in the efficacy of these institutions as misinformed and unrealistic, Weinstock asserted that such markets could neither relieve the pressure of the exploding production on the state's farmers nor reduce the cost of living for consumers.[70] The only project Weinstock undertook to assist consumers was the formation of a fish exchange in San Francisco. In 1915, the legislature had approved an appropriation of $20,000 for the state fish and game commission to examine the price of fish in California. The following investigation disclosed that prices were high, but not because of the machinations of a "fish trust" as some newspapers claimed. The fish business was a one-day-a-week proposition, for nearly all sales occurred on Friday. During the rest of the week an enormous wastage of fish ensued, with much of the catch being sold for fertilizer. Fishermen had to make enough profit on Fridays to cover losses on other days. Prodded by Weinstock, San Francisco's fish dealers voluntarily agreed to meet daily and set maximum prices. Organized as the Northern California Fish Exchange, the dealers also mounted an advertising campaign to encourage the consumption of fish throughout the entire week. State officials applauded these steps, for they felt the actions would both increase the consumption and lower the retail price of fish. These moves would also, they hoped, end wastage and insure the treatment of fish as "a natural resource" for the benefit of all the state's residents.[71]

When the state legislature convened in 1917, Weinstock moved to legitimize his actions. At his request Senator E. A. Luce introduced a bill drastically altering the duties of the market director. Under the terms of this proposal the market director was to concentrate upon organizing California's farmers into cooperative marketing associations. He was also to furnish advice on eastern market conditions and foster standardization movements. The measure said little about the state's consumers and contained no provision for the establishment of public markets. With this proposition Weinstock hoped to obtain legal sanction for shifting his attention from the state's consumers to the farmers.[72]

Luce's measure brought to the surface the growing unrest with Weinstock's policies. The failure of the market director to abide by the terms of his appointment, combined with his efforts to win sanctions for his change in policy, caused the pot of consumer discontent to boil over. The ensuing controversy pitted consumer bodies against farm organizations and raised fundamental questions about the role of the state government in the development of California's economy.

Groups of consumers quickly organized to spearhead an attack on the state market director. By the end of 1916, the residents of California's larger cities, hurt by the spiraling cost of food, had come to view the market director as their oppressor. Consumers in Berkeley formed a High Cost of Living Committee, which denounced Weinstock for ''organizing combines all over the state and boosting prices beyond reason'' and called for the defeat of Luce's bill.[73] Women's clubs in Southern California united as the Los Angeles Housewives' League. The league condemned the new market commission act and asked Governor Johnson to impose an embargo on all food exports from California as a way to lower prices within the state.[74] Municipal authorities supported these organizations. The Los Angeles city council demanded Weinstock's removal from office and urged Governor Johnson to set up a public market in their city.[75] The San Bernardino board of supervisors tried to drive speculators out of business by assessing food in storage at its full market value for tax purposes.[76] When an investigation revealed that 300,000 sacks of potatoes were being held off the market in San Francisco, that city's board of supervisors also considered raising taxes on warehoused foodstuffs. One supervisor complained that Weinstock had done nothing to help ''the consuming public,'' and called for the defeat of Luce's bill.[77]

Weinstock mounted a spirited defense of his work and labored for the passage of Luce's bill. Weinstock claimed that the 1915 measure had not actually required him to set up state-run markets; this provision, he incorrectly asserted, was only discretionary. At any rate, Weinstock continued, by organizing marketing associations he had lowered distribution costs and assured consumers of a steady food supply. He attributed price increases to the operations of speculators not yet driven out of business, the still imperfect system of distribution for agricultural products, inefficiency in home management, and shortages caused by the First World War.[78] California's farmers rallied to support Weinstock and backed Luce's measure. Local granges passed resolutions endorsing the proposed market commission, and the officers of cooperatives handling crops ranging from pigs to peaches spoke out on its behalf. The managers of the California Fruit Growers Exchange, the California Fruit Distributors, and more specialized marketing associations like the Walnut Growers Exchange journeyed to Sacramento to argue for the proposal.[79]

Luce's bill triggered a bitter legislative contest. Senators William Brown and J. W. Ballard of Los Angeles offered stiff opposition to the measure. Brown, who had pushed the 1915 act through the senate, hammered at Weinstock for misusing his power to establish "food trusts inimical to consumers." He demanded the removal of Weinstock from office and called for a return to the original intentions of the commission market act.[80] Ballard complained that the "commission cannot operate for the producer without hitting the consumer" and joined Brown in trying to block Luce's proposal.[81] Their efforts proved ineffective. After a prolonged struggle in committee and lengthy floor debates the market commission act won approval in the assembly by a margin of fifty-eight to eighteen and in the senate by twenty-seven to ten. As would be expected, most of the negative votes came from representatives of California's larger urban centers.[82]

Flushed with success, Weinstock moved quickly to implement the terms of the new law. He stepped up his efforts to establish cooperative marketing associations and again tried to link all of the state's farmers together in a single marketing organization. The provisions of the 1917 act relieved Weinstock of any obligation to establish public markets, and he ignored the state's consumers. As before he claimed that the best interest of consumers lay in assuring that agriculturalists remain in business and that this end could best be achieved by ensuring them of reasonable profits.[83]

As wartime shortages accentuated the problem of high prices in California, consumers renewed their quest to lower the cost of food. San Franciscans tried to establish a chain of privately operated markets at which agricultural produce would be sold to the public at cost. Although backed by such well-known and diverse figures as Rudolph Spreckles, the sugar king, John Neylan, the former chairman of California's board of control,

Daniel Murphy and Paul Scharrenburg, the president and secretary of the State Federation of Labor, Marion Delaney, the president of the Civic League of Women's Clubs, and Russella Ward of the San Francisco Federation of Women's Clubs, the scheme collapsed when its proponents failed to raise the required capital.[84] Across the bay former members of the High Cost of Living Committee headed new organizations in Oakland, Alameda, and Berkeley that called for Weinstock's removal from office and the regulation of food prices by federal or municipal authorities.[85]

Most galling to many urbanites was Weinstock's handling of the fish problem. In 1917, consumer bodies and the market director had worked together, in a rare show of fellowship, to secure passage of a law placing fish prices under Weinstock's control. By the terms of this act the market director daily set the wholesale and retail prices of all types of fish sold in the state. When the prices failed to drop as quickly as many had hoped, consumer groups charged Weinstock with being in the pay of a "fish trust," and by early 1918 the inhabitants of several cities were asking for the fitting out of municipally owned fishing fleets.[86]

City officials again backed the demands of consumers. The San Francisco board of supervisors started an investigation into the cost of food.[87] Oakland opened a city market that sold produce at cost and contemplated operating a municipally owned fishing fleet to supply it with food.[88] A plan to convert Lake Merritt, a nearby salt-water estuary, into a huge striped bass fishery from which citizens would be permitted to net their dinners free of charge also received serious consideration.[89] Los Angeles convened a grand jury to look into the cause of high food prices, and the Los Angeles district attorney examined the possibility of bringing antitrust proceedings against the Poultry Producers of Southern California, a cooperative marketing association set up with Weinstock's aid. However, other law suits, in which the market director appeared on behalf of the farmers, upheld the legality of cooperative marketing, and the district attorney dropped his charges.[90]

The rising chorus of protest found expression in the 1919 legislature. Senator Brown sponsored a measure revamping the duties of the state market director. Aimed at reducing food prices, it required the market director to establish state-run markets throughout California and forbade him from helping farmers form marketing associations.[91] In the same session Senator William Scott of San Francisco introduced a measure designed to lower the cost of fish. His bill transferred the market director's price-fixing authority to the head of the state fish and game commission and, in addition, empowered the commission to establish state-operated markets to sell fish directly to consumers.[92]

Familiar lines of cleavage appeared during the struggle over Senator Brown's proposal. Once again farmers backed Weinstock's work. Cooperatives selling milk, almonds, apples, eggs, peaches, raisins, pears, honey, alfalfa, and oranges denounced Brown's measure. By mid-February the Fresno *Republican* could accurately report that "the growers and producers of the state and especially of the San Joaquin Valley" had formed a "powerful offensive against the attempt to legislate the state market director out of office."[93] Just as predictably, groups of consumers and municipal authorities supplied Brown with the bulk of his support. Councilmen in Oakland and Berkeley passed resolutions favoring Brown's proposal, and Richmond's city attorney traveled to Sacramento to testify on its behalf. City officials, representatives of merchant bodies, and consumer advocates in the San Francisco area banded together as the Bay Cities Food and Fish Commission, which criticized Weinstock for having permitted an increase in food prices and sent representatives to lobby for Brown's act in the state capital.[94] In Southern California the Los Angeles Federation of Women's Clubs and municipal authorities came out in favor of Brown's proposition.[95]

Yet, consumers gained little from the legislature. As they had two years before, solons from California's agricultural areas outgunned those representing urban centers. The senate buried Brown's measure by the margin of twenty-four to nine, and a similar bill failed in the assembly, though by only four votes.[96]

Senator Scott's fish bill also became the subject of intense debate. Consumer groups throughout California backed the measure. More surprisingly, so did the state's fishermen. In a series of dramatic moves protesting Weinstock's pricing policies fishermen from San Diego to San Francisco went on strike.[97] They refused to take their boats out to sea until, as one of their spokesmen explained, prices were again "regulated by supply and demand" rather than by the whims of government officials.[98] Willing to use any method available to attack Weinstock, the fishermen gave their backing to Scott's proposal. The reason became apparent when the bill emerged from committee. In its amended form Scott's proposal authorized the establishment of a series of state operated fish markets but did not provide for price-fixing by any state official. Favored by the fishermen as a means of securing higher wholesale prices for their catches and by consumer groups as promising lower retail prices, the proposition met opposition only from the disorganized fish dealers and sailed through the legislature with few dissenting votes. However, Weinstock viewed the bill as an erosion of his authority and worked against it from its inception. When it passed the legislature despite his efforts, Weinstock convinced Governor William Stephens to kill it with a pocket veto.[99]

Far from abating, the attacks on Weinstock's action as market director intensified after the legislature adjourned. Consumer organizations never relented in their assaults. The San Francisco Bay Area's Mother and Parent Teachers Association condemned Weinstock for not clamping down on the soaring price of milk and called for his dismissal from office.[100] In Oakland and Berkeley consumers urged President Woodrow Wilson to intervene on their behalf and asked Governor Stephens to call a special session of the legislature to consider a new state market act.[101] In Southern California women's clubs endorsed Senator Brown's request for a special legislative session and began circulating petitions demanding that Weinstock be replaced by someone else as market director.[102] Municipal authorities also kept the pressure on Weinstock. The climax came in November, 1919, when mayors from 145 West Coast cities met in Sacramento to discuss ways to lower food prices. Dominated by the California delegation, this conference considered boycotting all products sold by cooperative marketing associations. Only Weinstock's timely intervention on behalf of the farmers thwarted this move. The convention did, however, pass resolutions proclaiming milk a public utility subject to governmental regulation and urging Governor Stephens to summon the California legislature into session to devise measures that would reduce the cost of living.[103]

Stephens rejected these entreaties. Acting upon the market director's advice, he refused to convene the legislature. When the mayors of Oakland and Los Angeles, rebuffed by this ploy, focused their energies upon a petition drive against Weinstock, the governor announced that under no conditions would he remove him from office. Political considerations influenced these decisions. As Hiram Johnson's political heir, Stephens hoped to avoid offending Weinstock who was one of Northern California's strongest Progressives. Then too, he recognized that the farm vote (and the state's farmers remained staunch supporters of the market director) was still potent in California.[104]

The consumer's revolt against high food prices came to a natural end. After a three-week-long illness that left his health seriously impaired, Weinstock retired from office in January, 1920. Governor Stephens, desiring broad-based support for his plans to reorganize the state government, disregarded Weinstock's advice that the manager of a cooperative marketing association succeed him as market director.[105] He chose a nonentity, Gilbert Daniels, the superintendent of the state motor vehicles department. Trying to conciliate both farmers and consumers, Daniels interpreted the powers of his office narrowly, and took care to offend no one.[106] He did not even publish an annual report in 1921. Daniels's timidity must have been a welcome change to California's consumers and probably did much to damp the fires of discontent. More important, however, was the drop in food prices. After rising steadily for five years, they fell dramatically throughout California, and by 1921 the cost of living no longer received attention from the state legislature.[107]

The struggle between consumers and farmers in California demonstrates the difficulty in viewing contests involving business legislation in terms of party politics. In fact, rifts cut across party lines. In the conflict between farmers and consumers geographic divisions proved crucial, with the legislators from the cities backing bills favored by consumers while those from agricultural areas supported measures desired by farmers. Even the leadership among Progressives split on these issues. Whereas Weinstock and Governor Johnson sided with the agriculturalists, other progressives from urban centers, especially Los Angeles and San Francisco, responded to the wishes of their constituencies, the consumers. As was often the case in California politics, party labels proved irrelevant in explaining the behavior of politicians. In particular, the fight over food prices raises the question of the validity of analyzing California politics in terms of "reform" and "reaction," for in no sense can the many pieces of legislation offered during the contest between farmers and consumers be considered "progressive" or "reactionary."[108]

The contest also raised questions, never completely resolved, about the role of the state government in California's economy. Most importantly, the conflict revealed, as would contests over other pieces of business legislation, that it was often impossible to benefit one segment of California's population without injuring another. The result was a jockeying for power by organized interest groups. As the most highly organized and first group on the scene, the agriculturalists won the initial victories, but they never achieved total hegemony over the state legislature. As consumers became increasingly organized, they won fuller consideration for their demands in Sacramento. Though originally at a disadvantage in terms of organization, consumers had several long-run advantages over agriculturalists. By 1915, California had become a highly urbanized state in which consumers of farm products clearly predominated over farmers in terms of numbers. Moreover, consumers succeeded, while farmers did not, in appealing beyond the bounds of narrow self-interest to win support for their cause. More than just high prices for food was at stake, consumer advocates claimed. The very health of the state's population became an issue; the San Francisco Bay Area's Mothers and Parent Teachers Association, for instance, accused the "milk trust" of stunting the growth of babies by hiking the price of milk. Possessing these long-term advantages, consumer organizations were eventually able to stop Weinstock's efforts to organize agricultural cooperatives and, had not the food issue died a natural death, would probably have won still further legislative victories.

3

The Oil Industry

California's oil men, like the state's fruit growers, encountered a bewildering set of difficulties thrust upon them by the rapid development of their industry. The opening of new fields in quick succession created a surplus production of crude oil in the early twentieth century, and the question of how to profitably dispose of their excess crude became the overriding concern of California oil men. The control of pipelines was intimately related to the problem of overproduction. Small-scale producers, who lacked the capital to construct their own networks, sought guarantees that they would be able to ship their crude through the lines of the state's larger concerns. Only with such assurances could they drill for oil without fear of bringing to the surface more than they could market. Finally, in addition to their economic problems, Californians had to adapt their technology to the scientific challenges met in exploration, drilling, and refining.

Oil men in other parts of the nation dealt with problems similar to those hindering Californians, but California's geographic isolation and the unusual chemical properties of California's crude accentuated the difficulties California producers faced. Because no pipelines connected California with the rest of the United States until the 1950s, the state developed as a separate oil province. California petroleum found few markets beyond the West Coast, and only rarely did Californians import oil from other regions.[1] The inability of Californians to send their petroleum east or secure out-of-state supplies widened any local disparity between the production and consumption of crude on the Pacific Slope.[2] The lack of options to which they could put their petroleum redoubled the vulnerability of Californians to the dangers of overproduction. The high viscosity of California oil further increased the handicaps under which operators labored.[3] As late as 1909, nearly two-thirds of the state's output was under 19°B., and as a result Californians refined a much lower percentage of their crude than did oil men in other areas.[4] The high sulphur content of their crude caused difficulties in refining not encountered in refining oil from many of the nation's oil fields. Combined with problems in discovery and drilling, the impurities in their crude led Californians to rely heavily upon scientific knowledge to rationalize their operations. By 1920, California possessed the most technologically advanced oil plants in the United States.[5]

Production Controls

Sustained large-scale production of petroleum began in California in the late 1890s, and a chronic imbalance between production and consumption characterized the California oil industry in succeeding years. In rapid order drillers brought in new fields in the upper San Joaquin Valley—the Coalinga, McKittrick, and Kern River. These discoveries boosted production from under 2 million barrels in 1897 to almost 30 million seven years later.[6] This increase far outran California's consumption needs, and the price received at the well for crude fell by over two-thirds.[7] As early as 1901, those in the petroleum business were reporting that ''the problem of securing a market'' was ''agitating the mind of the oil producer.''[8] Within three years operators had capped 424 wells and were holding 10 million barrels of oil off the market in tanks and open earthen sumps.[9]

However, Californians soon succeeded in developing new markets for their crude, and between 1906 and 1908 the demand for their oil outran supplies. On the West Coast, a coal-poor region with long distances and high transportation costs, it proved economically feasible to substitute crude petroleum for coal as a fuel, and Californians led the nation in this endeavor. In the first decade of the twentieth century railroads, public utilities, and some factories switched from coal to petroleum. By 1912, the Southern Pacific Railroad alone was taking 13 percent of California's annual output of petroleum.[10] As consumption exceeded supply, the price of crude rose, though not to the pre-1900 level, and the stocks of petroleum in storage dropped.[11]

New gushers brought in after 1909 shattered the hopes of oil men for continued prosperity. Production again outstripped consumption, and prices fell considerably.[12] In September, 1912, the Standard Oil Company of California, with 10 million barrels of crude in storage, ceased buying any crude of less than 19°B. This action led many smaller operators, whose only access to market was through the Standard's pipelines, to shut down, for the company refused to ship the oil of independents through its pipelines. By the end of 1912, 1,147 of California's 5,626 wells had been temporarily capped, and the state's closed-in production amounted to 25,000 barrels per day.[13] Most oil men suffered during the next three years. In spite of increased well closures, consumption caught up with production only in 1915.[14] Prices rose little, and many producers operated at a loss. Most of the smaller and some of the larger companies failed to cover their costs in 1914 and 1915, even after prices had recovered from the nadir to which they sank in 1912 and 1913. Only the outbreak of war, resulting first in larger exports abroad and then in increased domestic demands, brought higher prices to California's hard-pressed producers.[15]

The efforts of oil men to deal with the imbalance between the production and consumption of crude molded the structures of their individual companies. In times of excess production they first formed combinations, pools, and horizontally integrated companies to store and market their crude. When none of these attempts significantly altered the prices they received, the operators recognized that substantial profits in the oil business could be realized only in the carriage and refining of crude and the marketing of kerosene and gasoline. In their quest for security and profits, some then took the additional step from horizontal to vertical integration. By 1915, several of the loosely organized combinations had evolved into tightly structured firms that owned refineries and pipelines in addition to oil lands. Vertical integration less frequently occurred in the reverse manner. When crude was in limited supply, firms that had previously been involved only in transportation and refining entered into production as well. While profiting greatly from the overproduction of crude during much of the early twentieth century, those engaged in refining felt the pinch of crude shortages between 1905 and 1910 and in the years after 1915. To assure themselves of steady and ample supplies, they purchased and developed their own oil lands and pipelines.

San Joaquin Valley oil men led the early movements for combination. The larger producers in the Kern River and McKittrick fields formed the Associated Oil Company in 1901. Those joining the new corporation turned over their land and sales contracts in return for its stocks and bonds. Within two years the Associated had 600,000 barrels of crude in storage and was trying to make contracts at prices greater than those other companies received.[16] Even as the Associated began marketing crude, oil producers in other regions were setting up similar organizations. In 1904, the Pacific Coast Oil Company (a subsidiary of Standard Oil), with more petroleum in storage than it could refine, slashed its purchase price for crude and then stopped buying it altogether. To find a new market for their oil, operators in the Kern River field established the Independent Oil Producers Agency.[17] The agency leased the lands of its members and, in turn, licensed each member to develop its own properties. Those belonging to the association empowered its board of directors to dispose of all their crude for a five-year period. In 1907, producers in the Coalinga field followed suit with an organization modeled on the Kern River agency.[18]

None of these bodies achieved much success, for operators in some districts remained outside their ranks. Without control over all of California's fields they could neither curtail the state's burgeoning output of crude nor increase the prices obtained for it. Moreover, the agencies possessed no pipelines, refineries, or systems of distribution for gasoline and kerosene. They had to sell their crude to those few companies that specialized in these services, and the efforts of firms engaged in refining and selling finished products to keep the price paid for crude as low as possible added to the difficulties of the operators in the field.[19]

California producers learned from their early experiences and in later years moved in the direction of vertical integration, particularly when production again exceeded consumption after 1909. The Associated Oil Company took the first steps. In 1905, the firm bought a pipeline running from the Coalinga field to Monterey Bay, and three years later finished construction of a line from the Kern River district to San Francisco Bay. The Southern Pacific Railroad acquired control of the Associated in 1909, and from that point on the company's main function was to supply the railroad with fuel for its locomotives. However, as early as 1906, the Associated possessed refineries, and, since its lands produced more oil than the Southern Pacific could use, the firm marketed refined goods up and down the West Coast.[20]

Producers throughout California followed this example. In 1910, the Independent Oil Producers Agency and the Coalinga Oil Producers Agency merged, adopting the title of the first body. The new organization concluded long-term contracts to dispose of its members' crude through the Union Oil and Associated Oil companies. Oil men expected these agreements to stabilize prices and place the petroleum business "upon a dependable basis."[21] The agency also built extensive storage reservoirs in which to hold oil off the market in times of excess supply and tried to restrict the production of crude among its members.[22] The Independent Oil Producers Agency soon became, however, more than a marketing organization. In 1910 and 1911, it cooperated with the Union Oil Company in constructing a high-capacity pipeline from the San Joaquin fields to tidewater at Port Harford, and several years later it entered the refining business. In taking this course of action the agency adopted a restrictive membership policy and sought profits for its stockholder-members alone.[23] Still other producers in the Midway-Sunset, Lost Hills, Santa Maria, and Coalinga fields formed the General Petroleum Company in 1912. Though established first simply as a selling agency, within a few years the firm owned an extensive pipeline network and large-scale refineries. Conducting a wholesale business, it marketed its products throughout the Pacific Coast and much of the Southwest.[24]

Oil companies also achieved vertical integration through backward linkages. Having first entered the retail end of the oil industry, they later developed their own oil lands to escape fluctuations in the supply and prices of crude. The Standard Oil Company broke into the California market as a seller of kerosene and, despite its purchase of the Pacific Coast Oil Company in 1900, continued to rely upon others for the bulk of its crude during the opening years of the twentieth century. As late as 1904, its California subsidiaries produced only 120,000 barrels of crude petroleum. Its vulnerability to supply shortages led the Standard into the production of crude. Between 1906 and 1910, the company built up a producing department that searched for oil in untapped areas. Largely by drilling on its own lands the Standard climbed to first place among California oil producers by 1919.[25] The Shell Company of California (a subsidiary of the Royal Dutch Petroleum Company) evolved in a similar manner. Beginning as an importer of gasoline from Indonesia for California's retail trade, the Shell Company soon developed local sources of crude and refined goods. To avoid paying independent crude operators high prices and to assure itself of adequate supplies, the firm purchased producing companies in the Coalinga region that it then linked by pipeline to refineries on San Francisco Bay.[26]

Variations in California's crude output influenced the expansion of the Union Oil Company the least of any firm, but uncertainties affected even its growth. From its formation in 1890 Union Oil owned oil lands, pipelines, and refineries. However, in the face of the overproduction of crude in the early twentieth century, company officers placed growing emphasis on refined goods. In 1906, Union Oil began shifting from marketing fuel oil and asphalt to selling kerosene and gasoline, and these efforts were accelerated in later years.[27]

By the outbreak of the First World War five or six vertically integrated companies dominated the oil business in California. No single firm obtained a monopoly position in any phase of California's oil industry. Yet, this situation did not insure competition, for the companies reached agreements between themselves on prices and market territories. Oil men jointly drew up arrangements to end rate wars and circumscribe competition in both the fuel-oil and refined-products markets. The price of fuel oil varied with the output of crude, but, within limits set by fluctuations in production, most firms followed Standard Oil's lead in fixing prices. An investigator for the Federal Trade Commission reported that, as a result, prices in West Coast cities were "changed either simultaneously, or almost so, by the large marketing companies."[28] Firms retailing gasoline and kerosene entered into more elaborate agreements. Following a three-year price war, a group of small refiners in Los Angeles formed the Independent Petroleum Marketers Association in 1915, and the General Petroleum, Union Oil, and Associated Oil companies soon became members. Only the Shell and Standard Oil companies remained outside its ranks. The association set prices for refined products on the Pacific Coast, standardized customer classifications, and established market territories.[29]

Neither vertical integration nor agreements between firms could, however, completely alleviate the pressure of overproduction. Most small operators lacked the resources needed to integrate their firms, and the decision of the Independent Oil Producers Agency to restrict its membership deprived many of outlets for their crude. Even those belonging to the agency failed to escape the hardships resulting from the overproduction of crude, for the agency never developed sufficient refining facilities and had to rely upon more fully integrated firms to absorb some of the output of its members. Nor did pacts between companies solve the problems of the oil men. Some firms always violated the agreements, and price wars continued despite the best efforts to reach agreements.

Unable to restrict the production of oil by private agreements, independent oil men turned to the state legislature for help. They sought the passage of laws limiting the output of crude in California. They hoped that, as demand caught up with supply, the prices they received for their crude would rise. Geologists, state officials, and others concerned with the conservation of natural resources joined the oil men in pressing for legislation. They feared that the soaring production would quickly deplete California's oil reserves and pointed out that in times of excess supply, drillers would profit by leaving the oil underground until consumption balanced production.

Legislative action in California took place against the background of widespread concern about the nation's oil reserves. Geologists in the service of the federal government predicted that at the present rate of exploitation the reserves would be expended within twenty years. To a nation just coming to recognize that her natural wealth might not be inexhaustible, these warnings demanded remedial steps. Oil men in other sections of the United States faced the same problems as Californians, overproduction and low prices, and also called for limitations on the output of crude. When overproduction threatened the profits of Oklahoma natural gas men in 1913, they secured passage for a bill limiting the output from major pools. Oklahoma crude-oil producers won approval for a similar measure two years later. Texas oil men also invoked the aid of the state to help them out of their difficulties. In 1915, they pushed a bill through their legislature empowering the state corporation commission to close down any industry when there was danger of waste through overproduction.[30]

Petroleum engineers and state officials began the campaign to conserve California's oil. As early as 1912, geologists attached to the state mineralogist's office pointed out that the state's oil pools were limited in volume and, once depleted, could not be replenished.[31] After pondering a report prepared by three leading independent geologists in the same year, members of the Commonwealth Club of California urged officers of the state's oil companies to reduce their output of crude.[32] In 1913, a special commission appointed by Governor Hiram Johnson to study California's natural resources labeled many of the practices of the state's oil producers as wasteful and inefficient, and a year later the state mineralogist began issuing monthly bulletins on production and market conditions in an attempt to discourage further drilling.[33] As output continued to soar, the state mineralogist condemned California oil men in late 1914 for their "extravagence and wastefulness."[34]

Mark Requa, an independent petroleum engineer who became the head of the Oil Division of the Fuel Administration during the First World War, offered the most far-reaching analysis of the relation between overproduction and conservation. In a speech delivered before the American Institute of Mining and Metallurgical Engineers in 1912, he presented the arguments emphasized by the proponents of conservation. Requa declared that crude should be produced only when its sale price at the well equaled or exceeded the cost of bringing it to the surface plus a normal profit. He denounced the excess storage of oil above ground as both technologically inefficient (because of losses caused by evaporation and fires) and economically unsound (since large amounts of petroleum in storage depressed prevailing crude prices). Like most Californians, Requa defined conservation as the economic and efficient use of natural resources and judged waste in terms of private profits and losses.[35]

Long-standing demands for state legislation came to a head in 1915. As early as 1911, the legislators enacted a measure prohibiting the wastage of natural gas.[36] A year later some of the smaller Los Angeles oil men formed the Oil Conservation Association and drafted a bill providing for state regulation of petroleum production.[37] Nothing came of this proposal at that time, but, as excess supplies of crude continued to rise, oil men renewed their interest in legislation. By the winter of 1914–15, they were discussing measures for setting minimum prices for crude, creating a commission to regulate the drilling of new wells, and establishing ceilings on the profits of pipeline owners.[38] Finally, in April, 1915, Senator William J. Carr of Los Angeles introduced a bill in Sacramento designed to end the overproduction of crude. Similar to the Texas law enacted earlier in the same year, the measure defined waste as the production or storage of oil in excess of current consumption needs and empowered the state railroad commission to prevent such wastage.[39] In public hearings on his bill Carr spoke of it both as a way to stop evaporation losses suffered by supplies of crude held in storage and as a tool to abolish excess production.[40]

Senator Carr's measure split the ranks of the state's oil men. The small independent producers who sold their output of crude without refining it favored the bill. Many of them were operating at a loss and would have accepted any proposition that promised to boost the price of crude. As one noted, they were being "drowned in their own output." The bill's strongest support came from the Independent Oil Producers Agency whose president traveled to the state capital to lobby for its passage. Firms engaged in the finished products end of the petroleum business opposed the measure. Believing that its enactment would raise crude oil prices, they feared the measure might cut into their profits. Representatives of the Shell Company, which at this time depended upon other producers for much of its crude, denounced Carr's bill as "discriminatory and unjust" and threatened that, if it passed, their corporation would look elsewhere for investment opportunities. Even California's most highly integrated firms, the Standard and Union oil companies, still purchased substantial quantities of their crude from independent producers and probably worked against the proposal.[41]

Despite a favorable report from the committee on oil industries, Carr's measure failed in the senate by a vote of twelve to twenty-one. The divisions separating the different groups of oil men damaged its chances for success. Able to obtain support only from the small producers, Senator Carr found it difficult to convince his colleagues that his proposition was the best way to protect the state's oil resources, particularly since some of the companies opposing his bill had instituted conservation practices on their own several years before. Questions concerning the bill's constitutionality, especially the wide powers given the railroad commission, also detracted from its appeal. Finally, in mid-1915, the consumption of oil began catching up with production, and this unexpected occurrence undercut the arguments of those backing Carr's proposal. Within a few years wartime demands boosted the price of crude, and overproduction ceased to be an issue in state politics until the discovery of new fields again created surplus crude supplies in the mid-1920s.[42]

State Regulation of Pipelines

Like the fields discovered in Texas and Oklahoma, most of California's oil pools were far from centers of petroleum consumption, and the oil men had to devise a cheap and efficient way to ship their output to market. In the early days strings of tank wagons drawn by as many as forty braying mules hauled crude from wells in the San Joaquin Valley to the nearest railroads.[43] This method of transportation proved extremely costly and disappeared when the Southern Pacific and Santa Fe railroads completed spurs into the oil districts in the opening years of the twentieth century. Yet, railroad rates remained high even after the introduction of tank cars, and service was at times unreliable.[44] Shipment by ocean-going tankers and barges was more economical, and Californians pioneered in this type of transportation. However, even where such shipments were feasible, oil men had to first get their output to tidewater.[45] Pipelines provided the solution to the difficulties Californians faced, and, by 1920, the state's oil companies had blanketed California with five major systems of gathering and trunk lines.[46]

Oil producers found access to pipelines essential, for the costs of transportation by pipeline were far below those by rail, but they met numerous obstacles in shipping their output to market by this mode of conveyance.[47] Few operators possessed the capital needed to build their own lines. The Standard Oil Company's pipeline from the San Joaquin fields to its refinery at Richmond on San Francisco Bay required an expenditure of over $3,000,000, a sum few other firms could have raised.[48] Nor could the smaller producers rely upon competition among the companies owning pipelines to provide outlets for their crude. Many had connections with only one pipeline system. Before 1908, only the Standard Oil's lines served the Kern River, McKittrick, and Midway fields. Even after other firms constructed pipeline systems, lease arrangements, purchase options, price agreements, and interlocking directorships limited competition among the pipeline companies.[49] California's excess production of crude heightened these problems. Pipeline companies favored oil from their own wells in scheduling shipments when their lines were being utilized at full capacity. Moreover, some refused to transport any petroleum except their own. This policy could bar their facilities to independent producers, for in periods of excess production the pipeline companies often ceased purchasing any crude from outside sources.

Crude producers in other regions facing similar problems turned to their state legislatures and Congress for aid. From the 1870s on, oil men in the Appalachian fields sought laws making pipelines common carriers, and, as new fields opened, operators in them also pressed for regulatory legislation. The crude operators frequently blamed the pipeline owners for the low prices they obtained and worked for the common-carrier legislation as one way to increase their profits. Largely as a result of their agitation, Pennsylvania, New York, West Virginia, Kansas, and Ohio had, by 1906, declared pipelines common carriers. In 1905, the federal government also entered the picture. At the request of crude producers the Bureau of

Corporations investigated the oil industry, and a year later a section of the Hepburn Act empowered the Interstate Commerce Commission to regulate pipelines that crossed state boundaries.[50]

Californians began their campaign for state control in 1905. Senator E. J. Emmons of Kern County, one of the state's major oil regions, introduced a bill in the legislative session of that year proclaiming pipelines common carriers. Under its terms the state railroad commission was to supervise rates and conditions of service. Presenting his proposal at the end of five years of excess crude production, Emmons asserted that "under the present conditions the small producers" had to make "contracts with the Standard Oil for the sale of their oil at ridiculously low prices or else close down their wells." Only if pipelines were defined as common carriers could, Emmons claimed, firms like the Standard "be made to take the commodity offered for transportation from any person offering it." In the assembly J. R. Dorsey, also of Kern County, presented an identical bill, and its supporters employed similar arguments in its favor.[51] Opposition to these measures came mainly from the Standard Oil's subsidiary, the Pacific Coast Oil Company. B. C. Carroll, the firm's vice-president, appeared in Sacramento to fight the advocates of regulation. Like the opponents of regulation in other states, he argued that, because the pipelines had been built at private expense, they were private property not subject to state supervision. Carroll casually brushed aside claims that, since the legislature had granted pipeline companies the power of eminent domain and because they crossed public highways, pipelines could be regulated by the state.[52]

The opposition of the pipeline companies was persistent and effective, and the bills introduced by Emmons and Dorsey died without coming to a vote. The crude producers never mounted a well-organized drive on behalf of the measures. The subject was so new (the first long-distance line had been completed in California only two years before) that they lacked experience and knowledge in dealing with it. Moreover, confusion existed as to whether overproduction or transportation difficulties were hurting the small operators. Even many producers conceded that the surplus of crude rather than monopolistic control of pipelines was responsible for the low prices of their output, and this admission undercut the arguments of those backing Emmons and Dorsey.[53]

State regulation of pipelines again became a burning issue when crude production outstripped consumption in the years after 1909. The decision of Standard Oil, in September, 1912, to restrict its purchases of crude acted as a catalyst for those desiring legislation. Since the Standard refused to ship any petroleum other than its own, this move threatened the livelihood of many of the state's operators. Lacking adequate alternate lines, a large number capped their wells and organized to press for relief by political means. Led by Timothy Spellacy, a shut-down producer who headed the Mascot and Cresceus oil companies, they again sought the regulation of pipelines as common carriers.[54]

Turning first to the national government, the operators worked for supervision by the Interstate Commerce Commission. Although recognizing that none of California's pipelines crossed state boundaries, they pointed out that nearly all passed over public domain without proper authorization and urged federal officials to force a common carrier status upon them. Representatives of the Standard Oil Company moved to prevent such an eventuality by seeking an extension of an act of Congress that had given private pipelines rights-of-way through federal lands in Arkansas. In the maneuvering that followed issues became clouded and lost in committee hearings. The Standard failed to win approval for its measure, but the Interstate Commerce Commission declined to accept supervision of California's pipelines.[55]

Thwarted in Washington, the crude producers went to Sacramento. In 1913, Senator L. R. Hewitt of Los Angeles introduced a bill declaring oil pipelines common carriers under the jurisdiction of the state railroad commission. The producers strongly backed this measure and employed Francis Heney, an attorney who had gained renown for his prosecution of San Francisco's corrupt boss Abe Ruef, as their lobbyist. They asserted that since the Standard had stopped buying their crude, no sufficient outlets were available to get their crude to market. Competition among pipeline companies was, they argued, more apparent than real, for lease agreements, purchase options, and location differences had created a community of interest among pipeline owners. Not even the Independent Oil Producers Agency that, in conjunction with the Union Oil Company, possessed a line from the San Joaquin fields to Port Harford protected their interests. Spellacy testified that its restrictive membership policy and rigid price arrangements with the Union Oil Company had ended its usefulness to most independent producers. The operators had no qualms about the state's power to regulate pipelines. Since most pipelines had exercised the right of eminent domain and because all crossed public roads, the lines fell, they believed, within a realm of state supervision.[56]

Pipeline owners offered sharp resistance to Hewitt's bill. Though the officers of the Standard Oil Company avoided the fray because they felt any actions they took would be counterproductive, the executives of most pipeline companies showed less reticence. Representatives of all of the state's other major pipeline companies, including the president of the Independent Oil Producers Agency, testified against the common carrier measure. Some raised technical objections, that oil of varying degrees of gravity could not be transported in the same lines. Others asserted that the regulation of prices by the state would, in effect, deprive them of their property rights without due process of law and would, therefore, violate the fourteenth amendment to the United States Constitution. From these defensive positions the officers of pipeline corporations moved to the offensive. Far from assuring the existence of competition, a common carrier law would, they claimed, stifle it. Hewitt's proposal would fill up the pipelines of Standard's competitors with low-gravity oil, useless for refining and would, they stated, prevent successful competition in gasoline and kerosene.[57]

Despite the attacks by pipeline owners, Hewitt's bill became law. It declared oil pipelines common carriers whose rates and conditions of service were to be set by the state railroad commission. Two other measures gave the act clout. One required pipelines over thirty-five miles long that were not operated as common carriers to pay a prohibitive tax of fifty cents per barrel on oil transported across public highways. The other forbade any relations between railroads and piepline companies in restraint of trade.

Several reasons explain why legislation that failed in 1905 passed eight years later. The enactment of a law providing for state regulation of railroads and public utilities in 1911 helped pave the way for control of pipelines. Then, too, by 1913, government supervision of pipelines was more common. Oklahoma declared pipelines common carriers in 1909, and the Mann-Elkins Act strengthened federal control over interstate pipelines a year later. Most importantly, the refusal of the Standard Oil Company to purchase or transport the crude of independents clarified for many a hitherto confused question. The Standard's action focused attention on one aspect of the complex problem of the regulation of the production and transportation of petroleum. Gone were the doubts of those working for common carrier legislation in earlier years. By 1913, nearly all legislators believed that monopoly control rather than overproduction was the main problem. Finally, the crude producers succeeded in presenting their measure as one that would aid not just themselves, but the general public at large. Consumers, in particular, the crude operators averred, would benefit from decreases in the cost of oil carriage. As Spellacy often argued, the common carrier measure would prove "an effective check to monopoly" and "a wise and just measure for the good of producers and consumers."[58]

The crude oil producers realized that the passage of common carrier laws did not insure their enforcement. In the summer of 1913 the larger San Joaquin operators and some of the industrial consumers of fuel oil in the Los Angeles area organized the Oil Producers and Consumers League to safeguard their interests. The association planned to establish an information bureau that would report runs of petroleum by the pipeline companies and all orders that might be used to sidetrack the shipments of the smaller producers. Yet, only the Standard Oil Company agreed to operate its pipelines as common carriers, and the rates it charged, combined with the conditions it set for the use of its lines (one requirement was that only lots of 100,000 barrels or more would be handled), left the small producer little better off than before. The other firms waited to see how the railroad commission would administer the common carrier laws and refused to transport any crude but their own.[59]

After lengthy hearings and investigations the railroad commission announced its policy for the future in late 1914. Its members found that the state's leading pipeline companies had "secured the control and monopoly of the transportation of crude oil, petroleum and the products thereof from the San Joaquin Valley oil fields." To change this situation the commissioners ordered those firms to employ their lines as public carriers. However, the commission felt that the coastal oil districts presented substantially different conditions. Here many short lines connected the fields with the tidewater, and, because the commissioners believed real competition existed, they allowed these carriers to continue business as private concerns.[60]

Even before the railroad commission announced its findings the pipeline companies took legal actions to negate the common carrier laws. In 1913, the Associated Oil Company secured an injunction temporarily enjoining the railroad commission from enforcing the acts. Four years later the California Supreme Court, accepting the firm's claim that, since it shipped only oil produced on its own lands, it should be permitted to do business as a private carrier, ruled in favor of the Associated. In 1919, Standard Oil used a stockholder's suit against the company to have the federal courts strike down as unconstitutional the law that levied a fee on oil shipped across public highways in pipelines not operated as common carriers.

Thus, by 1920, legal decisions had dismantled most of the common carrier legislation enacted seven years before. However, with the relative decline of the San Joaquin oil districts and the opening of new fields closer to tidewater after the First World War, the topic of pipeline regulation receded in importance.[61]

Science and Technology

Exacerbating their economic problems were the numerous scientific and technical difficulties California oil men met in finding, producing, and refining their petroleum. California's scrambled rock formations baffled oil-seekers accustomed to the more predictable strata of other areas. The chemical properties of California crude made it extremely hard to refine, and, as a result, for many years most went to market as fuel oil. Probably the most vexing problem was how to keep water out of the wells, for in the early twentieth century the intrustion of water threatened the very existence of California's major fields. The oil men first tried to solve these problems independently or through voluntary cooperation. However, when it became evident that their private efforts alone would not suffice, they obtained the aid of state officials.

California oil companies led the nation in employing geologists to search for oil. In 1897, subsidiaries of the Southern Pacific Railroad established the first geology department in the petroleum industry, and two years later the Union Oil Company set up a similar division.[62] By 1915, all of California's major producers had geologists in the field looking for untapped pools and supervising production in the older ones. Discoveries increasingly depended upon knowledge about structural formations, anticlines and synclines, and less on finding surface indications. Despite the feelings of some pioneers in the business that scientists were about as useful "as tits to a boar pig," trained geologists had become an essential feature of California's oil industry by the outbreak of the First World War.[63] State agencies also provided sorely needed help in developing new discovery techniques. The state mineralogist's office issued bulletin after bulletin analyzing California's geology and pointing out signs by which oil fields could be recognized.[64]

From the earliest days of the California oil industry the high viscosity and impurities of the state's crude puzzled refiners. A chemist employed by the Union Oil Company in 1894 emphasized the uniqueness of California petroleum. "The trouble with California oil is," he asserted, that "no one knows anything about it."[65] A decade later a scientist attached to the state mining bureau lamented that the chemistry of California crude was still shrouded in "considerable obscurity."[66] State sponsored research and experiments by individual companies ultimately resulted in the development of successful refining techniques. The Union Oil Company hired professional chemists to find ways to distill kerosene in the early 1890s, and, in 1896, E. A. Starke, a powder-explosives expert employed by the Pacific Coast Oil Company, discovered how to rid California crude of its carbonaceous properties.[67] This breakthrough proved the value of scientific research and led to further work by company chemists and state officials. The California Bureau of Mining publicized advancements in bulletins distributed at state expense and in articles written for California's oil journals. The discovery of new uses for oil, especially as the base for gasoline, required continuous research to improve refining methods. The building of the Shell Company's refinery at Martinez in 1915 and 1916 highlighted the progress Californians had made. Using both European and American processes, it was one of the most advanced plants in the United States.[68]

The infiltration of water into their oil fields, more than any other technical problem, threatened the profits of California oil men. In many fields strata containing water existed above or below those holding oil. When drillers pierced the impermeable layers of clay or sandstone that separated the oil and water bearing sands, the water often seeped into the petroleum and rendered it useless for either refining or fuel oil. Because more than one company usually drew its oil from the same underground pool, water hit in one firm's drilling operations could easily hinder the work of others. By 1914, the damage was widespread. In the Coalinga field, which probably suffered the most, over one-quarter of the wells were producing more than 10 percent water. One operator, surveying the devastation around him, caustically remarked that the oil industry was "the most important water business in the state!"[69]

Because the larger companies had the most to lose from water damage and possessed the capital needed to experiment with ways to prevent it, they led the campaign to end the intrusion of water. In 1903, Union Oil crews devised methods of cementing well casings to stop the flow of water between different strata, and six years later Standard Oil adopted a similar process in Midway field. However, these efforts hardly made a dent in the problem. The neglect of a single company could let water into an entire field. Small operators working on a shoestring found the cementing processes prohibitively expensive, and in many fields only the larger firms could afford suitable casing. Abandoned wells presented a similar difficulty, for, unless they were correctly filled, they might also let water into the field. Since bankrupt companies lacked the funds to accomplish this task, complaints about improperly abandoned wells were chronic.[70]

Oil men soon realized that they needed police power to halt water intrusion, and political action began in 1903. In that year oil men obtained legislation that set standards for casing techniques, but, lacking any enforcement mechanism, the measure had little effect on drilling practices.[71] In 1909, the legislature strengthened this law with an act that held anyone letting water into his well liable for the cost of closing it. County oil commissioners paid by county funds were to administer the law. This measure failed to control the situation, for few counties appointed oil supervisors, and those who took office were overworked and underpaid. Small operators violated the law with impunity, and not even all the larger firms supported it, because some still felt the answer to their difficulties lay in their own individual efforts.[72]

During the next four years concern over damage to California's oil reserves mounted, and the larger companies established cooperative organizations to stem the flow of water. In early 1912, operators in the Sunset, Midway, and McKittrick districts set up the Kern County Oil Protective Association. Farther north, producers formed the Coalinga Water Arbitration Association. Both organizations were dominated by large firms that feared losing their investments due to damage caused by their smaller neighbors. The associations worked closely with county officers in correlating the well logs for each field. In this manner the oil men put together accurate descriptions of the strata that enabled them to predict at what levels they would hit water. Association members also advised each other on ways to shut off water. However, neither of the bodies proved successful, for without legal sanctions they could not force their regulations upon those who chose not to join.[73]

Recognizing the failure of voluntary cooperation, the larger producers returned to the state legislature. They desired legislation, because water infiltration cut into their present earnings. As the opposition of many of these same firms to legislation limiting crude production demonstrated, they cared little about conservation as an end in itself or even as a means to guarantee production in the future. Only when conservation promised quick dividends, would oil men back it. Because the drive to restrict the output of crude threatened the profits of their firms, they fought it. When, on the other hand, the intrusion of water reduced their income, they supported conservation measures designed to eliminate it.

State officials and petroleum engineers worked with the oil men in their campaign to end water damage. Mark Requa, a leader in the movement to limit crude production, also appeared in the vanguard of those who viewed water infiltration as a hindrance to oil conservation. In 1910, he pointed out that in the past it had been ''the eventual fate'' of all oil fields to be ''drowned in water'' and urged the major producers to adopt practices to avert this eventuality in California.[74] Two years later he expressed more concern. In a report prepared for the Commonwealth Club of California in 1912 he rated water infiltration as the number one problem facing oil men and called for the taxation of all producers to provide funds with which the state mining bureau could fight it.[75] The state mineralogist and Governor Johnson's conservation commission also recommended the enactment of new legislation to avoid further injury.[76]

In 1913, a legislative contest over measures to prevent water infiltration laid bare divisions within the California oil industry. The Kern County Oil Protective Association secured consideration for a bill drafted by its members. The proposal provided for the creation of oil districts headed by state officials empowered to take any steps necessary to keep out water. The oil men, who were to possess votes proportional to the amount of land they owned and actually had in production, would elect the officials. The larger companies, joined by conservation advocates, strongly backed this measure. Representatives of the smaller firms, however, presented sharp opposition to it. They pointed out that its voting arrangements discriminated against them and complained that they lacked the funds to comply with strict terms for cementing wells. Officers of the Kern County Oil Company, the F. C. Berry Company, C. F. Brant, Inc., and about one hundred other concerns presented a petition to the legislature denouncing the bill. Despite their protests, the measure unanimously passed both the senate and assembly. Governor Johnson, however, vetoed it. He recognized the danger of water damage, but he agreed with the small operators that the plan gave too much power to the large producers. For this reason he asked the oil men to rework their proposal for the next legislative session.[77]

Pressure for legislation increased during the following two years, and the oil men achieved success in 1915. After visiting the San Joaquin fields, R. P. McLaughlin, who headed the petroleum division within the state mining bureau, concluded that ''immense qualities of liquid wealth'' were being lost to ''the encroaching floods of water.''[78] Meetings between oil men and state officials generated broad-based support for a new measure.[79] The bill that emerged from these conferences called for the creation of a new department, the office of oil and gas supervisor, within the state mining bureau. The proposal empowered the supervisor, aided by deputies in the field, to secure well logs and any other information possessed by private companies on the question of water infiltration. Upon the complaint of three operators within one mile of any well the supervisor or one of his deputies would investigate the situation and recommend remedial actions. A board of three arbitrators (one appointed by the complainants, one by the well owner, and one by the state mineralogist) would examine and rule upon the supervisor's report. County superior courts could subject the board's findings to still further review. This complicated procedure with its many checks and balances both placated the small producers and promised relief for the larger companies. The bill obtained legislative approval with little dissent and quickly secured Governor Johnson's signature to become law.[80]

R. P. McLaughlin, the first oil and gas supervisor, worked closely with the oil producers in administering the new measure. He solicited their advice upon how to implement the law and employed "practical oil men" as his deputies in the fields. After his first year on the job McLaughlin reported that conditions were "almost ideal," largely as a result of "the hearty cooperation by a large majority of the oil operators throughout the state."[81] State Mineralogist Fletcher Hamilton also stressed the need for government-business understanding. He noted that although the oil and gas supervisor could compel the repair of wells letting in water, he hoped that the supervisor would act not "as a prosecuting officer, but rather as an advisory department to the operators."[82]

In its first few years of existence the office of oil and gas supervisor won only a partial victory over water intrusion. The department's advice helped individual operators, but the infiltration of water into California's major fields continued. The supervisor concentrated the work of his deputies in the San Joaquin fields and in 1915 and 1916 ordered that water be shut off in 414 wells in these regions.[83] However, regardless of the supervisor's claims about the cooperation of the state's producers, small operators evaded and appealed his orders. In some districts the damage done by water actually increased. In the Westside portion of the Coalinga field, for instance, drillers were making 29 percent water in 1916, but over 40 percent five years later. Despite the best efforts of the larger companies and state officials, the intrusion of water seriously hindered operations into the 1920s.[84]

As was true in California's other leading industries, oil men sought to solve their problems by a mixture of individual actions, voluntary cooperation, and state legislation. However, attempts to deal with the overproduction of petroleum, the regulation of pipelines, and water damage revealed more divisions than unanimity among the state's oil men. Rifts between large and small producers, refiners and producers, and the owners and nonowning users of pipelines quickly opened. The conflicts that developed within the oil industry could often be resolved only in the legislative arena. Many of the issues at stake, especially those involving conservation matters, attracted the attention of elements outside of the oil industry. In most cases those oil men who could best appeal for support beyond their own narrow interest group proved most successful in getting their way in Sacramento. Thus, the backing of independent geologists and of officials in the state mining bureau was of great help to those desiring strict measures to halt the flow of water into California's oil fields. By the same token, the smaller independent crude producers finally succeeded in having pipelines declared common carriers, at least in part, because they argued that taking such action would benefit oil consumers, not just themselves.

The contests over legislation to limit the output of crude and end the intrusion of water also shed valuable light on the attitudes of California businessmen toward conservation. Most oil men backed conservation measures only when they promised immediate benefits. In this respect they were remarkably myopic and took few precautions for the future. Only the larger companies performed any long-term planning, and even their efforts were, at best, rudimentary. Yet, most other California businessmen shared this outlook. The state's lumbermen supported conservation proposals for their industry only when assured that they would profit by doing so. Few businessmen considered the public consequences resulting from their actions. Instead, nearly all thought of conservation simply in terms of private gains or losses.

4

The Lumber Industry and Scientific Forestry

California lumbermen faced situations analogous to those troubling the state's farmers and oil men. As the number of trees cut mounted each year, production outran consumption. Confronted with rising costs at a time when the prices they received for their products remained steady, the lumbermen found themselves in a perilous situation. Yet, at the same time, the newly completed railroad network and, at a later date, the opening of the Panama Canal, promised a rosy future if proper marketing arrangements could be secured. Questions of conservation also concerned lumbermen and were directly related to their problem of overproduction. Lumber interests long recognized the advisability of fire prevention and reforestation measures, but they actively supported scientific forestry only when rising lumber prices and a scarcity of timber made it economically feasible and desirable.

None of the problems Californians encountered were completely new, for the rapid expansion of the lumber industry caused difficulties for lumbermen in all parts of the nation in the nineteenth century. Yet, although they faced few wholly unique situations, California lumbermen often devised original solutions, particularly with regard to conservation. When they reached the Pacific Coast, lumbermen could no longer migrate to new territories once they had logged over an area. In California and the other Pacific Coast states lumbermen reached their last frontier and, for the first time, had to grapple seriously with conservation issues. When they finally realized that American forests were of limited extent, California lumbermen pressed for novel forestry measures and land-taxation policies as the only way to guarantee the future survival of their industry.

Lumbermen and Overproduction

In the late nineteenth and early twentieth centuries Californians found themselves caught in a squeeze between rising costs and relatively steady prices received for their lumber. Between 1899 and 1916, the annual cut of pine and redwood in California nearly doubled, and lumbermen correctly blamed this rapid increase for preventing any significant rise in prices.[1] The prices of redwood and pine, while climbing temporarily during the rebuilding of San Francisco after the earthquake and fire of 1906, generally fluctuated little in the two decades before the outbreak of the First World War.[2] At the same time the costs of production soared. Logging operations required increasingly complex machinery. Donkey engines replaced oxen in yarding the felled trees, and steam locomotives took over the chore of transporting them to the mills. In the mills single- and double-band saws supplanted the older circular saws. Although mechanical improvements eventually increased the profits of the lumber companies, their initial impact was detrimental. Financed mainly out of current earnings, the innovations raised operating expenses. Mounting labor costs and the rising price of timberlands also bit into income. In a painstakingly detailed examination made for the Department of Agriculture in 1915, Swift Berry, a forestry expert, concluded that the prices pine men received barely covered their costs of production, and the same situation existed in the redwood industry as well.[3]

Overproduction and low prices had bothered lumbermen from the time their industry became a big business at the close of the Civil War, and the efforts of timber barons in other areas to deal with these problems fore-shadowed the actions of Californians at a later date. As their expenses rose in the 1870s and 1880s, many firms in the Great Lakes states turned to vertical integration. By controlling every step of lumbering, from felling the trees to marketing the finished products, company officials hoped to retain all the profits of the business for themselves. To capture economies of scale, company officers increased the size of their firms, and many of the smaller establishments merged. On the industry-wide level, lumbermen set up trade associations to control output, quality standards, and prices. Timbermen also sought government aid, especially tariff protection from Canadian imports. When they moved west and south in the 1890s and the opening years of the twentieth century, lumbermen tried to protect themselves in the familiar ways. Large, vertically integrated companies dominated the industry, and trade associations took on a new strength, particularly in the Pacific Northwest.[4]

Like their counterparts elsewhere, California lumbermen responded to the narrowing of their profit margins by restructuring their firms along the lines of vertical integration. Redwood companies that had once contracted with independent drivers to float their logs downriver to the mills took over this task themselves, and, as they logged off areas accessible to the river driving, they constructed railroads to transport their timber. In the early twentieth century the redwood companies also began building and operating their own coastal schooners to ship lumber to San Francisco and other points. In the Sierra pineries the same changes occurred. Independently operated flumes gave way to company-owned railroads as the chief means of carrying lumber. By the same token, firms that produced only unfinished lumber in the 1880s and 1890s expanded their operations to include drying kilns, planing mills, box factories, and sash and door plants. Lumbermen discovered new uses for what had once been considered waste materials; redwood bark and sawdust, for instance, found profitable markets.

Individual companies also increased in size. As early as the 1890s, reduced profits began forcing small concerns to merge or go out of business, and in the twentieth century this trend became still more pronounced. As the manager of California's largest lumber trade association pointed out in 1917, heavy capital investments made large-scale production "an economic necessity." The growth in individual sawmill capacity illustrated the tendency toward bigness. In 1900, small mills with circular or single-band saws still cut much of California's lumber, but two decades later large mills employing double-band saws clearly predominated. Although the total production of the mills greatly increased during this period, their number fell by one-fifth. By 1920, mills with an annual output of 10 million or more board feet apiece prepared 85 percent of California's lumber.[5]

The development of the Diamond Match Company in Butte County epitomized the movement toward vertical integration and bigness. Migrating from the East, the firm's officers started purchasing timberlands in 1902 and within a few years had acquired nearly 70,000 acres of mixed conifer woodlands in the Sierras. Relegating match production to the background, the company entered into all phases of the lumber business. The firm logged its lands with sophisticated equipment constructed in its own machine shops. From the forest the company's narrow-gauge railroads carried the felled timber to its sawmills and plywood and veneer factories near Chico. From this locality a thirty-two-mile standard-gauge line built by Diamond Match at a cost exceeding $1,500,000 connected the plants with the Southern Pacific's branch through the Sacramento Valley.[6]

Even the officers of such highly organized concerns as Diamond Match soon learned, however, that they could not insulate their firms from fluctuations in supply and demand by their own independent actions and formed trade associations to protect their market positions and profits. Selling specialized products and operating in an industry dominated by a few large firms, redwood lumbermen found it relatively easy to cooperate in the pursuit of common goals. Because their side of the lumber business contained many companies of all sizes manufacturing a multitude of products, pine men found cooperation more difficult. Yet, by 1916, even they possessed a comprehensive trade association dedicated to raising the prices members received for their goods.

Redwood men made their first significant effort to set up an industry-wide organization with the establishment of the Redwood Manufacturers Association in 1893. Organized at a time when, as one leading lumberman noted, "money has been and is being lost on every stick of timber produced," the association set monthly production quotas for member mills and published price lists for their products. The body also sought to enter eastern and foreign markets and obtained some reductions in transcontinental freight rates. Yet, the association lasted for only a few years. Prices and quotas, and the red tape involved in establishing them, caused innumerable disagreements. More importantly, several companies refused to join and consistently undercut the published prices. By 1898, the association had disbanded, and each mill was again "a law unto itself."[7]

Chronically low prices led to renewed efforts to organize the redwood business in the twentieth century. In late 1903, many of the larger firms formed the Redwood Manufacturers Company, which constructed a single large plant at tidewater in Contra Costa County. Controlling three-quarters of California's annual output of redwood, this company operated drying kilns to season wood, planing mills, and a sash and door factory. Aided by demands resulting from the rebuilding of San Francisco, the Redwood Manufacturers Company commanded high prices for its products through 1908. However, during the next few years consumption and prices dropped, and, in 1912, the Casper Lumber Company bought the facilities for its own use.[8] Lumbermen tried a different approach with the creation of the California Redwood Association in 1916. Composed of companies representing 80 percent of California's yearly cut of redwood, this body publicized the advantages of redwood in home construction and other uses. It maintained a sales agency in New York and established uniform grades of lumber to meet the specifications of East Coast buyers. The organization's manager also tried, with some success, to secure reductions in transcontinental freight rates. The California Redwood Association made no attempts to fix prices or production quotas, and, probably because it limited the scope of its actions, the association still exists today.[9]

Lumbermen in the pine regions were somewhat slower in forming trade associations. In 1896, the owners of seventy-four mills set up the Central Lumber Company of California to deal with the question of overproduction. Pine-mill capacity on the Pacific Coast at that time greatly exceeded consumption, and "ruinous competition" had, according to the president of the new establishment, driven prices below the costs of production. A loose confederation rather than an operating firm, the Central Lumber Company tried to fix uniform prices and grades for its members' products, but the organization disappeared within several years. Too many firms remained outside its ranks to make its price lists effective, and competition from Pacific Northwest lumber further eroded its power.[10] The collapse of the Central Lumber Company left the pine operators unorganized for over a decade. Finally, in late 1910, at a meeting called by the manager of the National Lumber Manufacturers' Association, they formed the Sugar and White Pine Manufacturers Association of California and Adjacent States. Designed only to define market territories for its members, the organization obtained no control over production and failed to raise prices.[11]

The pine operators, like the redwood men, made a new departure in 1916. Joined together as the California White and Sugar Pine Manufacturers Association, they concentrated on opening markets rather than fixing prices or production quotas. Their association trumpeted the values of western pine throughout the nation, and, in conjunction with the lumbermen of Idaho, eastern Washington, and eastern Oregon, enforced strict grading standards for its members' products. Representing nearly three-quarters of the pine lumber cut in California, the association also entered politics on railroad matters. In 1917, it sent exhibits to the national capital protesting a proposed transcontinental rate hike, and two years later its traffic committee worked for the passage of Albert Cummins's federal railroad bill. Moreover the organization, working in cooperation with other regional and national associations, circulated trade statistics and in this manner may have dampened price competition.[12]

Californians, like lumbermen in the Great Lakes states before them, discovered that neither the vertical integration of their companies nor the formation of trade associations could adequately assure them of profits in times of excess production. Single firms could not cope with industry-wide problems. Nor were trade associations completely successful. Tight organizations designed to limit output and fix prices failed, because they could never gain a monopoly over their markets. Some firms, desiring immediate profits or able to operate at a lower cost than their neighbors, always remained outside and undercut their prices. Looser associations set up to expand markets found it easier to attract members but did little better in raising prices. The increases that came after 1915 resulted more from wartime demands than the actions of trade associations. Coordination between the various regional trade associations could, perhaps, have helped solve the problems of California lumbermen, but only isolated instances of cooperation took place. California pine competed with pine from the South and the Pacific Northwest, and even redwood often had to contend with fir and pine from Washington and Oregon in many markets.

Although relying chiefly upon restructuring their firms and establishing trade associations as ways of solving their problems, Californians also worked through the state and federal governments. Lumbermen consistently sought tariff increases to protect forest products from foreign competition. In the early 1890s, lumbermen from the Pacific Coast and the Old Northwest fought attempts to place lumber on the free list. Despite their defeat on this issue with the passage of the Wilson-Gorman Act in 1894, Californians remained vocal advocates of a high tariff for the next several decades.[13] Both pine and redwood operators desired lower railroad rates to open new territories for their products. They supported state and federal railroad regulatory measures and frequently appeared before the California Railroad Commission and the Interstate Commerce Commission to request lower rates and better service.[14] Some California lumbermen also advocated the enactment of a "pure lumber" law by Congress in 1916. Inspired by the Pure Food and Drug Act of ten years before, it would have set standard grades for lumber sold anywhere in the United States. By improving the quality of their products, the lumbermen hoped to increase the consumption of their goods. Nothing, however, came of this proposal.[15]

California lumbermen further sought official sanction for the price-fixing and quota-setting activities of their trade associations. In this endeavor they faced the twin barriers of the Sherman Act and the Cartwright law, a California antitrust act modeled on the federal legislation. The lumbermen opposed the passage of the Cartwright Act in 1907 and worked for its repeal during the next legislative session. Thwarted in these efforts, they turned their fire on the Sherman Act. Though not troubled much by its provisions in the 1890s, they grew more concerned as progressive politicians began applying it to other industries in the twentieth century. Both the California Redwood Association and the California White and Sugar Pine Manufacturers Association worked for the modification of the Sherman and Clayton Antitrust acts. In 1918, they, along with other business groups throughout the nation, won a partial victory with the passage of the Webb-Pomerene Act. This measure allowed the formation of combinations among businessmen to meet the competition of foreign cartels in international trade. Even before the final passage of the bill the California Redwood Association set up a subsidiary agency, the Redwood Export Company, to push sales in the Far East, and by the early 1920s it was selling 10 percent of the nation's redwood overseas. Pine men, although they had worked for its passage, were slower to take advantage of the Webb-Pomerene Act. The California White and Sugar Pine Manufacturers Association appointed a committee to study European markets but took no further steps to enter them until the 1920s.[16]

The Movement for Scientific Forestry

Like most other forested states in the nation, California experienced a scientific forestry movement in the late nineteenth and early twentieth centuries. In California, as was usually the case elsewhere, the campaign for scientific forestry revolved around two major issues: the prevention and extinction of forest fires and the reforestation of cut-over timberlands. Both matters became entwined with the economic problems lumbermen faced, for lumbermen proved willing to adopt scientific forestry measures only when they promised to produce profits for their firms.[17]

It was farmers requiring irrigation and urban dwellers in water-poor regions, not lumbermen, that began the fight for scientific forestry in California. They did so out of a concern for their state's watersheds. Farmers in the Sacramento and San Joaquin valleys and orange growers in Southern California depended upon irrigation and viewed the destruction of forest watersheds by fires and logging as a threat to their livelihood.

Trees, they rightly believed, aided agriculture by absorbing rainfall, retarding stream runoff, and reducing soil erosion. City dwellers in the arid regions around Los Angeles, worried about municipal water supplies, employed similar arguments and joined the farmers in their quest for scientific forestry. These advocates of scientific forestry concentrated upon winning approval for legislation designed to prevent forest fires. Reducing the fire danger, they argued, should take precedence over reforestation and other conservation measures. It would be futile, they pointed out, to replant cut-over lands only to have them consumed in a holocaust a few years later.

Most lumbermen initially resisted forestry legislation as uneconomical, given the nature of their industry. Operating in a business characterized by excess supply and low prices, they opposed anything that threatened to raise their immediate costs of production. Many recognized that their logging methods and forest fires were wasteful, but they pointed out that as long as low prices prevailed and the stands of virgin timber lasted, it would be impractical for them to adopt more efficient techniques. As late as 1913, T. B. Walker, the owner of one of the largest tracts of pine lands in California, noted that "competition and adverse conditions kept the prices of common lumber below the profit point." He concluded that, as a result, lumbermen had no choice but to cut "only the finest trees and take only the best logs that would make clear lumber" and leave "the rest of the trees of those cut and the much larger number left uncut all subject to fire and decay."[18] Lumbermen also opposed forestry legislation, because they feared that state intervention in this sphere of activity might broaden to include other aspects of their businesses. They preferred to work, instead, through their own cooperative associations or with county officials on forestry matters.

California led most of the rest of the United States in setting up a board of forestry in 1885. Created by the actions of a loose coalition of agriculturalists, sportsmen, and nature lovers, the board accomplished little. Hamstrung by a lack of funds and technical knowledge, the agency passed out of existence eight years after its formation as a result of reductions in the state's budget.[19] Proponents of scientific forestry won few successes in the following decade. Several of the largest pine operators established skeleton fire patrols, but the vast majority of lumbermen trusted to chance and fought fires only when they threatened their mills. As one national forester explained, too much virgin timber remained for lumbermen to worry about the future.[20]

Scientific forestry advocates redoubled their efforts in the opening years of the twentieth century. The annual convention of the American Forestry Association meeting in Los Angeles in 1899 stirred up new interest, and at about the same time California's agricultural and horticultural societies formed several organizations dedicated to winning governmental support for conservation policies. The most important of these, the California Water and Forest Association, claimed 5,000 members. In 1903, this body secured a legislative appropriation of $100,000 for an examination of California's forest resources. The United States Forest Service, paid with these state funds, undertook the survey. Inaugurated personally by Gifford Pinchot, the investigation studied reforestation methods, ways to prevent forest fires, and cutting practices.[21]

The California Water and Forest Association next turned its attention to the formation of a new state board of forestry. At their annual meeting in the summer of 1904 the association's members directed their executive council to draft a fire protection bill. The council, in turn, referred the matter to E. A. Sterling, a national forester who had taken part in the 1903 survey. After conferring with representatives of the United States Forest Service and the Sierra Club as well as with members of the Water and Forest Association, Sterling drew up a measure calling for a four-man board of forestry headed by a professionally educated forester to be appointed by the governor. The state forester's main duty would be to prevent and extinguish forest fires, and for these purposes the bill empowered him to appoint an assistant forester and ten salaried district fire wardens. The state and the counties were to split the expenses of fire fighting and maintaining fire patrols.[22]

Sterling's proposal received ardent backing from a wide variety of sources outside of the lumber industry. Officers of the Water and Forest Association emphasized the necessity of halting the devastation of California's mountain watersheds. They claimed that soil erosion resulting from forest fires and poor logging practices had already clogged many streams with silt and that rainfall, instead of seeping into the soil to be gradually released for agricultural use, flowed out to sea in torrential floods.[23] Agricultural societies endorsed the stand of the Water and Forest Association and sent lobbyists to Sacramento to work for Sterling's measure. Chambers of commerce in towns and cities throughout Southern California, concerned about their water supplies, passed resolutions favoring the bill; and mining groups, worried about the depletion of lumber supplies essential for their industry, also came out for it.[24] The proposal's advocates, taking their cue from Gifford Pinchot, stressed that they had no intention of injuring the lumber business. Sterling, for instance, repeatedly emphasized that scientific forestry advocates desired not "to preserve in park form the trees now existing, but to cut them to supply the needs of civilization."[25]

Such assurances failed, however, to satisfy lumbermen, and most of them opposed Sterling's measure. Confusion about forest fires kept some lumbermen from backing the bill. A large number of them believed that small fires, whether set on purpose or accidentally, were beneficial, because they eliminated underbrush upon which larger conflagrations might otherwise feed. Many lumbermen also feared that the costs of the board of forestry would require increases in their property taxes, and they worked against the proposal for this reason. Representatives of the Southern Pacific Railroad, which owned large tracts of timberlands in Northern California, were particularly outspoken on this point. Still others, though willing to accept the expenses of fire protection, opposed Sterling's measure, because they viewed it as the opening wedge for state regulation of all aspects of their business. As events were soon to demonstrate, they preferred to rely upon county organizations or trade associations rather than state agencies to combat fires.[26]

Legislative committees emasculated Sterling's bill. The arguments of lumbermen before the committees proved effective, and few of the measure's original provisions remained intact. Many legislators agreed with the lumbermen that the proposal tried to do too much too quickly. They particularly disliked being presented with such a comprehensive, ready-made bill. The provisions for state taxation came under especially heavy fire, for legislators outside of timbered regions objected to charging all Californians for services that they felt would benefit only certain areas. The amended version of Sterling's bill still provided for a state board of forestry headed by a professional forester, but it severely restricted the forester's ability to combat fires. It contained no provisions for state fire wardens, and it strictly limited the funds the state could expend for fire fighting. Instead, the forester was instructed to cooperate with county officials and depend upon voluntary fire wardens. Governor George Pardee, an ardent conservationist, had to intervene personally to obtain passage for even this drastically altered measure.[27]

With the enactment of the Fire Protection and Forest Management Law California again took a place in the forefront of the nationwide movement for scientific forestry through state legislation. Minnesota had set up a state forestry board in 1899, and Wisconsin, after decades of neglect, followed suit four years later. Farther west, irrigationists in Colorado and Arizona were seeking legislation to shield their watersheds from damage, and lumbermen in Washington and Oregon secured state fire protection laws and formed their own associations to fight fires. In all, by 1905, some twelve states possessed forestry commissions of varying effectiveness.[28] Even with the changes made by the California legislature, Sterling's act surpassed those of most of the other states in scope and power.[29] Gifford Pinchot found ample praise for it. "If the counties will take advantage of the authority contained in the bill and appropriate a reasonable amount to pay for fire fighting, it will," he predicted, "rank in its practical effect higher than any other state forest law."[30] California conservationists, though worried about the delegation of power to the counties, also approved the law. Sterling felt that it signaled "the beginning of a new era in the forest movement in California," and members of the Water and Forest Association claimed that with it California "takes first place among the states that have attempted to deal with the problems of forest fires and forest management."[31]

The course of events shattered these high expectations. The state forester urged county officials to establish fire patrols as "a sound business investment" to reduce property losses and thus bolster their counties' tax bases, and, by 1912, twenty-two counties were cooperating in some manner with him. Yet, these efforts proved ineffective. As some conservationists had feared, the counties, strapped for funds, spent a minimal sum for fire protection. In 1912, for instance, they appropriated a total of only $10,995, and as a result fires blackened nearly 300,000 acres of brush and timberlands.[32]

Lumber companies, operating independently of the forestry commissioner, made only minimal progress in the direction of scientific forestry in these years. Diamond Match, the McCloud River Lumber Company, and some of the other major pine firms instituted or expanded fire protection programs, and a few of the larger redwood companies began constructing fire lanes and clearing out underbrush. Yet, even the actions of the most advanced firms were inadequate. The total annual expenses of the McCloud River Company for fire protection came to only $600, or less than four cents per acre; a single patrolman toured the company's vast holdings. Lumbermen also set up cooperative associations to fight forest fires, and, by 1913, three such bodies existed. The California Fire Protective Association, formed by some of the largest pine and redwood companies, was the most important. Inspired by similar bodies in the Pacific Northwest, the association carried on a publicity campaign against forest fires in newspapers throughout California and assisted in the establishment of county organizations of fire fighters. Yet, the efforts of the cooperative organizations, like those of the independent firms, proved inadequate. Surveys undertaken by the state forester in 1914 and 1917 revealed just how spotty the progress was. They demonstrated that all but a handful of the largest firms failed to take even the simplest precautions against forest fires. As several forestry analysts pointed out, lumbermen could not yet absorb the costs of scientific forestry. Excess mill capacity and overproduction continued to depress prices, and, as a result, few lumbermen felt that they could afford to experiment with fire prevention or efficient logging methods.[33]

Recognizing the defects of the 1905 Fire Protection Act, the state forester, prodded by agricultural groups, called for further legislation. State Forester E. T. Allen complained that his office could achieve little under existing laws and asked for changes as early as 1906.[34] A year later the Water and Forest Association and the state forester prepared measures designed to regulate the disposal of logging slash and increase the board of forestry's powers. However, lumbermen and large landowners claimed that they could not afford the expense of the bills and kept them from becoming law.[35] Pressure for forestry measures grew in the next several years. The National Irrigation Congress, meeting at Sacramento in late 1907, urged the state forester to examine private timber holdings on the watersheds of irrigable streams and set rules for lumbering operations on them. The state forester favored these proposals and, in 1909, again worked with farm organizations to obtain legislation enlarging the state's role in preventing forest fires and supervising logging methods. Introduced late, his bills disappeared in the crush of other business. At the succeeding legislative session the state forester obtained more control over the disposal of slash, but requests for additional funds and authority to combat forest fires died in committee.[36]

During the following two years agitation for forestry measures centered upon the work of the California Conservation Commission established by Governor Hiram Johnson in 1911. Inspired by the conservation efforts of Theodore Roosevelt and stemming indirectly from the conference of governors held in 1908, the commission investigated forestry proposals for the Golden State. In March, 1912, its secretary drew up a fire protection bill modeled upon British Columbia law, and later in the month the commissioners met with represenatives of the state's redwood and pine companies to discuss logging methods and fire protection.[37]

This three-day conference uncovered divisions of opinion between the pine and redwood lumbermen. Officers of many of the larger pine firms voiced a growing willingness to accept an increase in the state forester's powers. Although not completely breaking away from their past opposition to mandatory scientific forestry legislation, they did, at least, begin to see its value. Pine timber was particularly prone to fire damage, and pine lumbermen had just suffered through several bad fire seasons. As a result, the manager of the Sugar and White Pine Manufacturers Association pledged his organization's backing to additional legislation designed to prevent forest fires. Clinton Walker, of Thomas Walker and Company, and George Hoxie, who owned 20,000 acres of pine lands in Northern California, joined him in calling for new laws. The spokesman for the Southern Pacific Railroad, which had earlier opposed forestry measures, offered the most concrete plan for state action. He suggested that the state forester appoint salaried fire wardens throughout California and that the state should assume most of the costs of fighting fires. A tax levied on all properties within fire districts as defined by the forester would pay for these expenses. The redwood men, however, refused to sanction such a heightened role for the state. They claimed that their timber was less susceptible to fire damage than pine and that state legislation was, therefore, unnecessary for them. Redwood operators also used fire as an integral part of their logging process, and in the hearings before the conservation commission they defended their use of fire to dispose of slash even during the dry season, despite the fact that these fires sometimes ran out of control. Finally, they felt that, since the rivers running through their timberlands served few farms, the protection of their watersheds was not a legitimate concern of the state. Redwoods, they concluded, should be exempt from any legislation dealing with forest fires.[38]

Largely because of the publicity aroused by the hearings of the conservation commission, forest fire prevention measures again became major issues in the state legislature just prior to the outbreak of the First World War. In 1913, the conservation commission and the California Fire Protection Association jointly drafted a new fire protection bill. Although the measure increased state funding to extinguish forest fires, it continued the state forester's dependence on county officials and voluntary associations and restricted his freedom of action in other ways as well. State Forester

George Homans condemned this proposal and countered with a much stiffer measure of his own. The introduction of these two bills in the legislature resulted in a stalemate. This same deadlock, pitting the state forester against the lumbermen and the conservation commission, remained unbroken in the next two legislative sessions, and, as a result, no significant forestry measures won approval.[39]

It was the outbreak of the First World War, more than any other single event, that made scientific forestry, and, in particular, forest fire prevention measures, acceptable to California lumbermen. Throughout the prewar years most lumbermen had opposed strict scientific forestry legislation as too expensive, given the overproduction and low prices endemic to their business. The war dramatically changed this situation. It boosted demands for lumber and caused a sharp rise in the prices California lumbermen received for their products. These price increases made it possible, as lumbermen themselves pointed out, for lumber companies to afford at least rudimentary scientific forestry practices. The war furthered the cause of scientific forestry in other ways as well. Most importantly, it riveted attention on forests as resources essential for national security and made the prevention of their destruction a matter of public concern. Even lumbermen came to realize that the virgin stands of timber might be exhausted and expressed alarm at the rate at which forests were disappearing before fires and the woodsman's axe.

In California, officials from the United States Forest Service, lumber industry representatives, and faculty members of the University of California formed the Forest Industries Committee of California to deal with forestry problems arising in the war years. Working with State Forester Homans, who was its chairman, this group set up county fire-fighting organizations throughout the state. When these county associations failed to prevent particularly bad fire losses in 1918, lumbermen took the unprecedented step of joining the state forester in calling for remedial legislation.[40]

During the 1919 legislative session lumbermen and the state forester finally reached agreement on effective forest protection measures. The bills they jointly agreed upon passed both houses of the legislature unanimously and fundamentally altered California fire protection laws. Under their terms the state forester divided California into fire districts watched over by rangers employed by the state, and the state assumed the major costs of combatting blazes. The new laws did what Sterling's measure of

1905 had envisioned. They gave the state forester the authority and funds to provide fire protection for the entire state and ended his dependence upon cooperation with county officials.[41]

The links between the state forester and the lumbermen, forged in the heat of the war years, grew stronger in the 1920s. By this time most lumbermen had come to realize that unless they adopted scientific forestry practices they would soon exhaust their timber. The desire to avoid strict federal laws also pushed lumbermen into the arms of the state forester. Though discussed earlier, measures to regulate the lumber industry won serious consideration from Congress only in the postwar period. Many lumbermen hoped to block national legislation by demonstrating that they could work harmoniously with state officials, and some probably also felt that they could in this way gain the support of state foresters in their drive against federal legislation.

A meeting of California's major lumbermen with State Forester Homans in late 1920 foreshadowed the course forestry would take in succeeding years. The lumbermen unanimously passed resolutions calling upon the legislature to increase funds for the state forester's fire protection efforts, and both pine and redwood operators agreed to adhere to new strict guidelines on the disposal of slash. The same conference condemned the Capper Bill, a federal measure that would have established nationwide standards for lumbering, and called for its defeat by Congress. The state forester praised the lumbermen for their backing of his work and, in turn, went on record as opposing the Capper Bill. State officials cooperating with lumbermen could, he claimed, accomplish more in the way of scientific forestry.[42]

By 1920, lumbermen had drastically altered the position they held on fire prevention legislation. Whereas they had once opposed fire prevention measures as uneconomical, lumbermen came to accept and work for them. Blessed with good prices but threatened by the depletion of their virgin timber, lumbermen became leaders in the movement to prevent forest fires.

Developments in the campaign to reforest California's logged-over timberlands closely paralleled the evolution of the state's drive for fire protection legislation. Begun by the state forester backed by agriculturalists who were worried about their mountain watersheds, the campaign changed in nature in its later years. As had happened in the movement to prevent forest fires, it became a drive dominated by the lumbermen and concerned mainly with insuring the continued existence and profitability of the lumber industry.

When scientific forestry advocates began calling for reforestation in California in the opening years of the twentieth century, they considered two approaches to the problem. First, the state could purchase cut-over lands from private owners and reforest them; or, second, the state could, through tax incentives, encourage reforestation by the lumber companies. A third option—state management of virgin forest reserves with reforestation as trees were cut, an option being tried elsewhere at this time— received little consideration in California, mainly because the state had already sold most of its timberlands to lumber companies.[43]

The state forester and agricultural groups initiated the early efforts at reforestation. As early as 1904, members of the Water and Forest Association recognized the hurdle that the state's tax system placed in the way of reforestation. Each year lumbermen, rather than pay the annual property tax on their cut-over lands, forfeited thousands of acres to the state, for they felt they could not afford the expense of an annual tax on vacant land or second growth timber that might require thirty or more years to mature.[44] Rather than alter the tax laws, however, spokesmen for the association suggested that the state take over and replant lands abandoned for the nonpayment of taxes. The state forester backed this proposal and repeatedly called upon the legislature to appropriate funds for the reforestation of tax delinquent lands and the purchase of cut-over tracts still in private hands. Little came of these ideas. Concerned mainly with fire protection measures, neither the state forester nor the agriculturalists spent enough time or effort to get their proposals through the legislature, and they perished in committees.[45]

From these beginnings lumbermen assumed the leadership of the reforestation movement. A survey undertaken by the state forester in 1912 showed that many of California's larger lumbermen disliked the state's annual property tax and desired, instead, a yield or severance tax that would be levied on timber only when it was cut. Lumbermen also denounced the assessment of timberlands by county officials. This practice, they claimed, led to numerous inequities that only statewide audits could abolish. Condemning the yearly levy on timberlands, the state forester endorsed the lumbermen's petitions. Several of California's leading lumbermen, again backed by the state forester, repeated their requests at hearings before Governor Johnson's conservation commission and added that they now also favored state reforestation efforts.[46]

During the war years the lumbermen turned to Sacramento for aid. In 1915, the assemblymen from California's major redwood area introduced a bill appropriating funds for the state to buy cut-over lands for forest reserves. As amended in committee, the measure also instructed the state forester to develop a comprehensive plan for managing all state-owned timberlands along the lines of scientific forestry. Backed by the state forester and members of the conservation commission as well as lumbermen, the proposal passed both houses of the legislature unanimously, only to die at the hands of an inexplicable pocket veto from Governor Johnson.[47] Thwarted on this front, lumbermen turned their attention to tax reform. In 1917, they supported a bill to shift the power for setting assessments from county to state officials. This change would, they claimed, end differences between counties and result in uniform, predictable collections by the state. Opposition from county tax assessors and other local officials, however, defeated the measure.[48]

Lumbermen stepped up their drive for reforestation after the war. In 1920, a meeting of pine and redwood men with the state forester urged the state legislature to appropriate $150,000 for the forester to begin reforestation work. The legislature, then dominated by elements trying to cut state expenditures, refused this request. In the same session Assemblyman A. F. Stevens, a redwood lumberman, sponsored a constitutional amendment to separate the taxation of land from timber and to provide for a yield tax on timber. County officials, fearing the erosion of their tax bases, fought the proposal. Lumbermen and the state board of forestry were themselves divided on details of the plan, and it never came to a vote.[49] Conferences between groups of lumbermen and the state forester smoothed over differences during the next few years, and in 1925 lumbermen finally obtained their desires. A constitutional amendment to exempt second growth timber, as distinct from the ground upon which it stood, from taxation easily passed the senate and assembly. Backed by lumbermen's organizations, the state forester, and the County Assessors Association, it won approval in the following general election. The measure made it economically feasible for lumbermen to begin large-scale reforestation projects, and with its enactment the lumber industry took a long step in the direction of efficient production.[50]

The campaign for scientific forestry in California received its impetus from several sources. It began as a movement undertaken by farmers and others concerned with their state's mountain watersheds. Aided by state officials, most notably the state forester, these organized groups pushed the initial scientific forestry measures through the state legislature. In its later years the scientific forestry movement changed. As lumbermen came to dominate the movement, the emphasis on watershed protection (which, for instance, the federal Capper Bill would have furthered) yielded, for the most part, to considerations of continued profits within the lumber industry. As the prices they received rose after 1914 and as mounting demands threatened the last stands of virgin timber in the continental United States, lumbermen recognized the wisdom of sustained yield harvesting and worked to make it a reality. From a speculative and crudely exploitive industry, lumbering in California was emerging in the 1920s as a more rational business dominated by considerations of efficiency and order.

The adoption of scientific forestry by lumbermen was not, however, easily achieved. As was the case in the oil industry, divisions rent the ranks of the lumbermen well into the war years. The larger companies, which were interested in long-term yields, were more favorably inclined to scientific forestry than the smaller firms that often operated on a shoestring and sought short-run, speculative profits. Splits opened on other lines as well. Redwood men, who used fires as part of their logging process, were less willing to accept fire prevention measures than the pine operators who saw millions of dollars of damage done to their property by fire each year. Moreover, all lumbermen feared lest the movements for fire prevention and reforestation be expanded to encompass other aspects of their businesses as well. The support of lumbermen for scientific forestry came reluctantly and then only when such backing promised direct economic gains.

5

Railroad and Public Utility Regulation

In the early twentieth century California businessmen spearheaded movements to set up a new railroad commission with vastly increased powers and to bring public utility companies under state supervision. The driving force for railroad regulation came from emergent shipping interests desiring lower rates to expand their markets and from merchants seeking alterations in the state's rate structure to give them trade advantages over their rivals. Public utility officers led the campaign for state regulation of their firms. They hoped state supervision would help them both enlarge and rationalize their systems of public utilities to meet the needs of California's burgeoning population.[1]

The Movement for Railroad Regulation

The growth of new economic interests—agricultural cooperatives, integrated oil companies, and large lumber firms—provided much of the stimulus for railroad regulation. All of these business groups harbored grievances against the state's railroads, particularly the Southern Pacific. Each wanted better service and lower rates to allow them to tap larger markets for their goods. As their economic power increased, farmers, oil men, and lumbermen sought private redress for their problems, and their efforts to obtain satisfaction from the railroads helped pave the way for stricter state regulation.

California's agriculturalists held the most enduring complaints against the railroads and were among the first businessmen to challenge their economic and political grip on California. From the 1870s on, associations of fruit growers requested better service and lower rates. They enjoyed little success before the formation of comprehensive cooperatives to market citrus and deciduous fruits and, as late as 1895, proved unable to influence the state's leading railroads. Lengthy hearings held by the state railroad commission in that year resulted in only negligible relief.[2] Yet, little more than a decade later the citrus fruit men, by then thoroughly organized, secured a substantial reduction on rates for the shipment of oranges across the country. When the Southern Pacific and Santa Fe railroads tried to restore charges to their former levels in 1909, the California Fruit Growers Exchange successfully contested the proposed hike before the Interstate Commerce Commission. The deciduous fruit men followed the example of the citrus growers in 1911. After a week-long conference with the nation's transcontinental lines, they secured a large rate decrease on shipments to points east of Chicago.[3]

The actions of the state's oil companies also foreshadowed the course of future events. Though dependent upon the Santa Fe and Southern Pacific railroads for the carriage of much of their crude as late as 1910, the oil men had considerable resources of their own. In the early twentieth century, the larger firms exacted rebates totaling $200,000 annually.[4] Even the smaller operators wielded some power. In 1901, in a rare show of cooperation, the large and small producers obtained a 10 percent reduction of rates for the shipment of crude by the Southern Pacific and Santa Fe lines.[5] Four years later the oil companies nearly won approval from the state legislature for a demurrage measure setting strict requirements for the supplying of tank cars by railroads to producers of crude.[6]

California's lumbermen, particularly those engaged in the redwood trade, also held grievances against the railroads. In the 1890s, the lumber companies began searching for markets outside of California to relieve their chronic problem of overproduction. In doing so they collided with the railroads, for high transcontinental rates excluded them from eastern markets. Like the agriculturalists, the lumbermen tried to secure lower rates and better service through cooperative action. The trade associations of the pine and redwood operators won some concessions, but their inability to achieve total success insured that lumbermen would be active in the movement for stricter state regulation of railroads.

Discrimination in rates between localities and intercity rivalry for markets further spurred Californians toward tighter railroad regulation. As centers of population, commerce, and industry shifted in California, merchants in the affected areas often blamed the railroads for their troubles. Businessmen in towns with expanding hinterlands called for a change in the old rate structures to meet the altered conditions. Merchants in cities threatened by the new developments sought to bolster their positions by maintaining, or even increasing, the nineteenth-century rate differentials.

Both San Francisco and Los Angeles businessmen were displeased with parts of the state's rate structure. The losses suffered in their contest with Los Angelenos for the trade of the San Joaquin Valley led many San Francisco merchants to endorse stronger railroad regulation measures, for they felt that tougher regulation would result in rate differentials more favorable to their metropolis. Merchants in Los Angeles, though they had won much of the commerce of the San Joaquin Valley with the aid of the Southern Pacific, thought they had suffered at the hands of the line and joined their neighbors to the north in the demands for stricter state supervision. The fight to gain control of their harbor at San Pedro rankled most in the minds of Los Angelenos. In a twenty-year contest involving lengthy court battles and maneuvering in the state and national legislatures the Southern Pacific tried, for reasons of its own, to block Los Angeles's quest for a deep water port. Only in 1911 did the city gain control of its tidelands at San Pedro.[7] Nor did the Southern Pacific's rates always favor Los Angeles. In 1910, it cost as much to transport goods from Los Angeles to its port at San Pedro, a distance of 24 miles, as it did over the 126 miles separating Los Angeles from San Diego.[8]

Businessmen in other areas joined their counterparts in San Francisco and Los Angeles in condemning the policies of the Southern Pacific. Anxious to extend their cities' hegemony over the surrounding countryside, they laid the blame for any checks upon their progress, sometimes rightly but often wrongly, at the feet of the state's railroads. All asked to be designated as terminal points for transcontinental traffic, and between 1873 and 1910 the number of terminal points in California rose from four to ninety-seven. When the expected growth in trade often failed to materialize (partly because so many cities obtained the same privileges at the same time), the outraged merchants denounced the railroads.[9]

By 1909, the Southern Pacific had, in one way or another, antagonized most of California's businessmen. As an expert on railroad rates in California noted in 1922, the Southern Pacific could alter scarcely a single schedule without injuring some of California's merchants.[10] Local shippers compained of high charges and discrimination on intrastate shipments. Even those businessmen who cared primarily about transcontinental rates, over which a state commission could have little control, desired closer supervision of intrastate charges, particularly rates between points in the countryside and the terminal points from which goods began their transcontinental journeys.

State supervision of railroads in California started in the 1870s. The state constitution adopted in 1879 set up a three-man regulatory commission elected by district. Empowered to lower rates upon the complaints of shippers and to enforce uniform bookkeeping practices for railroads, the commission would, Californians believed, bring the state's lines to heel. The commission failed to fulfill these hopes. The Southern Pacific corrupted many of the commissioners, and even those who remained honest found themselves hampered by inexperience and the lack of expert knowledge. The complexities of rate-making particularly baffled them. Unfavorable court decisions further eroded the commission's effectiveness. Rulings by the United States Circuit Court for Northern California in 1896 and the Superior Court of San Francisco several years later severely limited the rate-fixing powers of the commission.[11]

With the failure of its first commission California fell behind other states and the federal government in railroad regulation. At the opening of the twentieth century reformers throughout the nation were calling for stricter regulation, and many states tightened their laws. By 1905, fifteen states had established railroad commissions empowered to set rates on their own initiative, and another eight possessed agencies allowed to change rates upon the request of complainants. Dramatic events in Wisconsin captured the attention of the nation. Business groups and politicians, led by Governor Robert LaFollette, overcame the intense opposition of the state's railroads to secure new regulatory legislation in 1903 and 1905. The laws, while not as far-reaching as LaFollette desired, established a commission to investigate abuses and set rates. The growing power of the federal government over interstate lines, like developments on the state level, underlined the need for new measures in California. In 1902, the Elkins Act forbade rebating, and four years later the Hepburn Act gave the Interstate Commerce Commission the right to fix maximum rates subject to judicial review.[12]

California's twentieth-century campaign for railroad regulation opened with federal and state investigations into railroad practices. In 1906, the United States Bureau of Corporations revealed that California's larger oil companies were receiving rebates on their intrastate shipments.[13] A year later Interstate Commerce Commissioner Franklin K. Lane uncovered further instances of favoritism. He found little evidence of rebating on interstate traffic but reported numerous instances of it on intrastate shipments.[14] These revelations goaded state officials into action. In 1908, the state railroad commission and California Attorney General U. S. Webb examined the conduct of the Southern Pacific and Santa Fe railroads. At public hearings the Traffic Association of California, an organization of San Francisco shippers formed in late 1907, documented many cases of discrimination.[15] However, because of the inadequacy of the state's laws, officials undertook no prosecutions. The results of these proceedings led Attorney General Webb to declare that the shippers were "practically helpless" and to call for an enlargement of the state's power over railroads.[16]

Efforts by the Southern Pacific and Santa Fe lines to increase their charges on transcontinental shipments in early 1909 set the tinder afire. A month before the proposed rates were to become effective the Traffic Bureau of the San Francisco Merchants Exchange lodged a protest with the railroads and threatened to appeal to the Interstate Commerce Commission. Several days later the Traffic Association of California called a meeting of shippers and merchants who would be affected by the hike. Businessmen from throughout the state attended the conference in San Francisco. Delegates represented California's leading agricultural associations and cooperatives, mercantile and manufacturing firms (particularly those of Sacramento and San Francisco), and the chambers of commerce of towns from all sections of the state. The convention endorsed the stand of the Traffic Bureau and pledged its support of that body. The meeting then passed resolutions condemning the rate increases and demanding an investigation by the Interstate Commerce Commission. The conference also denounced local charges and service. In fact, many businessmen complained more about the problems met in intrastate shipments than the difficulties and expenses of the longer cross-country hauls.

At the conclusion of its meeting the convention chose fifteen of its members, known collectively as the California Shippers Executive Committee, to examine local conditions and work for the creation of a stronger railroad commission at the coming session of the state legislature. The Executive Committee immediately began preparing for a Freight Rate Day protest. Just one week before the legislators convened in Sacramento groups of merchants and shippers in some fifty towns held rallies that criticized both instate and transcontinental rates and asked for intervention by the Interstate Commerce Commission and the state railroad commission. Many of these convocations further instructed their representatives in the state legislature to revamp the makeup and powers of the railroad commission.[17]

California's superheated atmosphere brought the 1909 legislative session to a boil. Governor James Gillette urged its members to enact regulatory legislation to keep California in step with the rest of the nation. Senator John Stetson quickly introduced a measure drafted by Attorney General Webb designed to give California one of the strongest state railroad commissions in the nation. Under the provisions of Stetson's bill, the commission could modify rates and freight classification schedules without waiting for the complaints of shippers. Moreover, the commission was to set absolute, that is, fixed or uniform, rather than just maximum rates. The proposal also allowed the commission to make physical evaluations of railroads to aid in determining rate bases. On behalf of the railroads, Senator Leroy Wright presented a counterproposal. Under its terms the railroad commission could establish only maximum rates (and, thus, railroads could continue to favor large over small shippers), and it could set these only if shippers questioned the reasonableness of the tariffs put into effect by the railroads. Wright's measure gave the commission no power to make physical evaluations of railroad property or define freight classifications. Nor was it as tough as the Stetson bill in providing for the punishment of those violating its terms.[18]

Merchants and railroad men soon clashed on these proposals. Shippers and merchants rallied to Stetson's measure. The Traffic Bureau of the San Francisco Merchants Exchange and the California Shippers Executive Committee agreed to work together for its passage. Seth Mann, a San Francisco lawyer who had earlier acted as counsel for the Traffic Association of California, represented them at public hearings in Sacramento. He argued that on intrastate shipments discrimination between shippers and places rather than the level of rates irritated businessmen the most. Speaking before the Senate Committee on Corporations he asserted that "stability of rates is more important to the shipper than the rates themselves." The Stetson bill, with its provisions for absolute rates, could alone, he concluded, provide the stability merchants sought. A little later, in an appearance before the Senate Judiciary Committee, he struck hard at discrimination between localities, which he labeled "the great railroad problem of the future."[19] San Francisco merchants, stung by their trade rivalry with Los Angeles, found this approach particularly appealing.[20] Spokesmen for the railroads, led by P. F. Dunn, an attorney for the Southern Pacific, countered these arguments by raising the issue of the constitutionality of the Stetson bill's provision for absolute freight rates. Interpreting the state constitution and legal decisions in a light favorable to their clients, they claimed that the railroad commission could be authorized to fix only maximum rates. This tactic worked. Largely because of the confusion on its legality, the Stetson bill failed to win approval; and, rather than lose everything, the merchant bodies reluctantly accepted Senator Wright's proposal incorporating the principle of maximum rates.[21]

The shippers did, however, secure passage for a mutual demurrage act to insure them of a constant supply of railroad cars. Two years before a car shortage at the height of the harvest season led the Southern Pacific to divert its cars from California which possessed no demurrage law to Oregon and Texas which did. This action infuriated the Golden State's fruit growers, and, in 1909, E. O. Miller of Visalia introduced a tough demurrage measure on their behalf. Oil men, who had long desired such a law, joined the fruit men in supporting Miller's proposal. Despite spirited railroad opposition, Miller's demurrage bill passed both houses of the legislature and became law.[22]

Businessmen and politicians intensified their demands for a new railroad commission during the next two years. At the end of its 1909 session the legislature held a series of hearings to examine railroad rates. The outcome was a senate resolution denouncing rate hikes by the state's express companies and railroads. The solons called upon the state railroad commission to extend the investigation and take whatever remedial steps it could. When the commission pigeonholed the issue, the legislators, sitting in special session in the fall of 1910, approved a resolution condemning the body's inactivity.[23] At their annual meetings and conventions fruit growers, lumbermen, merchant organizations, and other associations of shippers also continued to press for relief from the Interstate Commerce Commission and the state railroad commission.[24]

Political expression was given this continued agitation in Hiram Johnson's bid for governor in 1910. A progressive Republican, Johnson toured California in a flashy, red automobile and attracted crowds wherever he went by attacking the Southern Pacific "machine." Throughout his campaign Johnson emphasized, almost to the exclusion of other subjects, the need to free state government from the railroad's grip.[25] "The issue is," he repeatedly thundered, "shall the people of California take to themselves the government of the state or shall the Southern Pacific be continued in sovereign power?''[26] With Johnson's candidacy the movement for state railroad regulation assumed new dimensions. What had begun as a contest between California's emergent business groups and the state's established railroads broadened to include the general public as well. With this change, the campaign to place railroads under effective state control assumed a new urgency. Railroad domination of California, Johnson warned, was hurting, not just the state's economic development, but also the political freedom of its inhabitants.

Johnson's victory at the polls assured that railroad regulation would be the major topic facing the state legislature in 1911. In his inaugural address Governor Johnson urged the legislators not to let "the bogieman of the railroad companies, unconstitutionality" deter them from enacting a measure with the absolute rate principle.[27] A committee appointed by the Republican party drafted a bill based upon Stetson's proposal of two years before. Containing representatives of the merchant organizations of both San Francisco and Los Angeles, this body argued for the measure in much the same terms used to support the Stetson bill in 1909. Governor Johnson, relying upon arguments and figures supplied by the president of the San Francisco Merchants Exchange, sent the measure to the legislature with a ringing denunciation of railroad discrimination between shippers and places.[28]

In a move that puzzled political observers at the time and still defies definitive analysis today, the railroad men offered no opposition to Johnson's bill. Though they attended public hearings on the proposal, none spoke against it. As the chairman of the Senate Committee on Corporations noted, the railroad lobbyists exhibited "a spirit of bashfulness and backwardness" completely at odds with their behavior two years before.[29] Several reasons may account for this turnabout. The forces favoring strict regulation were more numerous in the 1911 legislature than in 1909, and their dominance, combined with Johnson's election, may have led railroad men to view tougher laws as inevitable. In addition, the main argument of those fighting the principle of absolute rates had been discredited. In a speech before the Commonwealth Club of California, State Supreme Court Justice Lucien Shaw declared that no legal foundation existed for the charge that absolute rates were unconstitutional, and proponents of Johnson's bill stressed this point in hearings on the measure.[30] Then, too, by 1911, railroad leaders may have felt that a law specifying uniform rates might actually work to their advantage by ending the costly rebates on intrastate traffic and by shifting the burden of defending the rate schedules of cities competing for the same trade from the railroads to the state railroad commissioners. F. G. Athearn, who headed the Southern Pacific's bureau of economics, asserted that "regulation is good for us" and came out in favor of the constitutional amendments embodying Johnson's proposal as "vastly superior to the articles of the constitution it is intended they should replace."[31]

Unhindered by railroad opposition, Johnson's measure sped through both houses of the legislature without dissent, and constitutional amendments incorporating the act's terms won ratification in the following general election. The new law gave California one of the most advanced railroad commissions in the country. Possessing all of the powers provided by the original Stetson bill of 1909, the commission would, Governor Johnson predicted, open "a new era wherein justice, fair dealing and the rights of the people shall prevail."[32]

The Campaign for Public Utility Regulation

Governor Johnson's measure gave the railroad commission control over only steam railroads, but within a few years further acts extended its jurisdiction to include nearly all public utilities in California. Developments in other parts of the nation directly affected the movement for state regulation in California. By 1911, New York, Wisconsin, Massachusetts, Texas, and at least seven other states had set up commissions to supervise the rates and services of utilities within their boundaries.[33] Public utility officers in California viewed the work of these commissions as beneficial to the public service corporations affected and campaigned for state regulation in California. They hoped that state regulation would end competition between their firms, enhance the value of their companies' stocks and bonds, and allow them to escape continual wrangling with county and municipal authorities.

Public utility men felt that state regulation would enable them to eliminate competition between their companies and thus insure the development of a unified, rational system of power and telephone networks in California. A wave of reorganizations and mergers in the opening years of the twentieth century left California blanketed with three or four major power companies, and the same trend was apparent in other public utilities. Company officers looked upon their firms as natural monopolies that should be protected from competition. They claimed that such a policy would benefit the public as well as their firms by ending the duplication of facilities, the costs of which were reflected in higher rate bases.[34] Closely related to the issue of competition was that of financing. The construction of regional and statewide utility networks to meet the needs of California's rapidly growing population proved extremely costly for the companies involved and greatly raised their demands for capital. They financed much of their expansion by bond flotations on the New York market, and many public utility men believed that the investigation and approval of proposed security issues by a state agency would increase their value and ease of sale. Most agreed with a San Francisco representative of an eastern brokerage house when he claimed that state regulation of public service corporations "almost without exception had a beneficial bearing on their securities."[35]

Public utility officers also hoped that state regulation would make it possible for them to end constant haggling with municipal authorities. They thought that city politicians, elected for short periods of time and having no special knowledge of the utility business, lacked the training necessary to reach equitable decisions on rates and service. Even worse, corrupt councilmen and mayors, public service corporation officers lamented, often demanded expensive payoffs to grant franchises or guarantee profitable rate levels. Graft prosecutions in San Francisco had, indeed, revealed numerous instances of collusion between corporate and city officials. The United Railroads of San Francisco paid $200,000 in boodle for a trolley permit in 1906. Nor did such arrangements always prove dependable. The Pacific States Telephone and Telegraph Company gave $51,000 to San Francisco's board of supervisors in 1906 to keep its rival, the Home Telephone Company, out of the city. The supervisors pocketed this sum and then granted the Home Telephone Company the coveted franchise in return for the still larger bribe of $125,000.[36] Fear of municipal ownership added to the distrust company officers had of city officials. Even before 1900, twenty municipalities had acquired ownership of their water systems in California, and in the first decade of the twentieth century twelve cities adopted charters permitting them to operate their own gas or electric plants. State regulation would, public utility men felt, knock the wind out of the sails of municipal ownership advocates and remove this threat to their businesses.[37]

John Britton, vice-president of the Pacific Gas and Electric Company, initiated the drive for state regulation with a lengthy article in California's leading financial journal in early 1909. State regulation would, he claimed, solve many problems for public utility officials. Writing just after graft prosecutions in San Francisco, Britton blamed the corruption on the greed of the supervisors and warned that without state regulation "each corporation would be at the mercy of as pitiless a pack of howling destroyers, as would the lonely traveller on the Siberian steppes be against the gaunt and hungry wolves.'' Besides freeing themselves from the grip of venal politicians, state supervision would, according to Britton, help public utility officers restore public confidence, and particularly the faith of investors, in their companies. Only a panel of experts (Britton wrote with favor on the commissions of Massachusetts, New York and Wisconsin) chosen by the governor would, he believed, be able to decide "mooted questions" of financing, rates, and franchises in "calm deliberation and not in political heat." Finally, Britton concluded that only by the creation of such a body could public utilities escape "that unreasonable demon and destroyer, Municipal Ownership."[38]

Public utility officers throughout California quickly joined forces to back Britton's stand. At the 1909 meeting of the Pacific Coast Gas Association, the vice-president of the Los Angeles Gas and Electric Company called for state supervision "on account of the growing desire on the part of our city governments to regulate our affairs."[39] Several months later officers of the Pacific Gas and Electric Company again came out in favor of state control modeled upon the commissions in Massachusetts, Wisconsin, and New York. These agencies, company officials observed, were "composed of specially qualified men of known integrity" and set rates influenced by neither "sentiment nor partisanship, by neither gallery nor graft."[40] In 1910, the president of the Pacific Coast Gas Association denounced municipal authorities as "pirates" and urged the establishment of a state commission to "insure us fair rates and a much more settled condition as to competition, thus enhancing the value of our securities."[41]

The Pacific Lighting Company, the Los Angeles Gas and Electric Company, and the Pacific Gas and Electric Company set up a committee to lobby for state regulation at the coming legislative session, and in 1911 these efforts bore fruit.[42] Constitutional amendments preparing the way for supervision of public utilities by the state railroad commission passed the legislature and won approval in the following general election. After their enactment Max Thelen, an attorney for the railroad commission, inspected railroad and public service commissions in eleven states throughout the nation. John Eshleman, the president of the California Railroad Commission, then embodied Thelen's findings and suggestions in the Public Utilities Act that he and several members of the state senate drafted. This proposal increased the size of the railroad commission and extended its authority to cover power and light companies, street railroads, telephone and telegraph companies, and public wharves. Under the measure's terms the commission was empowered to grant franchises, set rates and conditions of service, and investigate proposed securities issues of the state's public utilities.[43]

The Public Utilities Act received wide publicity and came under lengthy discussion at hearings before the railroad commission. All of the public utility officers attending these hearings favored the measure. However, representatives of California's largest power and telephone concerns sought modifications. They feared that under the bill's provisions it would be impossible to set different rates for the same product sold under different circumstances. Electric company officers felt, for instance, that they would have to charge mountain towns, which were close to the source of energy, the same rates as other areas farther away. Some also requested that stock and bond issues already authorized by their companies be excluded from inspection by the railroad commission. Thelen and Eshleman assured them that rates could vary according to the different classes, conditions, and locations of service. However, they rejected pleas that securities authorized previous to the passage of the proposal be excused from the provisions of the bill. After meeting with the railroad commissioners, John Britton of the Pacific Gas and Electric Company and Tirey Ford of the Sierra and San Francisco Light and Power Company declared that "we are glad to be regulated for our own sake" and lent their support to the measure.[44] The inclusion of a section allowing incorporated areas to maintain supervision of public utilities within their boundaries mollified city officials and municipal ownership proponents. As originally drawn up, the bill required all cities to hold elections at which voters would decide whether or not to transfer the regulation of their utilities to the state. However, the proposal was amended, at the insistence of city officials, to require elections only if three-fifths of a city's board of supervisors or 10 percent of the voters requested it. Otherwise, utilities serving incorporated areas would remain under municipal control.[45]

Encountering almost no opposition, the Public Utilities Act easily secured approval from a special session of the state legislature and went into effect in March, 1912.

California's public utility officers praised the new law; in fact, their only criticism was that cities would still be able to regulate their own utilities. The general agent of the Pacific Telephone and Telegraph Company declared that "from the first this corporation has been in favor of a central, high powered, high salaried, long term commission" and expressed regret that "the framers of the law, contrary to the urging of the utilities interested, saw fit to weaken the commission . . . by one sided, elastic provisions in connection with the retention and surrender of certain powers by municipalities." The act would, he predicted, make it easier to market public utility securities and limit wasteful competition between companies.[46] Pacific Gas and Electric officers echoed these words. Lamenting only that the commission lacked "complete control similar to the other progressive states where so much has been accomplished," they urged all public utility men to "hail this new law with acclaim and play a part in insuring its successful operation."[47] In his presidential address to the Pacific Coast Gas Association in 1912, William Baurhyte, vice-president of the Los Angeles Gas and Electric Company, voiced the same ideas and like the others felt "it is unfortunate" that the Public Utilities Act "still permits municipal regulation under certain conditions."[48] The secretary of the Southern California Edison Company called the Public Utilities Act a "long step [forward]" and emphasized that it would provide "absolute stability of our securities and protection from unnecessary competition."[49]

In the next few years, company officials campaigned to place those public utilities located in cities under state control.[50] Max Thelen, then president of the railroad commission, drafted a bill embodying their desires in 1915. In open hearings representatives of the Pacific Telephone and Telegraph Company and the Home Telephone Company urged the speedy passage of the measure as "necessary for the preservation of the peace of every public utility in California."[51] Public utility officers obtained their wishes; the railroad commission received complete jurisdiction over all, except municipally owned, public utilities in California.

The Activities of the Railroad Commission

Between 1911 and 1915, the new railroad commission demonstrated a liveliness not shown by its predecessors and laid down guidelines that would be long followed in California. The commission investigated 4,040 complaints; by way of comparison only 113 complaints had been disposed of in the preceding thirty-two years.[52] In resolving the cases before it the commission tackled three major problems: the setting of reasonable railroad and public utility rates, the establishment of standards of competition for these concerns, and the investigation of proposed securities issues of those companies under its jurisdiction.

In most cases the commission relied upon the expense of providing service in setting rates and had, therefore, to face the question of determining which costs should be included in rate bases. The commissioners considered two possibilities: the original cost of constructing the physical plant and the present cost of replacing that plant. Breaking with precedents established by the United States Supreme Court and other state regulatory bodies, the California Railroad Commission found the replacement cost method unsatisfactory. If it were used as the rate base, the public service corporations would, the commissioners reasoned, benefit unjustly from any appreciation in the value of lands and other properties they held. A rise in the value of a utility's property would raise the expense of replacing it and hence justify an increase in rates.[53] Therefore, the commissioners applied the original cost method in determining most rate bases.[54] The commission took particular care to avoid including watered stock or false construction expenses in estimating rate bases. For instance, it cut the rates of the Southern Pacific Railroad and its tributary lines in Kern County on the grounds that company books had inflated the costs of building the railroads.[55]

The commission also brought competition under state supervision. The commissioners sought to eliminate discrimination in rates between localities and shippers, for they reasoned that these types of discrimination formed artificial barriers to trade and felt that they unjustly benefited some businessmen at the expense of others. While acting against what they viewed as unfair discrimination, the members of the railroad commission adopted the stance of many "New Nationalist" progressives that railroads and public utilities were natural monopolies and should, therefore, be protected from competition in their spheres of operation. By limiting competition the commissioners hoped to end what they felt was the inefficient duplication of facilities by public utilities. The commissioners were quick to point out that the costs of duplication were ultimately borne by consumers in unnecessarily high rates. By the same token, the commissioners viewed rate wars as detrimental to the best interests of both the utilities and the consumers and sought to dampen them. "Vigorous competition with violent voluntary rate reductions," the president of the railroad commission explained, often led to "consolidation and subsequent increases in rates above all previous levels."[56]

Under the prodding of local merchants and businessmen, the commission first worked to abolish discrimination in rates and service. The policy-making decision in this field pitted Los Angeles against the Southern Pacific and San Pedro railroads. In 1911, the Los Angeles Board of Harbor Commissioners challenged the justness of rates on the branch lines of these railroads between Los Angeles and its harbor at San Pedro. In the ensuing investigation the railroad commission found that charges for the carriage of goods from Los Angeles to San Pedro and San Diego, which was much farther away, were identical. Declaring that "we believe it is the duty of any rate-making body to eliminate artificial conditions," the commissioners lowered the rates between Los Angeles and San Pedro.[57] Further rulings upheld and expanded the implications of this decision. In 1912, after lengthy hearings, the commissioners acceded to the wishes of San Francisco merchants by reducing rates for the transportation of their products into the San Joaquin Valley.[58] The commission also acted to end rebating and other forms of discrimination among shippers. It denied the application of the California Western Railroad to carry the timber of several lumber companies at lower rates than those charged their competitors in return for right-of-ways through their properties.[59] Similarly, the commissioners refused to allow railroads to raise the minimum carload weights for the shipment of concrete pipes, because they felt that such an increase would favor large over small manufacturers.[60]

To foster the growth of efficient public utility and railroad networks in California the railroad commission sought to limit competition between the various systems. Arguments of efficiency persuaded the commissioners to let the Pacific Coast subsidiary of the American Bell Telephone Company purchase the Home Telephone Company of San Francisco and other independents throughout California. The commission granted approval, its bond expert explained, "in the interest of vastly improved service and a correspondingly decreased rate."[61] Following the same policy, the commissioners denied the Oro Electric Company permission to compete with the Western States Gas and Electric Company in serving Stockton. Stockton's officials backed the Oro Electric Company's plea as offering "real competition in the bidding for public lighting" and asserted that the rates it proposed would be lower than those of the Western States.[62] Nonetheless, the commissioners refused to grant the franchise to the Oro Electric, because they thought that Stockton already received adequate service and that competition would lead to an unnecessary duplication of facilities.[63]

For similar reasons the state railroad commissioners supported the Southern Pacific Railroad in a lawsuit brought by United States Attorney General James McReynolds to dissolve the line's connection with the Central Pacific Railroad. McReynolds claimed that the links between the two railroads were stifling railroad competition on the West Coast. The California Railroad Commission countered with the argument that dissolution would "impair the efficiency of what is now a strong and unified transportation system." Many of California's commercial and shipping organizations backed the stand of the railroad commission and, in 1923, the Interstate Commerce Commission ruled in favor of the Southern Pacific.[64]

The railroad commission also facilitiated the sale of new securities by public utilities and railroads, while, at the same time, protecting investors from shaky or fraudulent projects. Examination of their securities by the commissioners probably aided company officers in placing new flotations. Within the first nine months of its operation the new railroad commission approved over $50,000,000 of stocks and bonds for public utilities alone, and by the beginning of 1915 $500,000,000 in securities had won authorization. Not all companies, however, received permission to issue securities. When the United Railroads of San Francisco applied for the right to float bonds, an investigation by the railroad commission revealed that the corporation was already overcapitalized. Until the firm agreed to set up adequate sinking funds and eliminate a fictitious surplus from which dividends were being paid to the detriment of equity, the commission prohibited further bond sales. The commissioners emphasized that their supervision of securities benefited everyone. "The public is protected," explained the commission's bond expert, "by an insurance that service shall not be impaired nor rates raised merely to pay interest on excessive debt." The investor secured "a more careful safeguard of the securities which are issued." Even the public utilities gained, he thought, "by the pressure of an outward force to keep their debt down."[65]

Shippers and merchants responded favorably to the actions of the railroad commission. Oil men praised the commissioners for lowering the rates of the Southern Pacific in the upper San Joaquin Valley. The editor of California's leading oil journal stated that this reduction signified that an "era of justice seems to have been ushered in." Fruit growers and merchants in the San Joaquin and Sacramento valleys obtained numerous local rate adjustments, and the railroad commissioners often appeared on their behalf in cases pending before the Interstate Commerce Commission. Lumbermen were also pleased with rate decreases. San Francisco merchants, though they believed still larger reductions were in order, approved of the lowering of rates between their city and points in the San Joaquin Valley. Los Angelenos were, predictably, incensed by these cuts, but the decrease in freight rates to and from their port at San Pedro at least partially appeased them.[66]

Public utility and railroad officers, while often disturbed by specific rate reductions, found much to praise in the work of the railroad commission. They singled out the commission's policy of stopping rate wars and its certification of new securities for special commendation. In 1914, John Britton, then president of the Pacific Gas and Electric Company, lauded the commission for ending "unrestrained competition" and declared that "the prevention of . . . the destruction of capital is one of the greatest works of a commission, and I am happy to be able to say that it has been the dominant note of the commission of this state." He added that the commission, by ruling on stock and bond offerings, had "done in two years more to inspire the investor with confidence in California securities than all the gilt-edged promises of promoters in the years past."[67] The manager of the securities department of the Northern Electric Railway spoke in a similar vein. The commission had, he thought, "enhanced the value of . . . securities" by withholding approval from "any project financially unsound or wildly speculative in its character."[68] William Herrin, the vice-president and former political manager of the Southern Pacific, also praised state supervision. Writing three years after the passage of Governor Johnson's railroad act, he noted that "the cut-throat competition between railroads by means of rebates was in some measure responsible for the uncertain conditions of railroad finance" and doubted that any "railroad manager would agree to dispense with government regulation at the cost of returning to the old conditions."[69]

As was frequently the case with other pieces of business legislation, the struggle over railroad regulation exposed deep divisions within California's business community. Everyone favored regulation; the issue turned on what kind of regulation. California's new business groups—especially agriculturalists, lumbermen, and oil men—first sought private redress from the state's railroads and, when these efforts proved inadequate, supported stiff measures to bring the lines to heel. In this endeavor they were joined by local merchants seeking to uphold or win trade advantages for their towns or cities, as the battle between San Francisco and Los Angeles amply demonstrated. The railroads, recognizing that some type of supervision was unavoidable, pressed for weaker proposals that would have left the rate-making initiative in their hands.

The contest over railroad regulation was, then, essentially a battle between competing business interest groups. In this regard, it closely resembled the struggle for scientific forestry measures that, in its early days at least, pitted business farmers against lumbermen. This fact does not, however, mean that the general voting public was unimportant in the drive for railroad regulation. It was, for the businessmen and shippers ultimately won success by appealing beyond their own interest groups for support. Though the movement for railroad regulation was of long standing in California, it came to fruition only when Hiram Johnson's campaign for governor provided the state's emergent businessmen with a popular vehicle to carry their grievances to audiences throughout California. By emphasizing the threat the Southern Pacific political "machine" posed to political democracy, Johnson dramatized the issue of strict railroad regulation and hastened its arrival in California.

The movement for public utility regulation revealed more unanimity of purpose. Nearly all of California's public utility officers pressed for state supervision, had the same goals in mind, and were instrumental in obtaining passage for the Public Utilities Act. Yet, they probably could not have achieved success had the state's legislators viewed this law as inimical to the utilities' customers and, indeed, it would be wrong to see too sharp a dichotomy between the best interests of the utilities and the general public. Though in the matter of rate-making consumers gained at the expense of the public utilities by the commission's decision to use the original cost instead of the replacement cost in establishing the rate bases, all profited from the commission's policy on competition. By protecting public service corporations within their fields of operation, the commission both strengthened the financial positions of the utilities and prevented rate wars and the duplication of facilities that, as the commissioners frequently pointed out, added to the charges levied on consumers.

6

Banking and Bank Legislation

Adequate banking services, no less than transportation facilities, were needed for California's economic development. With the changes in the state's economy came increased demands for credit, capital, and a more flexible money supply by farmers and businessmen. As the various sections of the state became increasingly interdependent, it also became necessary for bankers to improve connections among themselves and with financiers outside of California. Finally, the growing complexity of the state's businesses led banks to begin providing a full range of banking services—savings, commercial, and trust—rather than specializing in a single type.[1]

As agriculture based on irrigation developed and the petroleum and lumber industries became big businesses, the capital and credit requirements of Californians soared. New banks sprang up to supply the credit facilities, and, as in the rest of the United States, most of these institutions were state rather than national banks. These state banks generally possessed less capital than the national banks, and most were located in the countryside, especially in the interior farm valleys and in Southern California. By 1905, the assets of banks outside of San Francisco rivaled those of the metropolis. Because their prosperity was usually closely linked to the local economic situation, the country banks were often forced to close their doors or declare bankruptcy during recessions or depressions. These failures disturbed the larger-city bankers, especially San Franciscans, for they believed that any bank failure shook public confidence in all banks, including their own institutions. How to increase the supply of capital and credit for businessmen while reducing bank failures and generally stabilizing banking in their state became an overriding concern for many California bankers.[2]

With the spread of banking into new areas within California, the establishment of dependable communications among California bankers became a pressing problem. The main difficulty lay in reconciling the often divergent aims of country and city bankers. The need for mutual understanding between these two groups increased when country bankers began depositing their reserves with San Francisco rather than New York banks.[3] By the same token, the maintenance of regular connections between California bankers and their correspondents on the eastern seaboard assumed a new significance.[4] The national marketing requirements of California fruit-growers particularly heightened the dependence of California bankers on their eastern correspondents. In times of financial panics the actions of eastern bankers could imperil California institutions, and Californians became increasingly concerned with protecting their banks from national economic fluctuations.

Changes in California's banking structure matched the growing complexity of the state's and the nation's economy. Banking became more complicated as banks took on new functions. As was happening in New York and elsewhere, California institutions began providing a full range of services: savings, trust, and commercial banking. When trust companies invaded the field of commercial banking, the commercial banks retaliated by entering the trust business. By 1909, nearly all of California's banks were engaging in more than one form of banking.[5] This practice further upset banking conditions, for damage to one type of banking often had repercussions in other areas. The failure, for instance, of a bank's commercial department could well cause trouble for its savings department. These circumstances presented yet another difficulty for California financiers: how, in the competitive situation that existed, to offer a full range of banking services without impairing the soundness of their institutions.

California bankers faced, then, a set of interrelated problems. They needed to supply their state's industries and agriculture with capital and credit without endangering the solvency of their banks. It sometimes proved impossible to obtain both of these goals, and many bankers opted for stability at the expense of credit expansion, much to the dismay of some businessmen. Second, California bankers sought to improve relations among themselves and tried to insulate their institutions from national economic fluctuations. Finally, California bankers recognized the necessity of presenting a complete line of banking services for businessmen. Yet, at the same time, they feared that the expansion of banking services might undermine a bank's financial soundness and felt that steps should be taken to prevent too rapid a growth in this direction.

Unlike many European nations, the United States did not possess a central banking system that could have dealt with these problems. Prior to the passage of the Federal Reserve Act in 1913 the United States had a mixed banking system composed of both state and national banks. National banks were chartered and regulated by the federal government and were empowered to issue their own bank notes. State governments chartered and supervised the state banks. Although for all practical purposes the state banks could not issue bank notes, they possessed certain advantages over the national banks: lower reserve and capital requirements, the ability to make loans on land, and a general laxer form of government regulation. With little central control, America's post–Civil War banking system was inherently unstable, and economic expansion and diversification in the 1880s and 1890s exacerbated the instability of the system.[6]

Lacking a central banking system, California bankers, like their counterparts throughout the United States, tried to cope with their difficulties through a mixture of private actions and state legislation. Bankers in San Francisco, Los Angeles, and other cities set up clearing houses and later a statewide trade association to help them solve their problems. Bankers also took the lead in initiating and securing passage for banking legislation at Sacramento, particularly after the financial panic of 1907. And, in an attempt to alter their relationships with each other and the general public, bankers began to define themselves as professional men with duties and obligations to the rest of society.

Banking Associations

California bankers initiated private efforts to solve their problems with the formation of the San Francisco Clearing House Association in 1876. In the early 1870s, California banks settled accounts in gold, an awkward and risky method of doing business. The clearing house eliminated the need for trundling bullion through the streets of San Francisco, for representatives of member banks met daily to exchange and cancel drafts drawn upon each other. With the rapid spatial development of their city resulting from a land boom in the early 1880s, Los Angelenos also felt the need for a clearing house, and, in 1887, they established an organization modeled upon the San Francisco association. Like the San Francisco Clearing House, it sped transactions among member banks, some of which were by this time separated by considerable distances.[7]

Considerations of convenience rather than a concern for the stabilization of banking dominated the nineteenth-century work of these clearing houses. Bankers showed little disposition to control the business practices of their fellows. Making credit and capital available to business and agriculture was more important to most financiers than the soundness of their state's banking system. The San Francisco Clearing House neither set capital requirements nor demanded financial examinations for banks seeking admittance to its ranks. Moreover, nonmembers could clear through the association by using the services of banks that belonged. The clearing house possessed well-defined procedures for the expulsion of members in perilous financial straits, and the power of expulsion could have been an effective tool in policing the city's commercial banks. However, the directors of the clearing house took no actions against banks in unsound conditions. Nor did they try to aid any of the banks in trouble. At least partly as a consequence of these policies several clearing-house banks were forced to close their doors in the hard times of the 1890s. Virtually the same story was repeated in Los Angeles. Eager to build up their area, most bankers could countenance no restrictions on their freedom of action. Only a few of the larger bankers wanted the Los Angeles Clearing House to impose discipline and high business standards upon its members, and, as in San Francisco, nothing came of these suggestions until the twentieth century.[8]

In setting up clearing houses Californians were imitating actions already taken by bankers elsewhere, but neither the San Francisco nor Los Angeles clearing houses assumed all of the functions of their counterparts in eastern cities. Besides easing the settlement of accounts between their members, clearing houses outside of California sometimes sought to relieve monetary stringencies in financial panics by issuing loan certificates collectively backed by their members, which then circulated as money. This procedure began in New York in the 1860s and had become widespread by the 1870s and 1890s. Clearing houses also often fostered standard banking practices. Some, for instance, set uniform interest rates paid depositors and charged for collections. California bankers, concerned more with rapid economic growth than with economic stability, took few steps in these directions in the nineteenth century.[9]

It required the panic of 1907 to fundamentally alter the nature of California's clearing houses. While still retaining their role of expediting financial transactions, the clearing houses now assumed new functions as well. They tried to moderate financial disturbances and enforce uniform banking practices. They issued clearing-house loan certificates to member banks and scrip for public use to compensate for the lack of money and to protect banks from runs by their depositors. These procedures had been adopted by eastern bankers at an earlier date, but Californians soon went further. To prevent bank failures in the future the clearing houses toughened their regulation of institutions using their services and appointed highly paid inspectors to periodically check the financial soundness of their members. In these actions Californians were preceded only by New York bankers who had initiated periodic inspections of clearing-house banks several years before.

The panic of 1907 caught Californians in a vulnerable position. Few bankers expected the crisis, and none anticipated the shortages of specie that quickly developed. Banks in New York, Chicago, Boston, and Philadelphia informed their Pacific Coast correspondents that they would not be allowed to withdraw funds on deposit with them. The eastern banks agreed to pay drafts drawn upon them only with clearing-house loan certificates. These actions proved especially harmful to California bankers, for they had just placed the returns of a large fruit crop in New York banks. Strapped for funds, sixteen California banks closed temporarily, and four failed, one with liabilities exceeding $8,000,000.[10]

Clearing houses throughout the state tried to blunt the impact of the crisis. San Franciscans led the way. Upon depositing acceptable securities with a loan committee, clearing-house members received certificates that they could use to settle clearing-house accounts, thus freeing their limited supply of specie to meet the demands of their depositors. To satisfy business needs for a circulating medium the San Francisco Clearing House supplied scrip in amounts of from one to twenty dollars. Banks desiring it placed clearing-house loan certificates with the loan committee and obtained scrip in return. At one point member banks had $12,339,000 in clearing-house loan certificates and $6,784,929 in scrip outstanding.[11] Bankers throughout California dealt with the panic in a similar way. The Los Angeles Clearing House issued $2,022,000 in loan certificates and $3,396,650 in scrip. Bankers in other cities relied upon clearing-house notes, and some certificates circulated even in Nevada.[12]

The panic of 1907 also led clearing houses to tighten their controls over member banks. Both the San Francisco and Los Angeles associations toughened their membership requirements. To belong to the San Francisco Clearing House banks now had to pass inspection by an entrance committee and possess a paid-in capital of $500,000 (nonmembers operating through clearing house banks needed a capital of at least $200,000). The Los Angeles Clearing House set its capital requirement at $200,000.[13] For the first time the clearing houses made provisions to regularly check the financial soundness of their members. Any bank using clearing-house loan certificates in San Francisco had to acquiesce in a weekly inspection of its books, and this detailed scrutiny continued after the panic. In 1908, the clearing house hired a full-time examiner at the princely annual salary of $15,000 to inspect all member banks at least once each year. He reported any discrepancies to a central committee that then decided whether to aid the bank in trouble or expel it from the clearing house.[14] The Los Angeles Clearing House appointed an examiner in the same year, and he operated on terms similar to those of the San Francisco inspector.[15]

Bankers hoped that the clearing houses would stabilize their industry, and the associations partially realized these desires. Examinations in Los Angeles revealed, according to the president of that city's clearing house, that many institutions were "of a mushroom character, illy [*sic*] organized as to personel [*sic*], under-capitalized, addicted to unethical methods." To change this situation the clearing house enforced new rules adopted in 1908, and this move helped touch off a wave of mergers and liquidations that led to the closing of thirteen of the city's forty-six commercial banks. The resulting banking structure proved strong enough to weather the crisis of 1914 with only a single bank closing. Furthermore, in the one case of failure, the clearing house reimbursed all the depositors of the member bank that failed. The collapse of any bank, those belonging to the organization agreed, should be avoided, because it lessened public confidence in banking as a whole.[16] In San Francisco, too, the power of examination and the threat of expulsion gave the clearing house real power, since, as one San Franciscan noted, for a commercial bank exclusion amounted to "financial suicide." While it is difficult to accurately measure the impact of the clearing house's actions upon San Francisco banking, it is worth noting that many bankers felt its new rules and inspections would prevent bank failures in the future. Most agreed with one of the city's leading financiers, when he observed in 1909 that "the feeling of security in dealing with our neighbors'' made clearing house examinations ''worth all that it costs.''[17]

Businessmen were ambivalent in their attitude toward these efforts to stabilize the state's banking structure. They generally applauded attempts to eliminate bank failures. Yet, their approval was tempered by concern lest these actions restrict the amount of credit and capital available for business expansion. When they could not obtain the funds they desired, businessmen often blamed the bankers. Insurance men and other businessmen in Los Angeles accused that city's clearing house of acting as an artificial barrier to entry into commercial banking. They asserted that it was ''almost impossible for another bank to start business in Los Angeles, so carefully has the Clearing House guarded its interests.'' They claimed that clearing-house members were discouraging the formation of new banks because ''the more banks, the more their power would have been jeopardized, and the less would be their profit'' and feared that such actions might impede the growth of local industry.[18] San Franciscans voiced similar complaints. The California Promotion Committee, a heterogeneous group of San Francisco businessmen, accused California bankers of not making enough credit available for new enterprises and of refusing to purchase the bonds of new companies like electric street railroads. The committee blamed this conservative attitude for forcing promoters to turn to New York for funds.[19]

Some of this criticism was probably valid. Businessmen, and not just fly-by-night speculators, incurred difficulties raising capital in California. The organizers of public utility and street car companies found themselves particularly hard-pressed. When expansions, reorganizations, and mergers took place in the early twentieth century, the promoters were almost invariably forced to travel to eastern money centers to float new stock and bond issues.[20] This difficulty in raising money was, of course, one of the main reasons public utility officers desired state regulation of their companies, for they hoped inspection by the railroad commission would enhance the value of their stocks and bonds. Other industries also depended upon eastern capital for development. The lumber industry, in particular, relied upon eastern capital. Much of the development of California's lumber industry came from the influx of eastern capital and firms (like the Diamond Match Company) that moved into California in the 1890s and early twentieth century.[21]

Although never completely successful in reconciling financial stability with financial expansion, California bankers proved more capable of regularizing transactions among themselves. The growth of banking in new areas underlined the need for a statewide banking organization in California. The growth of small state commercial banks to finance the development of agriculture in the state's interior seemed, according to many Californians, to demand some sort of central regulation. Only such control could, they believed, rationalize relations between bankers in different regions and stabilize the banking industry throughout California. Bankers facing similar problems in other areas of the United States established state or regional trade associations, and, by 1890, eleven state associations existed. Californians followed their lead with the formation of the California Bankers Association in 1891.[22]

From its earliest days the California Bankers Association worked to improve relations between country and city bankers. In the early twentieth century it established a par checking system for the entire state. Californians were in the forefront of this nationwide movement; only New York bankers were more advanced. As California's economy became increasingly complex, its residents needed to be able to cash checks wherever they were. Yet, most city bankers accepted drafts drawn on country banks only at a heavy discount. This practice particularly irked country bankers, because bankers in Los Angeles and San Francisco honored each other's checks at par. During the 1890s, country bankers tried to win acceptance for their notes at face value, or, failing in this matter, to secure approval for a uniform schedule of rates charged for cashing checks. In 1901, they succeeded. California Bankers Association members agreed to cash each other's checks at par, without any discounting or service charges. The organization also ironed out difficulties country bankers encountered as depositors in San Francisco institutions. Problems involved in these transactions became frequent as country banks began placing parts of their reserves in San Francisco rather than New York banks. The association sought to fix standard interest rates offered correspondents and uniform daily balances required of them. The California Bankers Association brought together bankers from different regions in still other ways. In 1902, it created a protective committee that circulated information about bank robberies, and ten years later it started purchasing office equipment for its members, usually receiving a 10 percent discount from the manufacturers.[23]

The California Bankers Association also established a group banking system and tried to set up a network of clearing houses to stabilize banking conditions in California. With the differentiation of the state's economy, the consideration of distinctly regional topics became increasingly urgent for California's bankers. To fill this need the California Bankers Association formed a number of local associations. The first group of this system (which the bankers labeled "group banking") began holding meetings in 1912, and within eight years six other groups existed. Besides discussing local problems, these bodies standardized bank forms and, in a few instances, established uniform interest rates paid depositors and charged borrowers. Some considered hiring inspectors to examine the financial soundness of their members.[24] Still more significant were efforts to found a statewide clearing-house system. Following the panic of 1907, the members of the California Bankers Association voted to set up ten regional clearing houses. Each would employ examiners to investigate the financial integrity of their members, and a central board elected by the state's bankers would lay down guidelines for the clearing houses to enforce. Hailed as a way to "prevent improper or unsafe conduct upon the part of any bank within the state," the plan won approval at the 1909 California Bankers Association convention. Yet, despite this auspicious beginning, the scheme never materialized, for bankers discovered that they could attain their goals more thoroughly and easily through legislation.[25]

As their failure to set up a state clearing-house system indicated, bankers realized that only measures having the force of law could adequately solve their problems. Clearing houses and other organizations might help, but because membership in them was voluntary, they could not provide the complete answers. What they could not adequately achieve by private actions many bankers hoped to accomplish by legislation.

Banking Legislation

From its inception the California Bankers Association worked for the passage of banking legislation at Sacramento. Most historians dealing with American banking legislation in the late nineteenth and early twentieth centuries have focused their attention on national developments. This emphasis is understandable, for federal legislation, the Aldrich-Vreeland Act and the Federal Reserve Act, did fundamentally alter banking in the United States. Yet, developments on the state level also proved important. In California bankers labored for bills to stabilize their state's banking system and protect their institutions from danger during financial panics, sometimes at the expense of extending credit and capital to farmers and businessmen. In addition, bankers pressed for measures regulating the expansion of multipurpose banking.

Bankers were not the only architects of California's banking laws. State officials, politicians, and various groups of businessmen influenced the legislation. Nor did bankers always agree upon the shape of legislation. Rifts often separated city from country bankers. They sometimes divided upon the issue of whether economic stability or rapid economic growth was more desirable, with city bankers usually taking the first and country bankers the latter point of view. Legislation also pitted bankers against each other on functional lines. Commercial and trust bankers, each of whom was trying to invade the other's domain, sought to use legislation defining multipurpose banking for their own ends. Yet, despite such splits, bankers played the predominant role in drafting California's bank laws. By hammering out their differences at the meetings of the California Bankers Association they often achieved near unanimity of purpose and as a result were able to establish the form of banking legislation in California. The California Banking Commission may have been, as the historian Gerald Nash has suggested, a "good example of how a public agency was shaping enterpreneurial techniques of private business" in the early twentieth century, but it was the bankers who determined the scope and nature of the duties and powers of the commission.[26]

Bank failures during the mid-1890s dramatized the need to modify banking legislation in California. California's three-man board of bank commissioners proved incapable of dealing with the depression. Inadequate laws and lax regulation contributed to widespread bank failures in 1893 and 1894, with only Kansas surpassing California in the number of closings. The failures of the Pacific Bank and its affiliate, the Home Savings Bank, attracted the most attention. Systematically looted by their officers, these institutions had passed examinations by the state bank commissioners in 1892.[27] Bankers moved quickly to obtain legislation to prevent a recurrence of such events. At their convention in 1894 members of the California Bankers Association passed resolutions calling for measures to establish tighter state control over insolvent banks, set cash reserves for commercial banks, and fix capital requirements for savings banks. The state bank commissioners, who took part in the debates, wanted to go even further. In addition to the association's recommendations, they desired laws abolishing overdrafts and completely separating savings, commercial, and trust banking in California.[28]

Meetings between a committee of the California Bankers Association and the bank commissioners smoothed out differences, and, in 1895, the commissioners sponsored bills in Sacramento on behalf of the bankers. As the president of the California Bankers Association explained in a letter to the organization's members, public hostility to bankers made it unwise for bankers to demonstrate open support for the measures. Such efforts, he cautioned, might well hurt their cause. Bankers should instead, he urged, leave public backing of the proposals to the commissioners.[29] This strategy succeeded, and the contours of the resulting legislation showed that the bankers rather than the commissioners had dominated the discussions on bank laws. Proposals setting capital requirements for savings banks, increasing the authority of the bank commissioners over insolvent institutions, and requiring savings banks to retain part of their profits as reserve funds won approval from the state legislature and became law. Nothing was said, however, about separating the different types of banking, the major concern of the bank commissioners.[30]

The response of bankers to the legislation revealed divisions within their ranks. City bankers felt that additional laws would further strengthen and stabilize their state's banking structure, and at the 1895 convention of the California Bankers Association they persuaded country bankers to support a resolution condemning bank overdrafts. Los Angeles and San Francisco financiers, backed by the state bank commissioners, also urged that loans to an officer by his own institution be prohibited or limited to small amounts. Country bankers from Santa Rosa, Dixon, Fresno, and Stockton opposed this suggestion. Because small towns usually contained only a few banks, any statute of this type would, they argued, make it difficult for bankers to raise capital for business ventures in which they might be involved. Proposals against loans to bank officers might, they concluded, retard the economic development of their areas.[31]

With the return of prosperity in the late 1890s the demand for new bank laws temporarily dissipated, but the issue of credit expansion reappeared, in a new form, in 1905. In that year the state legislature considered a bill that would have lowered the capital requirements for banks in small towns. Legislators from California's inland farm valleys and small towns favored the measure. They claimed that merchants and farmers in newly developing regions sometimes lacked adequate credit facilities and that this situation hindered their economic growth. Opponents of the bill argued that the proposal would lead to "banks springing up like mushrooms" and that it would "make our banking institutions weak and unstable." The measure passed the senate, but, because of the intervention of the California Bankers Association, it failed in the assembly. The association's large-city bankers worked against the bill, for they feared that undercapitalization might cause bank failures in times of financial stress. Some country bankers approved of the measure; but others opposed it, for they had no desire to encourage the creation of competitors. Despite the defeat of this bill, the issues it raised were to recur in later legislative sessions.[32]

Two years later the panic of 1907 transformed banking laws throughout the United States. Its impact on national legislation is well known. The crisis led to efforts to create a more elastic money supply and prevent bank failures. The Aldrich-Vreeland Act of 1908 authorized national banks to form national currency associations in times of need. Banks belonging to such associations could issue new notes backed by commercial paper or selected types of bonds, thus increasing the available money supply and easing financial stringency. The Aldrich-Vreeland Act also set up the National Monetary Commission to recommend changes in the nation's monetary and banking laws, and this investigation ultimately resulted in the passage of the Federal Reserve Act five years later.[33] While these developments were occurring, changes were also taking place on the state level. California led the way in new state-banking legislation.

The failure of the California Safe Deposit and Trust Company supplied the catalyst for action in the Golden State. Founded in 1889, this institution was, according to one contemporary, "a hustler for deposit accounts." By offering higher interest rates than other San Francisco banks it boosted its deposits from $2,142,000 in 1903 to $9,303,532 just four years later. The bank's officers grossly mismanaged these funds, and, when the San Francisco Clearing House refused to bail them out, the institution folded. Its closing deprived 20,000 depositors of over $8,000,000 in savings.[34] With this event, the president of the California Bankers Association correctly observed, "a stigma was cast on every bank in the state."[35]

Bankers and politicians moved quickly to change banking practices in California. The state legislature set up a commission of six senators and assemblymen to examine banking in California and to report recommendations for legislation at the 1909 session. At the same time the California Bankers Association appointed a committee to investigate remedial legislation.[36] Meetings between the legislative commission and committees set up by the California Bankers Association eventually led to the enactment of the Bank Act of 1909, which remained the state's fundamental piece of banking legislation for some twenty years.

The 1908 meeting of the California Bankers Association, which the legislative commission attended, laid the foundations for future legislation. Discussions at the convention revealed agreement among nearly all bankers on some subjects. With the mismanagement of the funds of the

California Safe Deposit and Trust Company fresh in their minds, all felt that banks should stop making loans to their officers (except directors) and the association passed a resolution asking for legislation on this matter. Most also believed that the reserve requirements of commercial banks should be raised, and they called for a law setting them at 15 percent of deposits. Legislation on these points, bankers argued, would help make their institutions safe from failure and thus restore public faith in banking.[37]

Proposals for the separation of different types of banking aroused more controversy. Big-city bankers, including nearly all the financiers of San Francisco, Los Angeles, and Sacramento, favored strict segregation of the deposits and capital of commercial, savings, and trust banks. They pointed to temptations facing a commercial bank to use the deposits of a savings affiliate in its own business and concluded that only trouble could result from connections between essentially different institutions. Their arguments made little impression upon country bankers. Country bankers conceded that separation might strengthen the structures of large-city banks. Yet, they feared that in smaller communities separation might retard economic progress. They claimed that where deposits were small segregation would make "it impossible to have any bank there at all." As a San Jose banker noted, "large cities can specialize in all branches of business as provincial districts can not." Divisions opened on other lines as well. Trust bankers, who were then entering commercial banking, proved reluctant to back any measure that might limit their future actions. Commercial bankers, who were trying to keep trust bankers out of commercial banking, were more amenable to separation. Because of these cleavages the association failed to reach agreement on this subject. A resolution calling for the severance of ties between commercial, trust, and savings banks split the convention and suffered defeat in a close vote.[38]

Regardless of these divisions, bankers clearly felt that they should be the group to administer any new pieces of banking legislation, and at no time was this attitude more apparent than in the meeting's consideration of the future composition and duties of the state board of bank commissioners. Nearly all bankers wanted to replace the board of bank commissioners with a single superintendent of banks. By centralizing power in one man, bankers hoped to end the uncertainties stemming from the overlapping jurisdictions and actions of the commissioners. They probably also felt they could assure the selection of a superintendent sympathetic to their interests more easily than the appointment of an entire board. J. A. Graves, a well-known Los Angeles financier, suggested that the governor choose the superintendent from a list of five names supplied by the California Bankers Association, and this proposal won instant approval at the convention. Some bankers urged, in addition, that the superintendent rely exclusively upon clearing-house inspectors to examine the financial condition of California banks.[39]

Few groups presented alternatives to the ideas of the bankers. Members of the legislative commission objected only to the method of selecting the superintendent of banks. Pointing out that the American Bankers Association did not advise the president upon whom he should appoint as controller of the treasury, they felt it was improper for the bankers to suggest the man to regulate themselves.[40] The Commonwealth Club of California discussed proposals for new legislation and reached some of the same conclusions as the California Bankers Association. The club called for measures establishing a superintendent of banks and prohibiting loans by banks to their officers. Unlike the bankers, however, the Commonwealth Club also requested legislation dissolving all links between commercial, trust, and savings banks.[41]

At the close of its 1908 meeting the California Bankers Association appointed a committee carefully chosen to represent the bankers of San Francisco, Los Angeles, and the interior to work on legislation. Members of the commission appointed by the state legislature asked the bankers' committee to prepare a law suitable to themselves that would also provide absolute protection for depositors. At four meetings during the next few months the committee drew up an act embodying many of the resolutions passed at the 1908 bankers convention.[42] The measure created the position of state superintendent of banks. Appointed by the governor (but not from a list supplied by the bankers), he would hold office for five years at an annual salary of $7,500. His main duty would be to examine the financial soundness of California's banks at periodic intervals. The proposal forbade banks to make loans to their own officers (except directors) and limited loans given any one person to a sum equaling one-tenth of the bank's capital. The bankers reached a compromise on the separation of different types of banks. When an investigation revealed that three-quarters of California's banks engaged in more than one sort of banking, they concluded that to limit banks to one type of service would be "revolutionary, impractical, and contrary to business practice." Instead, they drafted a plan for what they called "departmental banking." Under this scheme an institution could take part in all forms of banking if it segregated the assets, capital, and deposits of each. These requirements meant, for instance, that a bank could not use the deposits of its savings department for loans granted by its commercial department. Both commercial and savings banks were to possess a minimum capital of $25,000. If an institution engaged in both, each department was to maintain this amount. The capital requirement for trust companies was set at $100,000.[43]

The commission of legislators altered this proposal little and offered it to the legislature in early 1909.[44] With the strong backing of both the bankers committee and the legislative commission, the measure met scant opposition in Sacramento. Only one modification won approval. Legislators acceded to pressures from some country bankers and small-town businessmen to reduce the capital requirements for banks doing a savings and commercial business to $25,000, rather than that amount for each department.[45] The state legislature considered only one other bill dealing with banking, a measure that would have assessed all banks 1 percent of their average daily deposits to create a fund with which to pay off the depositors of any bank that failed. The bill was modeled upon an Oklahoma statute passed in 1907. By 1918, eight western, midwestern, and southern states possessed such laws.[46] However, California bankers denounced the proposal as "socialism, thinly disguised," and "simply an absurdity," and their opposition killed it in committee.[47]

Bankers in California and the nation praised the Bank Act of 1909. The president of the California Bankers Association noted that "the committee [the bankers' legislative committee] did its work well" and was pleased that "the bill as drafted by them was practically the same as the one passed by the legislature."[48] John Drum, the California Bankers Association's chief lobbyist, also characterized the measure as ably embodying the wishes of the bankers.[49] Most financiers agreed with him and often reserved special commendation for the creation of the office of superintendent of banks. The secretary of the American Bankers Association lauded Californians for the passage of the act, and the legislatures of other states requested copies of it.[50]

Governor James Gillette appointed Alden Anderson as superintendent of banks, a choice popular with California's bankers. A former assemblyman and lieutenant governor, Anderson possessed ample banking experience as president of the Capital Banking and Trust Company of Sacramento, vice-president of the London Paris National Bank in San Francisco, and director of the California National Bank of Sacramento. Upon taking office, Anderson outlined an approach to regulation designed to win approval from the state's bankers. "I expect to advise with others," he declared, "whom I know to have been conservative, who have been honest and who have been successful in the banking affairs of the state." Anderson moved to enforce the Bank Act, but, as he phrased it, he allowed "change to be . . . evolutionary, in aid of which all possible assistance is being given." Financiers applauded the superintendent's "reasonable and judicious attitude," and praised him for appointing only men recommended by bankers as bank examiners.[51]

Although generally satisfied with the Bank Act of 1909, bankers, working in close cooperation with the superintendent, prepared several modifications for the 1911 legislative session. As they had done two years before, members of the California Bankers Association set up a committee to draft the bills. After meeting with Anderson, the committee drew up measures that the superintendent then introduced in the legislature. Passed with little debate, the bills altered the 1909 law in several ways. Most importantly, they set new capital requirements for both commercial and savings banks. The chronic conflict between city and country bankers was ended, at least temporarily, by fixing the requirements according to the population of the towns in which the banks were located: $25,000 for towns of under 5,000; $50,000 for those of 5,000 to 25,000; $100,000 for cities of 25,000 to 100,000; $200,000 for centers of between 100,000 and 200,000; and $300,000 for larger metropolises.[52]

Anderson continued as superintendent until Governor Hiram Johnson replaced him in 1911. Johnson evicted him from office only after a lengthy legislative battle that resulted in making the tenure of the superintendent of banks dependent upon the pleasure of the governor. Governor Johnson dismissed Anderson for several reasons. Johnson condemned Anderson for failing to enforce the Bank Act, and there was substance to his criticism. Anderson had allowed some bankers to violate parts of the acts, particularly those sections dealing with departmental banking, and he granted special favors to others. Political motives, however, also prompted Johnson's moves against the superintendent. As the choice of conservative Republicans for governor in 1910, Anderson had run against Johnson in the primaries, thus incurring his wrath, and Johnson was not the type of person to forgive past injuries.[53]

W. R. Williams, the governor's new appointee, denounced Anderson's administration, but he maintained his predecessor's ties with bankers. In late 1911, the new superintendent charged that during Anderson's tenure "the whole system of state control has been permeated by discrimination, inequality in administration of the law and the granting of special privileges." He reported that banks had loaned large sums to their officers and had violated the provisions for departmental banking with impunity.[54] Williams clamped down on these practices, but he continued to work with bankers on legislative matters. In his 1912 report he called for changes in the Bank Act, and in the same year the president of the California Bankers Association toured the state to find out what amendments bankers desired. As in the past, a committee of bankers and the superintendent drafted legislative proposals. Passed by the legislators without debate, the measures increased the powers and flexibility of the superintendent of banks in a number of ways.[55]

The Bank Act of 1909, as amended in subsequent years, remained California's fundamental banking law until the 1930s. Together with the actions of bank organizations it brought a new measure of stability to the economic situation. Despite the continued founding of state banks, few failed in the decade after the law went into effect. Most weathered the shock of the outbreak of the First World War quite well.[56] Although other factors, the passage of the Federal Reserve Act and the general increase in prosperity after 1907, contributed to the improvement, the Bank Act helped bring order to banking in California. The impact of the Bank Act on the provision of credit and capital for the state's farmers and businessmen is hard to judge. Certainly, California businessmen claimed that credit was scarce after 1909, and it appears that there was some truth to this complaint. Yet, the act did not retard the founding of new banks in California. The number of state banks in California grew from 506 in 1908 to 843 in 1933, and their capital increased from $483,000,000 in 1900 to $3,250,000,000 in 1930.[57] Equally important, new banking methods made credit and capital more available to Californians from about 1910 on. Even before the First World War branch banking, pioneered by the Bank of Italy, began easing the credit situation, and in the 1920s this trend continued. Based in San Francisco, the Bank of Italy established branches throughout the state's interior farm valleys and then in Southern California. In doing so it combined the advantages of the stability of a strong city institution with those of country banks in touch with the needs of local farmers and merchants.[58]

The Professionalization of Banking

"Banking is a profession," declared the president of the California Bankers Association in 1905. "If theology is the science of religion, if

medicine is the science of the human body, if law is the science of justice,"
he continued, "then banking is the science of finance."[59] Like other
American businessmen, California bankers tried to win acceptance of
themselves as professional men in the early twentieth century.[60] In this
way bankers hoped to foster better relations with the general public, and
especially with the state's businessmen, improve relations among themselves, and win support for their legislative programs in Sacramento. To
achieve these ends bankers established new educational facilities, codes of
business ethics, and social organizations. In their speeches and, though to
lesser degrees, their actions, bankers demonstrated a growing awareness
that they were an integral part of the larger society around them and that
they owed certain obligations to their communities.

As their business became more complex, bankers required an increasingly sophisticated education. In the first decade of the twentieth century a
number of American universities offered business courses, and both Stanford University and the University of California took steps in this direction.
Addressing the 1907 convention of the California Bankers Association, a
Stanford professor of economics commented upon the fragmentation of
American business. "Modern business has become so specialized," he
observed, "that it represents a distinct profession or rather group of
professions." Noting that universities presented courses in railroad transportation, factory organization, accountancy, insurance, and foreign
commerce, he urged that they also set up programs in banking.[61] Despite
the efforts of the universities, most of the education of bankers took place
outside their doors. Yet, bankers recognized that learning on the job no
longer sufficed, and, in late 1903, the American Institute of Banking, a
national organization, opened a San Francisco chapter. Within a decade
five other California cities possessed branches. By 1920, the Los Angeles
group was the fifth largest in the nation, and only the New York chapter
surpassed San Francisco's membership of 1,800.[62] Supported in part by
the state's clearing houses, the California chapters offered both theoretical
and practical instruction. In 1909, the San Francisco organization engaged
a Stanford professor to lecture on corporations, money systems and markets, trust problems, and negotiable instruments. A decade later its program had expanded to include political economy, international trade,
public speaking, elementary banking, French, Spanish, business English,
commercial law, foreign exchange, credits and accounting. Few other
chapters had as wide a range of subjects, but most offered a fair variety of
courses. All gave examinations and conferred certificates upon those who
completed their programs.[63]

As professionals, bankers tried to devise and uphold codes of business ethics. Although never totally successful in this endeavor, they made considerable progress. The clearing houses imposed stringent rules on all institutions using their facilities, and their membership included the most prominent commercial banks in California. The California Bankers Association, while possessing little formal control over its members, operated through legislation to upgrade the state's banking practices.

Organizations established to further education and foster uniform codes of business conduct also brought about an increase in the group cohesiveness of bankers. Each convention of the California Bankers Association featured elaborate social functions for the delegates and their wives, and one of the reasons the association initiated group banking was so that "bankers of the various districts would become better acquainted with each other."[64] The chapters of the American Institute of Banking provided many opportunities for closer social contact among bankers. They held dances, smokers, clam bakes, river excursions, picnics, and amateur plays. Their members competed against each other in adding-machine contests, track and field meets, debates, and baseball games. By 1916, the San Francisco chapter possessed committees on athletics, auditing, education, entertainment, forum, library, public affairs, publicity, and thrift. As one San Franciscan noted, "many warm friendships have been made through the institute."[65]

Bankers sought to gain consideration for themselves as experts capable of dealing with society's economic problems, and they realized that they could obtain such acceptance only if they played an active role in the development of their communities. As early as 1895, one financier described bankers as "public custodians" and asked his fellows to recognize the existence of a mutuality of interest between bankers, depositors, and borrowers. In the twentieth century these ideas became more clearly defined. Jess Stoddard, a prominent Los Angeles banker, noted, in 1914, that banks were "more and more being regarded as quasi-public institutions" and claimed that a bank "should recognize an implied obligation to use its loanable funds . . . as will best protect and foster the industries that make for the general welfare." Bankers argued that they were more than "simply the representatives of stockholders" and contributed bank funds to local projects and charities. J. M. Elliot of Los Angeles requested that the stockholders of his bank set aside a sum that he could use for such purposes. James Lynch of San Francisco endorsed this plan, for he believed that a bank was "an entity, a person, an individual" that had "a duty to the community." Country bankers adopted this attitude more slowly, but, by 1920, they had joined their city correspondents in financing and organizing boys clubs throughout California.[66]

Bankers partially succeeded in securing approval for their status as professionals. Their acceptance as experts by the public helps explain why their legislative programs passed in Sacramento with almost no opposition. Even businessmen who suffered from bank closings and failures during the panic of 1907 looked to the bankers to prepare and administer new legislation. In 1908, a leading San Francisco businessman addressing the Commonwealth Club urged that bankers be allowed to choose the state superintendent of banks. He noted that the state medical society recommended the state medical examiner and that the California Architects Association chose the state architect. "If doctors and architects can suggest," he queried, "why can not bankers also?" Another businessman added that the superintendent should rely upon clearing-house examiners to inspect the state's banks. Professional competence could be achieved only in this way. As he put it, "it seems to me the best regulators of banks are bankers . . . this is simply on the line of having the business overlooked by an expert, one who understands the business thoroughly." Not all businessmen, however, were satisfied with the actions of bankers. Some continued to complain, right up to the First World War, that bankers took little part in community affairs and that they failed to provide funds for community projects. Others objected to the paternalism implicit in the bankers' position. Few Californians agreed, for instance, with the assertion of one financier that bankers should be "the balance wheel" that would "prevent any [social or political] movement from going too far in one direction."[67]

To solve the problems caused by economic changes in their state, California bankers formed cooperative associations, labored for the passage of state legislation, and sought recognition as professionals. Though never totally able to reconcile their sometimes contradictory goals, bankers achieved a considerable degree of success in their endeavors. Clearing houses expedited transactions among their members and sought to protect them from the effects of financial panics. The California Bankers Association improved relations among bankers and worked for banking legislation at the state capital. The Bank Act of 1909 and its later modifications were largely the creation of bankers. Finally, bankers won growing acceptance for themselves as professionals, skilled in their specialty and, like doctors, lawyers, or clergymen, owing fairly definite obligations to the rest of society.

The changing image Californians had of their state's bankers helps explain why bankers generally succeeded in getting their way in the state legislature. The senators and assemblymen were themselves mainly business and professional men who were coming to view bankers as experts possessed of special knowledge in their fields of endeavor. In this situation the legislators were often willing to defer to the bankers as those who were best qualified to propose solutions for financial problems. Other factors were however, also important in the bankers' legislative victories. Most significantly, the bankers, when able to heal their splits, composed a highly organized interest group well able to make their wishes known in the state capital. The California Bankers Association maintained full-time lobbyists in Sacramento, and the organization's officers frequently traveled to the capital city to express the desires of the body. Yet, as in the case of the Public Utilities Act, the legislators viewed the Bank Act of 1909 as being in the public interest as well as in the best interest of the business group it most closely affected. Indeed, had not the measure promised protection for depositors, it would probably not have passed in Sacramento. As the various committees set up by the California Bankers Association and the commission established by the state legislature argued, the Bank Act would aid both bankers and depositors by stabilizing economic conditions in California. In the eyes of the bankers and legislators, at least, the public and private interests of their state could be neatly subsumed.

7

Investment Banking and the Blue-sky Law

As in savings and commercial banking, California's economic expansion required changes in the state's investment banking. The need for credit and investment capital by California's booming businesses placed grave strains upon the Golden State's stockbrokers and investment bankers. In the late nineteenth and early twentieth centuries, they found themselves faced with the dilemma of trying to provide financing for their state's rapid economic growth, while, at the same time, attempting to impose some sort of order upon California's highly fluid economic situation. Working through both private actions and state legislation, the brokers and bankers, often joined by other businessmen, sought to reconcile these divergent goals.

Voluntary Supervision of Securities Sales

Stockbrokers and investment bankers undertook the first efforts to supervise securities sales in California. Through their state's stock exchanges stockbrokers made some attempts to police the financial soundness of corporations offering new issues for sale on their boards. Investment bankers formed local chapters of the Investment Bankers Association of America, which tried to drive shady investment companies out of business. When, however, it became apparent that their work alone would not end fraudulent securities transactions, most investment bankers and stockbrokers took a leading part in the drive for a tough blue-sky law.

Californians formed stock exchanges soon after the granting of state-hood in order to facilitate capital transactions. Stockbrokers operated in San Francisco as early as the 1850s, but they worked in an informal manner, and prices were, as one pioneer dealer later remembered, "not all regular nor [*sic*] uniform."[1] The discovery of immense silver deposits in Nevada's Comstock Lode and the subsequent high volume of trading in mining issues led to the formation of the San Francisco Stock and Exchange Board in 1862. Thirteen years later the Pacific Stock Exchange opened its doors, and, in 1882, brokers founded the San Francisco Stock and Bond Exchange. Though the major function of these organizations was to mobilize capital for mining concerns, by the 1870s and 1880s, they were also listing the securities of insurance, gas, railroad, steamboat, water and telegraph companies.[2] As in San Francisco, the first stock exchanges in Los Angeles owed their existence to mineral strikes, in this case the oil discoveries of the 1890s. In the early twentieth century the Los Angeles Stock Exchange absorbed other bodies to become the leading exchange in Southern California, and it was soon dealing in industrial, railroad, and public utility issues.[3]

From their earliest days, most stock exchanges possessed the power to police new issues of securities. Before agreeing to list a firm's securities, exchange members could insist upon investigating the company's financial soundness and future prospects. If anything were found amiss, the brokers could deny it a listing and, in this manner, exclude questionable issues from trading.[4] The San Francisco Stock and Exchange Board originally required a majority vote of its members to place a security on the list called, and, in 1874, it set up a standing committee to examine all new applicants. In the 1880s, the exchange ordered mining companies to report all dividends paid on capital stock, and late in the decade its members adopted a resolution empowering its president to employ an expert accountant to inspect the books of firms traded by the organization. The failure of a company to allow such an investigation could result in a suspension of its listing.[5] The San Francisco Stock and Bond Exchange also maintained a committee to examine the affairs of corporations desiring listings, and, by 1885, it was calling upon San Francisco's street railroads for monthly financial statements.[6] Exchanges in Southern California followed the example of the San Francisco bodies. In 1916, the president of the Los Angeles Stock Exchange asserted that a listing should be a "moral guaran-tee" of a stock's value and began tightening listing requirements. Within a few years the exchange had a committee that examined the affairs of companies applying for listings and maintained a bureau of information to supply the public with reliable data about new security offerings.[7]

The stock exchanges made, however, little use of their power to withhold listings in the nineteenth century. Like commercial bankers in the same period, they cared more about rapid economic growth than economic stability. Some brokers even abetted swindles. In fact, in its early years the San Francisco Stock and Exchange Board, composed of forty brokers, had an unsavory reputation, and the more conservative businessmen of the city labeled it "the forty thieves." One historian, using records now destroyed, noted that many of the issues listed by the exchange in 1876 either paid no dividends or were fraudulent and concluded that the examinations made by the exchange were "a sham."[8] This could well have been the case, for the brokers made considerable sums by agreeing to list new firms on their exchanges. Listing fees ranged as high as $2,000, and the brokers, unwilling to pass up such windfalls, probably made only perfunctory investigations into companies' assets and intentions.[9]

Only in the early twentieth century did the exchanges begin denying questionable or unstable concerns access to their boards. The San Francisco Stock and Bond Exchange, for instance, refused to approve first mortgage bonds floated by one of the largest corporations in California, for in examining the deed of trust securing the bonds, the exchange's investigatory committee found that the issue was not a first, but a collateral, mortgage. Its only backing was the stock of other companies, which had already encumbered themselves with first, and in some cases, even second mortgages. Not until the firm's officers agreed to change the name of the bonds did the exchange allow trading in them.[10] The same trend appeared in Southern California. By 1918, the president of the Los Angeles Stock Exchange could report that in the previous year his organization had rejected as many listing applications as it had accepted.[11]

Investment bankers also tried to regulate the sale of securities in California. Like the exchange brokers, they realized that transactions in fraudulent or overly speculative stocks and bonds would injure their standing with the public and make future trading more difficult. Californians (eleven San Franciscans and three Los Angelenos) composed one of the largest state contingents at the formative convention of the Investment Bankers Association of America in 1912.[12] The organization worked to suppress irresponsible dealers and to educate the public "so that they will know a sound security when they see it." Californians felt the need for control most urgently. Cyrus Pierce of N. W. Halsey's San Francisco office explained the reason to the Sacramento chapter of the American Institute of Banking. The promoters of land development schemes, especially in Southern California, finding themselves unable to move their securities through reputable bond dealers, were, he complained, either forming new investment houses of their own or selling their stocks and bonds directly to the public. To halt such actions, which they viewed as undermining their businesses, nearly all the leading investment bankers in Los Angeles and San Francisco joined the association.[13]

Stockbrokers and investment bankers soon found that their work by itself could not end fraudulent practices. As late as 1915, J. A. Graves, the vice-president of the Farmers and Merchants National Bank, found it necessary to urge members of the Wall Street Club of Los Angeles "to scrutinize with the greatest care every bond issue you attempt to sell" and to warn them that commissions received for any transaction would be "but a small compensation" for the loss of reputation suffered by dealing in shoddy securities.[14] A year later the manager of the Los Angeles Stock Exchange estimated that three-quarters of the local business was still taking place outside the exchange, either on the curb or over the counter, and was, therefore, subject to no regulations.[15] The same situation, though to a somewhat lesser degree, existed in San Francisco as well. Nor did members of the Investment Bankers Association of America succeed in weeding out black sheep from their ranks. Shady practices continued despite their best efforts.

The Movement for a Blue-sky Law

Recognizing that their private efforts to police securities transactions were only partially successful, many stockbrokers and investment bankers worked for the passage of a blue-sky law providing for state regulation of their businesses. They were not, however, alone in their desires. Several different groups, for different and sometimes conflicting reasons, wanted the enactment of such a law. In fact, a wider variety of interest groups probably labored for the blue-sky law than for any other single piece of business legislation in California.

The state mineralogist actually began the campaign for legislation to end phony stock sales in California. The oil and other mineral discoveries of the late nineteenth and early twentieth centuries required new capital investments to defray the expenses of development, and the state mineralogist feared that the failure of unsound enterprises would frighten off funds needed by bona fide companies. Upon receiving complaints from investors in 1901, he investigated some of the schemes and discovered that many mining corporations "were making gross misrepresentations" of their finds. He also believed that "swindling operations" were scaring capital away from investment in legitimate concerns. To combat this trend he began legal prosecutions with the post office for mail fraud and within a year had obtained several convictions.[16] These actions won the praise of the *Mining and Engineering Review,* one of the state's leading mining journals. At the end of 1903, its editor reported that the muddied waters of mining investments were clearing and that California would soon "be open for investors who wish to become interested."[17] Progress by means of court cases, however, proved costly and time-consuming, and, in 1904, the state mineralogist called for the passage of laws "to deter these sharks [promoters of fraudulent mining companies] from further operations in this state."[18]

The 1905 session of the state legislature approved a measure based upon the state mineralogist's recommendations. It forbade false advertising by mining companies and provided for a fine of up to $5,000 and a two-year term of imprisonment for those convicted of this crime.[19] Within a year the state mineralogist asserted, somewhat prematurely, that "the glittering and exaggerated statements which were so plentiful in the published advertisements and prospectuses of some mining companies before the law went into effect are no longer seen."[20] Many of the state's miners and oil producers favored this act and supported the regulatory efforts of the state mineralogist. In 1912, the California Miners Association passed a resolution requesting the legislature to appropriate more money for the state mining bureau to "examine any probable fake or 'wildcat' mining organizations affecting mining properties within the state."[21]

When Hiram Johnson won election as governor, he added a new impetus to the movement for a blue-sky law. In his decision to press for legislation Johnson was influenced by events occurring beyond California's boundaries. By this time the movement for state blue-sky laws had become national in scope. States were moving from noncoercive to semicoercive and coercive means of executing securities regulations. No longer content to simply depend upon statutory requirements, legislatures empowered state officials to enforce their laws and in some cases set up new government agencies to administer them. Kansas led the way with the passage of a stringent act in 1911. Johnson conferred with the governor of Kansas to discuss his state's experiences in securities regulation in 1912 and came away from the meeting convinced that California needed a strong blue-sky law.[22]

California's more conservative financiers and real estate men shared Governor Johnson's sentiments. As early as 1903, the president of the California Bankers Association urged his fellows to exercise restraining hands on new securities issues. He noted that although bankers could not prevent the flotation of inadequately secured stocks and bonds "so long as the supply of paper keeps up and the presses are in good order," they could bring pressure to bear by refusing to loan money on them. In 1912, these ideas took a more definite form. In that year the secretary of the California Building and Loan League appeared before the annual convention of the California Bankers Association to ask for aid in pressing for legislation regulating the state's investment companies and securities sales. In response to this request the convention of bankers passed a resolution condemning the "allurements and misrepresentations of stock promoters" and instructed the association's legislative committee to work with the Building and Loan League to secure the enactment of a blue-sky law like that in force in Kansas. Partners in some of California's leading investment houses, once convinced that it would "not hamper legitimate business," also came out for a blue-sky bill, for they hoped it would aid in securing capital for the expansion of California's railroads, electric power plants, and irrigation systems.[23]

Progressive politicians favored the blue-sky proposal for different reasons than most businessmen. Although not oblivious to the capital needs of their state, they stressed the benefits of a blue-sky law to the small investor. As one put it, the measure would protect the "man or woman, who by industry and economy gathers a little more than is required for immediate use and desires to invest it."[24] Progressive newspapers and journals praised the bill in the same terms. The editor of the Sacramento *Bee* expected the blue-sky law to end "the monstrous evil . . . of the sale of stocks and bonds of corporations without adequate assets to give security to investors."[25]

With broad-based business and political support, Governor Johnson had Senator Lee Gates of Los Angeles and John Eshleman, the president of the California Railroad Commission, draw up a measure modeled on the Kansas blue-sky law. In drafting the legislation Gates and Eshleman took cognizance of the wishes of the businessmen it would affect. They took special care to confer with representatives of the Los Angeles Realty Board and the California State Realty Federation in preparing Johnson's bill.[26]

Yet, despite their efforts, some businessmen fought the proposed blue-sky law. The California Association of Investment Corporations offered the most vehement resistance. The moving force behind this organization was the Los Angeles Investment Company, a speculative holding company with real estate, agricultural, and industrial ventures in Southern California. Charles Elder, the president of the Los Angeles Investment Company, also headed the California Association of Investment Corporations. The association maintained lobbyists in Sacramento to work for a weaker measure as substitute to Johnson's proposal. In addition, its officers sent out circulars to bankers, real estate promoters, and other businessmen denouncing the governor's bill for giving too much power to state officials.[27]

Regardless of these actions, Governor Johnson's bill easily became law in 1913. It provided for a commissioner of corporations to examine each new issue of securities offered for sale in California. The commissioner could deny any company the right to float its stocks and bonds in the state; only those securities already coming under the jurisdiction of other state agencies like the railroad commission were exempted from this provision. The law also gave the commissioner "general supervision and control" over investment houses and brokers. More specifically, he was to license all brokers who operated in California.[28] In a closely related move the California Bankers Association, joined by some real estate corporations, won approval for an amendment to the Bank Act of 1909, which gave the banking superintendent the power to examine all bonds submitted by corporations for investment by state banks.[29]

Businessmen throughout California applauded the passage of the blue-sky law. By May, 1913, the *Coast Banker,* California's foremost financial periodical, could accurately report that the law was generally regarded in the financial world as "a very satisfactory measure."[30] A Fresno businessman speaking before the Commonwealth Club in San Francisco explained why many businessmen favored the new act. He noted that though the blue-sky law would eliminate corporations "formed for the sole purpose of defrauding the public," it would further the development of legitimate enterprises. "The standing of a corporation that incorporates under the provisions of this act," he continued, "will be enhanced by the certificate of the commissioner of corporations." The investor, he believed, would be more willing to place his capital in such a company "knowing that some competent person, whose business it is, has investigated its plan of business and manner of incorporation."[31]

Only the California Association of Investment Corporations openly opposed the measure. Shortly after its passage, the organization began a drive to invoke a public referendum against the blue-sky law. Its officers charged that the law would allow the political party in office to build up a political machine by the use of patronage, and that the measure would discourage the entrance of new industries into the state. If the referendum defeated the blue-sky law, the association intended to present its alternate bill as an initiative proposition. The weapons of reform would be turned upon the reformers![32] The organization secured enough signatures on its petitions to hold the referendum. Then scandal blighted the efforts of those seeking repeal. In late 1913, the Los Angeles Investment Company failed and went into bankruptcy. The stock of the corporation plummetted from $4.50 to $0.40 per share, wiping out the savings of over 20,000 investors, most of whom were retired citizens living in Los Angeles. An investigation by a federal grand jury revealed that the firm's officers had systematically milked the company's funds for their own use. The board of directors and president of the corporation, Charles Elder, were indicted, tried, and sentenced to prison terms.[33] A stockholders committee set up to recover as much of the company's assets as possible sent out circulars urging shareholders to "VOTE TO SUSTAIN THE BLUE-SKY LAW." The flysheets noted ruefully that "Elder made a bitter fight against the law" and claimed that his "operations would have been impossible had this law been in effect a few years ago."[34]

With its opposition discredited, the blue-sky law won approval in the referendum election by a wide margin of votes, and, in 1917, the legislature extended its jurisdiction to the resale of stocks and bonds in California.[35]

The Enforcement of the Blue-sky Law

Once Californians upheld the blue-sky law at the polls, the commissioner of corporations clamped down on questionable securities transactions. He limited the amount paid sponsors for the sale of new flotations and severely restricted the issue of promotion stock without tangible support. When he permitted the sale of stocks backed by intangibles like inventions, the commissioner required that the certificates be placed in escrow until they began paying dividends. Between 1915 and 1920 he handled stocks with a par value of $326,956,000 in this manner. To prevent the undercapitalization of new companies the commissioner required that a minimum amount of capital be actually paid up within a prescribed period of time. If the firms could not obtain adequate financing, the commissioner dissolved them and returned their funds to the investors. Fraudulent concerns—Sission's Diving Bell, Berry's Airship Company, firms purporting to manufacture wave motors and gold-making machines—were forbidden to raise funds in California. During the first four years of the blue-sky law's operation the commissioner of corporations denied 274 companies the privilege of selling securities in California, and, in 1918, he reported with pride that corporate financing in his state had assumed a new "degree of sanity and stability."[36]

The commissioner repeatedly stressed that his regulatory efforts would benefit California's legitimate businessmen and further the state's economic growth. The deputy commissioner explained to members of the Los Angeles Chamber of Mines and Oil in early 1915 that the aim of the department of corporations was "to encourage legitimate industry which will upbuild the state and develop its resources, meanwhile driving the wildcatters and fraudulent speculators out of the field." The commissioner made the same point in his first biennial report to the state legislature. "Money saved from ultra-hazardous and impracticable ventures means," he asserted, "that more capital is available for enterprises which reasonably promise returns." Besides exposing phony promoters, and thus making more capital available for genuine companies, the commissioner of corporation took other steps to help the state's entrepreneurs. As the commissioner pointed out, he assumed "the initiative to aid corporate business wherever possible, by suggesting legislation to meet changing conditions." In 1917, for instance, he secured passage for a law allowing the organization of California corporations with shares of stock of no par value. The staff of the state corporation department also offered to act as advisors to those just going into business or expanding their spheres of activities, and many businessmen conferred informally with them about their plans.[37]

In late 1917, the corporation commissioner, speaking to the San Francisco Commercial Club, summarized his actions during the past two years and defined the purpose of the blue-sky law in a way that must have caused some progressives to wonder if it was the same measure they had fought for. The commissioner said nothing about the need to shield small investors from manipulations. Rather, he described the law simply as a way to further the development of legitimate business in California. He began by declaring that the "purpose of the department of corporation commissioner is not to be repressive, but is one of putting scientific business methods into government.'' He noted that in applying the blue-sky law he had tried to be ''as little onerous as possible'' and that permits for new securities flotations had been readily granted to firms whose management was ''fair, reputable . . . and competent.'' The commissioner concluded that the blue-sky law was ''a business law for business people'' and that it was designed simply to keep ''crooked businessmen . . . from getting into competition with decent business people.''[38]

The conduct of the commissioner won the approval of California's business leaders, especially members of the state's financial community. Bankers particularly liked the work of the commissioner and helped secure an extension of his powers in 1917. Some even suggested placing all of the state's land sales under his jurisdiction. In 1916, the president of the Los Angeles Stock Exchange lauded the blue-sky law and lamented only that a more stringent measure were not in force. Two years later the manager of the exchange called the attention of its members to ''the ever increasing volume of business being transacted in high class investment securities through the Southwest'' and praised the efforts of the commissioner of corporations in ''curbing the activities of ruthless promoters,'' which made this improvement possible. The California members of the Investment Bankers Association of America also looked with favor upon the efforts of the commissioner to eliminate unscrupulous securities dealers. In 1918, the commissioner of corporations could accurately state that the blue-sky law ''has met with general commendation and hearty cooperation on the part of legitimate brokers and businessmen.''[39]

Government-business cooperation with regard to the blue-sky law reached a climax in 1919. When a stock promoter challenged the blue-sky law in the courts that year, managers of California's leading investment banking houses voluntarily subscribed ''a substantial sum'' for the employment of a special counsel to aid the state corporation department in defending the measure. For this assistance, which proved successful, the commissioner praised them as ''progressive businessmen'' who had helped in ''the splendid work of the past six years in keeping out of this state the trashy funds originating in other states.''[40]

The campaign for the blue-sky law illustrated the diversity of support that a single business measure could engender. For stockbrokers and investment bankers its passage spelled the successful conclusion of long-standing efforts to upgrade and rationalize their businesses. Commercial and savings bankers, along with businessmen involved in a wide range of activities, viewed the measure as a way to mobilize capital for California's rapidly expanding industries. Like the public utility officers who supported the Public Utilities Act in 1912, they hoped state regulation of securities would speed the economic development of their state. Finally, progressive politicians worked for the blue-sky law for a still different reason. For them the protection of the small investor was the primary concern.

Yet, while the campaign for the blue-sky law derived its backing from a wide range of sources, it also disclosed cleavages among California's businessmen. As in the case of banking legislation, capital requirements divided businessmen into opposing, if often ill-defined, groups. The more conservative businessmen, who, nonetheless, had an urgent need for new investment capital, favored the proposal because they felt it would help funnel additional funds to their companies. On the other hand, some businessmen saw state regulation of securities transactions as a threat to their existence and worked against the blue-sky law. In particular, officers of speculative, and sometimes fraudulent, real estate and land investment firms viewed the chaos resulting from changes in California's economy as an opportunity to be fully exploited for their private gain. They feared the restrictions a blue-sky law might place on their actions and fought the measure tooth-and-nail.

8

The Insurance Industry

From practically the earliest days of statehood California possessed an insurance industry composed of companies chartered in the state, branches of foreign firms, and companies incorporated in other states but doing business in California. Fires that swept through San Francisco in the early 1850s convinced Californians of the need for protection, and, by 1857, four English and two eastern fire insurance enterprises had entered the state. The next decade saw a rush of eastern companies to California, and twelve local firms also began operations. Despite a high rate of turnover, local concerns continued to play an important role until rate wars in the 1890s practically eliminated them.[1] Life insurance companies also opened offices in California at an early date, and the struggle between the big three—the New York Life, the Equitable, and the Mutual Life of New York—added a fillip to the expansion of life insurance in the state. By 1885, the three accounted for about half of the policies in force in California. Two decades later, however, their share of the market had dropped considerably. Other eastern firms filled the state's demand for life insurance, for until after 1905 only one California company existed in California, and it failed to keep pace with the demand for insurance.[2]

California's rapid urbanization, combined with the commercialization of agriculture and the growth of big business, brought changes to the insurance industry. Insurance men tried to blunt the impact of the new conditions through the formation of trade associations and state legislation.

Although they proved capable of solving many of their problems, the insurance men never succeeded in eliminating friction between themselves and other businessmen in California. The clash of interests became most pronounced in legislative struggles over measures designed to harness the funds of insurance companies for the economic development of California. As in the case of bankers, insurance men found themselves besieged by state officials and businessmen desirous of using their reserves and savings to build up California.

The Problem of Competition

Violent competition disrupted the nation's insurance industry in the late nineteenth century, and California became the storm center of the struggles on the Pacific Coast. Fire insurance men found themselves particularly hard hit and led a drive to dampen the rampant competition. However, they found themselves hampered in their efforts by the quest for what seemed to be two opposing goals: a high volume of business and economic stability. They wished to increase their companies' shares of the market and were willing to use almost any means at their disposal to achieve this aim. Yet, at the same time they longed for security and an end to the more virulent forms of competition. Rate wars in the 1880s and 1890s bit deeply into their profits, and neither agents nor managers wanted such conflicts to continue in the twentieth century.

Fire insurance men first sought to control competition with the establishment of the Pacific Insurance Union in 1884. Within a year of its founding all the agencies in California had joined; and, by 1888, its jurisdiction extended over Montana, Idaho, Utah, Oregon, and Washington. The association tried to set uniform rates charged by the insurance companies. However, despite some initial success, the Pacific Insurance Union proved incapable of eliminating cutthroat competition. A rate war in Oakland led to a suspension of the Union's tariff and the rewriting of that city's risks at figures much lower than the former rates. Local contests also developed in other communities, and, as a result, the premiums received by companies for their business dropped precipitously.[3] The Pacific Insurance Union could not survive such competition. Many of the firms belonging to it either merged, went into bankruptcy, or withdrew from business in California. Between 1890 and 1895, the number of companies writing fire insurance in California fell by over one-half. Many of those firms remaining left the Pacific Insurance Union; in 1894 alone, twenty companies withdrew from its ranks. Last minute efforts to save the organization by requiring monetary pledges from its members to prevent rebating and rate-cutting failed, and, in early 1895, the Pacific Insurance Union disbanded.[4]

Unwilling to accept the loss of profits resulting from unrestrained competition, fire insurance men formed a new organization, the Board of Fire Underwriters of the Pacific. Like insurance trade associations in other regions, the board fixed uniform rates for companies belonging to it, outlawed rebates, set commissions for agents, and, through a nonintercourse clause, forbade reinsurance or other types of business with nonboard firms. These efforts to limit competition proved stillborn, for several of the most important companies refused to join the new compact. One company even brought suit against the board in the federal circuit court in San Francisco. Its attorneys accused the board of being "a gigantic combination organized for the purpose of controlling the fire insurance business of this coast," and demanded its dissolution. They struck particularly hard at the board's nonintercourse rule and charged that its members were trying to destroy the business of the independents. Lawyers for the board admitted that the association regulated rates to prevent "reckless" competition but denied accusations of conspiracy, coercion, and intimidation. The court decided in favor of the board, but it did prohibit fraudulent advertising designed to undermine the position of those firms remaining outside its ranks.[5]

The board proved incapable of stifling rate-cutting and rebating, and, in late 1895, under the pressure of the independents, it suspended its tariff for California. A general rate war ensued, with the hottest contests taking place in San Francisco, Los Angeles, and Oakland. As the San Francisco manager of the Transatlantic Fire Insurance Company lamented, these years constituted "a period of demoralization—almost approaching a state of chaos." Fire insurance companies saw their profits dwindle as the premiums received for new business fell and losses on the rising number of poor risks they accepted rose.[6]

Insurance men finally restored a semblance of order with the reorganization of the Board of Fire Underwriters of the Pacific in 1897. Now joined by nearly all the firms doing business in California, it regulated rates, policy forms, commissions for agents, agency appointments, and business with nonboard companies. The board forbade rebates, and its officers established an effective apparatus for the detection and punishment of violations.[7] This time the association proved more successful in stabilizing rates. New companies entered California, and both premiums and profits increased. In 1906, a general agent described the Pacific Coast as the "one green oasis in the desert of insurance waste in the United States." Yet, all was not well in the new Eden. Rate wars, though now localized, still occurred. In 1901, insurance men reported that competition in Santa Anna had "reached an unbearable extreme." In Los Angeles the contest begun in 1894 lasted for a full decade, and farther north in Visalia a rate war raged without interruption from 1910 to 1915.[8]

If fire insurance men could not end what they considered excessive competition, life insurance men encountered even more trouble in this respect. The nationwide struggle among the big three insurance companies grew particularly fierce in the Far West. Then too, the method of rating required less cooperation among life than fire agents. Life insurance men relied upon standard actuarial tables and consequently had no need to lay down uniform rules governing the writing of risks. Nonetheless, life insurance men set up trade associations that, while never as strong as the Board of Fire Underwriters of the Pacific, established some guidelines for competition.

In their headlong rush for business, life insurance men resorted to a wide range of "unfair" business practices. Company managers paid their local agents high commissions, parts of which the agents then used as rebates to acquire new customers. In the mid-1890s, the larger eastern companies signed an antirebating agreement to eliminate this expense, but, when the president of the Equitable withdrew his firm from the compact in 1899, it collapsed. Within a year refunds of 30 percent had become common on the Pacific Coast, and rebating continued well into the twentieth century. Fraudulent advertising also bothered those in life insurance. Agents sold assessment insurance on the pretense that it was straight life insurance and engaged in a multitude of other forms of misrepresentation. Such behavior frequently resulted in litigation that some insurance men condemned for "bringing odium upon the company contesting," and for letting "the bottom drop out of life insurance in that community for an indefinite period." Company officers viewed twisting (the enticement of policyholders from one company to another) as a still more serious vice. Since the combination of commissions paid to agents and office expenses often exceeded the premiums received on first-year policies, insurance companies usually made a profit only on return business. In the 1890s twisting threatened even these receipts. Agents, desiring the high commissions on new business, lured policyholders from contending firms, and the lapsing of policies after the first year became a serious problem that cost companies several million dollars annually in California alone.[9]

Like the fire insurance men, life insurance agents and managers established trade associations to control competition. Northern California insurance men formed the San Francisco Life Underwriters Association in the 1890s to combat rebating, the payment of excessive commissions, and agent-stealing. Southern Californians made similar efforts with the establishment of the Los Angeles Life Underwriters Association in 1904. Finally, Sacramento agents set up an organization in 1910, which also joined the campaign to lessen competition. None of the efforts of these organizations proved very effective, however; and rebating, twisting, and agent-stealing continued almost unabated. As late as 1907, a leading insurance journal reported that the life insurance business in California was still in a "very disorganized condition."[10]

During the first decade of the twentieth century insurance men came to recognize the limitations of their trade associations and sponsored legislation in Sacramento forbidding rebating and twisting. The state legislators also debated the merits of giving the state insurance commissioner the power to set uniform rates in California and discussed bills designed to permit the formation of new types of insurance companies. The many contests over insurance measures uncovered rifts as well as cohesion within the insurance community. Company managers and agents in the field could usually agree upon the need to end rebating and twisting, but they clashed on state rating proposals. As might be expected, insurance companies already established in California fought measures for the formation of new firms that would compete with their companies.

After several preliminary skirmishes, insurance men mounted a major effort to push a bill forbidding rebating through the state legislature in 1913. Drawn up by the California branch of the National Fire Insurance Agents Association, the measure also had the backing of the Los Angeles Fire Underwriters Association. To further restrict competition the California State Association of Local Fire Insurance Agents urged speedy passage for a bill limiting insurance companies to two local agents in cities of less than 100,000. The Board of Fire Underwriters of the Pacific, faced at the time with several local rate wars, backed both measures. With overwhelming support in insurance circles, the bills passed the assembly and senate, only to meet with a veto from Governor Hiram Johnson. He refused to approve bills that he felt would benefit insurance companies without helping consumers. Unless the state were empowered to fix insurance rates, Johnson would countenance no measures limiting competition.[11]

The same scenario was reenacted two years later. During the opening days of the 1915 legislative session members of the Los Angeles Life Underwriters Association met with the state insurance commissioner to draft a bill prohibiting rebating and twisting. After conferring with the Los Angeles body, the chairman of the Senate Insurance Committee introduced this measure in the legislature. The bill passed both houses, and the life and fire associations of Los Angeles spearheaded a campaign to win Governor Johnson's approval.[12] Yet, the governor again vetoed the proposal. Johnson pointed out that unless state control of rates accompanied the abolition of rebates the measure might hurt policyholders by preventing agents from passing on part of their commissions to them. He concluded that the bill "does not give one penny of benefit to any man insuring in the State of California" and refused to sign legislation that he believed was so "wholly favorable to the companies and those engaged in the insurance business."[13]

While the abortive drive for an antirebate law demonstrated a high degree of unity among insurance men, the struggle over state fire-rating measures revealed lines of cleavage. Company officials fought all attempts to transfer the power over rates and the evaluation of risks to the state. Lobbyists for the Board of Fire Underwriters of the Pacific traveled to Sacramento on numerous occasions to argue against any proposals that would have eroded the power of their organization. Local agents, on the other hand, hurt by rate wars and frequent breakdowns of the board's discipline, supported state rate-fixing bills as a way to stabilize their end of the insurance business and, they, too, labored in Sacramento to win acceptance for their position.

The results of San Francisco's earthquake and fire initiated efforts to secure state supervision of insurance rates. To recoup losses resulting from the disaster, the Board of Fire Underwriters of the Pacific increased its tariff for San Francisco by one-quarter and began rerating all California risks. The attempts of some firms to escape paying their fire losses and the bankruptcy of others further hurt the standing of insurance companies in the eyes of the public. San Francisco Mayor James Rolph denounced the actions of insurance men, and a widely circulated report prepared by Matthew Sullivan for San Francisco's Mission Promotion Association, a local improvement body, condemned the Board as "a formidable trust which is responsible for the extortionate rates of insurance."[14]

Following several years of indecisive action, the drive for state control of insurance rates climaxed in 1913. Working together, Rolph and Sullivan drafted a bill outlawing all types of rate-fixing compacts. Strongly opposed by both insurance agents and underwriters, the measure failed to win legislative approval. Most of those favoring state regulation placed their hopes, instead, on a bill introduced as a progressive measure by Senator William Kehoe. Kehoe's proposition required fire insurance companies to use tables of hazards and classifications of risks prepared by the state insurance commissioner in drawing up their rating schedules. Unlike the Sullivan bill, Kehoe's measure recognized the need for uniform rates to prevent rate wars, but at the same time it gave the final power over rates to a public official rather than a private organization.[15]

The struggle over Kehoe's measure exposed divisions between insurance men. The Board of Fire Underwriters of the Pacific fought the bill with all the resources at its command. The head of its rating bureau, augmented by an army of lobbyists, labored diligently in Sacramento to defeat the bill. Local agents, however, initially favored Kehoe's measure as a way to decrease competition and raise their profits. The California State Association of Local Fire Insurance Agents maintained a committee in Sacramento to work for the measure and sent circulars to businessmen throughout the state pointing out that Kehoe's bill would prevent discrimination in rates.[16]

The Board of Fire Underwriters of the Pacific won the contest. As the struggle over the proposal became heated, board members brought pressure to bear upon their agents to change their views. Noah Adair who headed the association of local agents lost his agency. The actions of those belonging to the board secured the desired effect, and within a few weeks the association had reversed its position to oppose the Kehoe bill. In spite of the backing of California's leading progressive newspapers and Senator Kehoe's oft-repeated declaration that his measure would reduce insurance costs and thus save millions of dollars annually for the insured, the bill failed in a tied vote in the senate.[17] Resurrected in 1915, Kehoe's measure suffered the same fate as two years before. The local agents of Southern California were, according to one insurance journal, "red-hot" for the state rating scheme. However, the Board of Fire Underwriters of the Pacific continued to fight it and managed, despite a favorable committee report, to kill it in the senate by the count of fourteen to twenty-four. After this defeat the measure was never revived.[18]

Legislation dealing with the formation of new types of insurance companies in California uncovered still more divisions between insurance men. The well-established stock fire companies opposed measures to liberalize laws dealing with the founding of mutual fire insurance organizations. By the same token, the mutual life insurance companies tried to use state legislation to restrict the activities of their new competitors, assessment life firms. The mutual life and stock fire companies argued that the newer types of firm were financially unstable and apt to fail in times of crisis. The state insurance commissioner, disregarding conclusive proof to the contrary, aided the more established firms in these contests.

Mutual life firms sought to combat the popularity of late nineteenth-century assessment life schemes through state legislation. Throughout the 1890s, they worked with the state insurance commissioner to extend state control over the assessment organizations and to slow their expansion in California. In 1891, the insurance commissioner obtained passage for measures laying the groundwork for state regulation of assessment companies. Three years later Commissioner M. R. Higgins, noting that the growth of assessment schemes had been tremendous, called for still tougher laws, and the 1895 legislature enacted the desired modifications. Probably because assessment companies declined in importance during the last years of the nineteenth century the commissioner made no further efforts to increase his power over them.[19]

Stock fire insurance companies, also aided by the state insurance commissioner, sought to prevent the passage of legislation allowing the formation of mutual life insurance ventures. In 1895, the intervention of the Board of Fire Underwriters of the Pacific killed a measure permitting the establishment of mutual companies, but two years later a more limited proposition for the incorporation of mutuals in rural areas won approval. In 1903, the mutuals sought permission to write risks in towns as well as country regions, but the combined opposition of the stock companies and the insurance commissioner blocked this move. The losses some policyholders suffered in the San Francisco earthquake and fire increased public insistence for the liberalization of mutual fire insurance laws, and, in 1907, the legislature broadened the types of risks mutuals could accept. The stock firms, however, quickly regained their poise and, with the assistance of the insurance commissioner, defeated additional steps in this direction two years later. Insurance Commissioner Myron Wolf even called for the repeal of the 1907 laws. Only in 1911 did measures further enhancing the legal status of mutual firms win approval. Backed by Progressives as a way to check the rates of the stock companies, the bills passed the legislature and were signed into law by Governor Johnson.[20]

As these legislative struggles demonstrated, a spirit of cordiality characterized the relationship between the well-established mutual life and stock fire insurance firms and the state insurance commissioners. Few of the commissioners tried to increase their powers over these companies. In 1888, Commissioner J. L. Wadsworth claimed that "the introduction of numerous bills" at each legislative session "tends to disturb well settled underwriting principles" and declared that "the present laws upon our statute book meet nearly, if not all, requirements of the business." Commissioner Wolf echoed these sentiments fifteen years later. "The laws of this state," he asserted, "are well settled, and the insurance people are honest, law-abiding people." Only Commissioner Andrew Clunie showed antagonism toward the insurance companies, and personal considerations probably motivated his actions. Appointed in 1897, he soon began harassing the larger life companies, especially the big three. The attorney for the New York firms recommended the employment of a special counsel to settle the cases. When the companies chose Thomas Clunie, the commissioner's brother, to represent them for a monthly fee of $250, Andrew Clunie's attacks lessened and then ceased.[21]

Part of the explanation for this business-government coziness may be that the office of insurance commissioner became something of a steppingstone to a position as an insurance company executive. After M. R. Higgins retired as commissioner in 1896, he became second vice-president for the largest life insurance company chartered in California. When M. M. Rhorer stepped down as deputy insurance commissioner after twenty-five years of service, the San Francisco Life Underwriters Association held a testimonial dinner in his honor and presented him with a purse of $1,100. Many of San Francisco's foremost bankers and insurance men endorsed Myron Wolf's application for the position of commissioner in 1902, and, upon his resignation from office eight years later, Wolf accepted the vice-presidency of an insurance company in San Francisco. J. E. Phelps, who took over as commissioner in 1914, had been a local agent in Los Angeles and vice-president of the California State Association of Local Fire Insurance Agents. As one insurance journalist noted with approval, he was not an iconoclast and would do nothing to upset existing conditions. In all, three of California's five insurance commissioners between 1890 and 1915 either had been or would become insurance men.[22]

The Rationalization of the Insurance Business

Even as they wrestled with the problem of competition, California insurance men encountered difficulties resulting from the growing complexity of their state's economy. Urbanization and industrialization, and the new life styles these processes engendered, forced insurance men to rationalize their businesses. Fire insurance men sought to devise scientific methods of rating risks and worked together to hammer out reinsurance and loss-adjustment agreements. Both fire and life insurance men labored to standardize insurance policies.

Devising accurate methods to rate fire risks was a chronic problem in California, for economic and social conditions were in such a state of flux that insurance men could not build up a body of statistics to use in formulating probabilities. Urbanization and the consequent increase in conflagrative hazards, the adoption of new building materials and methods, and the introduction of electric and oil-burning engines in industry thwarted rate-makers who tried to depend upon past experience. In 1902, William Saxton, the dean of special fire insurance agents in California, summed up the changes insurance men had to deal with. The old-timer, he observed, "floated from rough board, shake roof, cloth and paper, tallow candles to rustic shingle roof." By way of contrast, he noted that the modern agent had to deal with "the skyscraper, acetylene gas, and electricity."[23]

Insurance trade associations set up rating bureaus to cope with these problems by fixing standard or uniform charges. These bodies first set rates on what they called the "tariff" basis. This method considered only three variables in arriving at charges: the class of construction of a building, the occupation carried on inside it, and how close the building was to other structures (exposure charge). In 1869, the San Francisco Board of Fire Underwriters specified four classes of exposures and about 200 occupations, and local agents possessed considerable leeway in setting rates. Eighteen years later the Pacific Insurance Union recognized five exposure charges and nearly 400 occupations, and detailed rules limited the freedom of local agents. By 1912, the Board of Fire Underwriters of the Pacific listed 550 different uses for buildings and had promulgated twenty-five general rules for agents to follow in setting rates.[24] Even this increasing refinement in setting rates fell short of the needs of many insurance men. On the one hand, some agents complained that they could not understand the twists and turns in the labyrinth of rate-making. On the other hand, many felt the rates, which normally covered entire states or even larger areas, needed further modifications to take local conditions into consideration.[25]

A new method of setting rates, which insurance men labeled "schedule" rating, won acceptance in the late nineteenth and early twentieth centuries and provided a partial solution to the troubles encountered in tariff rating. While retaining the same variables as the tariff system, schedule charges also took into account the general fire danger prevailing in the spots to which they were applied. Schedule rating did not, however, increase the authority of local agents, for surveyors from the Board of Fire Underwriters of the Pacific continued to make their rounds checking rates. By 1909, the Board employed eight electrical engineers, seven engineers to supervise sprinkler systems, thirty daily report examiners, and thirty rating supervisors. Although insurance men never eliminated all inequalities, rate-making became an increasingly systematic science in which guess work had little place.[26]

Insurance men also standardized the adjustment of fire losses. Since policyholders usually insured their property with more than one firm, the companies had to devise ways to apportion losses among themselves. This situation often resulted in acrimony. Insurance men found it hard to determine the amount each firm owed, and the expenses of adjustment were large, sometimes as high as 5 percent of the actual damages suffered. Then too, on some occasions one company, desiring to appear generous to the insured, forced hasty and unnecessarily costly settlements upon the others. Continued complaints led the Fire Underwriters Association of the Pacific, an organization of special agents and adjusters, to set up a committee to study the problem. The committee's report of 1879 urged that companies act in harmony and not seek competitive advantages by lax settlements. However, only with the adoption of what became known as the "Kinne Rule" six years later did adjusters finally reach agreement. This formula provided guidelines for the apportionment of losses and established standards for the division of adjusting expenses. With few modifications it remained in effect well into the twentieth century.[27]

Because few fire insurance companies wanted to be held liable for all of a large loss, they reinsured parts of their policies with other firms. Like fire adjusting, reinsurance raised a number of ticklish questions. Efforts to draft a standard reinsurance contract failed in the 1890s, but insurance men achieved some success in the next decade. In 1901, the Board of Fire Underwriters of the Pacific and the Fire Underwriters Association of the

Pacific created a joint committee to draft a uniform contract. This committee presented its findings two years later. Although the contract embodying the committee's suggestions never won total acceptance, it did help rationalize this branch of the insurance business.[28]

Campaigns for the adoption of standard life- and fire-insurance policies provided the most dramatic manifestations of the drives for efficiency and rationality. New York state's investigation into life insurance in 1905 and the San Francisco disaster a year later aroused public interest in the matter. Policyholders came to view standard policies as a way to protect themselves from insurance companies trying to avoid paying their losses. Insurance men also favored standard policies, for they saw in standardization a way to rationalize their businesses. Yet, few insurance men wanted to go as far in this direction as most policyholders, and the resulting conflicts between the desires of the insured and the insurance companies set the stage for a series of lively legislative contests.

By the early twentieth century life insurance policies had become quite confusing, and efforts to standardize them led to legislative battles in Sacramento. Persons seeking life coverage could choose from a myriad of policy types: industrial, level premium, semitontine, and all shades in between. To attract new business California companies even offered combinations of life, health, and accident insurance. The Armstrong Investigation into life insurance in New York revealed that many policyholders failed to understand complicated clauses of their policies, and after the investigation a conference of governors, attorneys general, and state insurance commissioners met in Chicago to prepare a model standard-policy law. In 1907, California's insurance commissioner sponsored this measure in Sacramento. However, officers of insurance companies chartered in California successfully blocked its passage. They feared that the bill would outlaw the new types of policies they were pioneering and that it would thus deprive them of their most potent weapon against the competition of the larger eastern firms. The legislators heeded their arguments and, believing they were protecting a home industry, defeated the bill.[29]

Fire insurance policies matched the confusion of the life policies, and early attempts to standardize them failed. In the 1870s and 1880s, fire policies were unwieldy affairs that contained lengthy and sometimes contradictory printed and handwritten clauses. Some firms adopted the standard New York form in the 1890s, but many discrepancies remained. In 1899, the California legislature considered bills that would have made the New York policy obligatory for all companies operating in California.

When, however, the Board of Fire Underwriters of the Pacific advised the solons that similar proposals in other states had been declared unconstitutional, they dropped the measures.[30]

The San Francisco earthquake and fire focused public attention on standard policies and laid bare the conflicting interests of the insured and the insurance companies. When some firms tried to escape paying fire losses on technicalities in their policies, San Francisco merchants organized a policyholders league to press the claims of its members and to work for standard-policy legislation. In 1907, the league presented a standard-policy measure for consideration in Sacramento. Though claiming that they favored "any legislation calculated to render insurance contracts more uniform and easier of comprehension," members of the Board of Fire Underwriters of the Pacific opposed the bill. They argued that the proposal needed further work to iron out rough spots and threatened to withdraw their companies from California should the act become law. Despite this threat, the legislature passed the bill. The insurance men then brought pressure to bear on Governor James Gillette, and the governor, who claimed that he disliked several riders attached to the measure, vetoed the bill.[31]

Continued pressure from both San Francisco businessmen and the insurance companies kept the issue of standard policies alive. In December, 1907, Governor Gillette set up a special commission to investigate the problem. Composed of the insurance commissioner, representatives of San Francisco's merchant bodies, and William Dutton who headed both the Fireman's Fund Insurance Company and the Fire Underwriters Association of the Pacific, the commission prepared a compromise measure acceptable to both the insurance men and the merchants. In 1909, the commission secured its introduction into the state legislature. After amending the bill, against the wishes of the insurance men, to provide for indirect as well as direct fire losses, the legislators gave it their approval, and the measure soon became law.[32]

Insurance Companies and Economic Development

Contests over state regulation of insurance company funds exacerbated the other conflicts between insurance men and California businessmen. By the late nineteenth century, insurance companies possessed large amounts of capital that could be invested to stimulate a region's economic growth. California businessmen and legislators hoped to prevent insurance companies from extracting more from their state in premiums than they returned to it in the payment of losses and investments. To achieve this end California legislators passed laws specifying the types of investments firms incorporated in California could make and even considered regulating those of eastern and foreign companies. The solons also enacted measures establishing deposit requirements for firms operating in California.

Long-standing complaints that eastern companies operating in California were draining the state of capital led to efforts to supervise their investments for the benefit of home industry. In 1894, the New York Life bid on a $500,000 state bond issue because of criticisms that it had no investments in California. In the same period the Prudential entered the state's loan business, and the Mutual placed a large deposit with the Bank of California. By 1897, Insurance Commissioner Clunie could report that California was losing little insurance money to eastern centers. Many businessmen, however, reached different conclusions and thought that the insurance companies should do more to aid their industrial and commercial ventures. In 1907, the Texas legislators approved a measure requiring insurance firms to invest three-quarters of the reserves generated by Texas business in Lone Star securities. Two years later Californians drew up a similar bill; but they never introduced it in the legislature, perhaps out of fear that, as had happened in Texas, the large eastern insurance companies would leave the state. In 1915, a nearly identical proposal died in committee.[33]

Despite the lack of legislation on this matter, the investments of eastern companies in California rose sharply in the early twentieth century. In the years after the Armstrong Investigation the firms were particularly vulnerable to public criticism and found that they could improve their public images by investing in the same areas in which they sold policies. Then, too, investment opportunities in California widened as the state's economy developed, and insurance executives probably recognized that they could earn more on capital in the Far West than in most other regions. By 1911, the Pacific Coast led all but two other sections of the country, the Southwest and the Northern Plains, in the percentage of insurance reserves derived from the area's premiums being reinvested in the region. California money was staying at home, and Californians were drawing upon capital accumulated elsewhere, most notably in New England, for the development of their state.[34]

Legislators also tried to tap the savings of insurance companies incorporated within California. The requests of California insurance men for a wider range of investment opportunities and the desire of local businessmen to channel insurance funds into their state's industries transformed the laws governing the investments of California insurance companies. Before 1905, insurance firms could place their funds in federal bonds, the note issues of all states, the municipal and county bonds of California and Oregon, certain types of real estate loans, and (with the exception of life companies) the bonds of corporations chartered both inside and outside California. Legislation passed in 1905 liberalized the types of investments allowed. Insurance companies could now purchase the securities of counties and cities anywhere in the nation, and the new laws relaxed restrictions on property loans and legalized loans made on policies. Life insurance firms could, for the first time, acquire corporate securities, and stocks as well as bonds won appróval for purchase. This last provision, however, had a catch. Because they wanted to use insurance funds to further the economic development of their state, the legislators stipulated that the insurance companies could buy only the securities of corporations chartered in California. The same trends continued in later years. By 1913, the legislature had added the bonds of school and irrigation districts to the list of investment possibilities, timely provisions for a state with a swelling population and an agricultural system dependent on irrigation.[35]

Finally, legislators sought to encourage California's growth by setting deposit requirements for insurance companies. In 1895, the solons considered a proposal requiring all insurance companies doing business in California to place $200,000 of securities with the state treasurer. The securities could consist of the bonds of the national or any state governments and the notes of California municipal or county governments. Proponents of the bill, who included California insurance men already under the jurisdiction of a similar measure, argued that the bill would protect policyholders from losses and help stem the capital drain to the East. Out-of-state life and marine firms, however, won exemption from the proposition, and, as passed by the legislature, the bill applied only to fire companies. Disliking the exclusion of life and marine companies, the governor vetoed the bill and called for the enactment of a more stringent law. Nothing came of such pleas until the 1906 disaster revived public interest in deposit legislation. Several foreign firms, unwilling to pay the losses they incurred, withdrew from California leaving their debts unsettled. To discourage such actions in the future the 1907 legislature passed a measure requiring a $200,000 deposit from all foreign companies. The firms could place this sum with any state treasurer, not just California's, and the range of permissible securities was wide. This act dissatisfied many Californians. Insurance Commissioner Wolf believed, for instance, that at least part of the deposit should be in the hands of California officials and that some of the securities should consist of California issues. Nonetheless, the measure won the governor's approval and became the law regulating the deposits of foreign companies for over a decade.[36]

The Professionalization of Insurance Men

Like bankers, insurance men looked upon themselves as professionals and hoped that the professionalization of their business would dampen competition, help speed their efforts at rationalization, and improve their image with California businessmen. As early as 1879, one of the state's leading fire insurance men urged his fellows to end "charlatanry, backbiting and all manner of envy" for the sake of "our profession," and, by 1910, the president of the Fire Underwriters Association of the Pacific was describing his calling as "a combination of business and a profession." To gain public acceptance as professionals, insurance men tried to work out codes of business ethics, set up schools to provide professional education, and increase their social contacts with one another.[37]

The insurance trade associations sought to establish standards of "fair" business practices, for many insurance men wanted to control the abuses of competition they viewed as unseemly for professionals. At the height of the rate wars of the 1890s, the secretary of the Fireman's Fund condemned "the tendency of the day in changing our profession from a science to a mere barter and trade proposition" and called for a return to higher standards. The organizations of insurance men labored to end rate wars, rebating, fraudulent advertising, and the stealing of agents and, though never totally successful, made some progress in these areas.[38]

Reflecting the growing complexity of California's economy, the insurance business grew increasingly specialized, and insurance men came to require a broader, professional education. At the opening of the twentieth century, six universities in the United States offered insurance courses. The University of California was among the leaders in this field. By 1904, it presented classes on the actuarial problems and mathematics encountered in insurance work, and in later years its program expanded in detail and scope. Insurance men relied, however, primarily upon their own organizations for education. The Fire Underwriters Association of the Pacific and the life insurance organizations provided forums at which insurance men could present papers and debate current business topics, and such discussions played an important role in the development of uniform reinsurance and fire-adjustment agreements. Most ambitious were efforts to create an institute for the education of fire insurance men in San Francisco. In 1905, the Fire Underwriters Association of the Pacific set up a school modeled upon insurance institutes in England. The first of its kind in the United States, the school gave a ten-week series of lectures covering many facets of fire insurance. The 1906 disaster halted plans for expansion, but attempts to revive the courses proved partially successful when the Insurance Institute of America established a Pacific Coast branch in San Francisco five years later. The Fire Underwriters Association of the Pacific also entered the field again in 1914 with bimonthly lectures on reinsurance, the California standard policy, schedule-rating, and other insurance topics.[39]

Organizations that brought insurance men together for educational purposes promoted social intercourse among them as well. Insurance men founded the Fire Underwriters Association of the Pacific to "promote harmony" between managers and special agents, and, by 1881, the organization's president could speak of its members as forming "one large insurance family." The rate wars of the mid-1890s partially dispelled this feeling of fellowship; but, by 1897, several agents could again ascribe the establishment of "enduring personal friendships" to the association, and some predicted these social contacts would help check competition in the future. During the opening years of the twentieth century, Los Angeles and San Francisco fire insurance men organized "ponds" of the Ancient and Honorable Order of the Blue Goose, a national social organization. In 1910, San Franciscans also set up a local club for agents and adjusters "to wear away the rough edges of distrust," and Los Angelenos followed this example several years later. Life insurance men exhibited less social cohesion, but their trade associations provided a source of some social contacts. At their annual banquets in Los Angeles and San Francisco the revelers told stories, shared experiences, and sang popular songs of the day.[40]

Despite their various efforts, insurance men failed to win professional acceptance they sought. As legislative contests over such matters as policy standardization demonstrated, the interests of insurance men and other businessmen often clashed. The inability of insurance men to harmonize their goals with the needs of California businessmen helps explain their rejection as professionals. In this context it is worth noting that bankers, who more fully reconciled their aims with those of California businessmen, were more successful in winning wider recognition for themselves as professionals.

Like so many other California businessmen, the insurance men sought, through the campaigns to dampen competition, their drives to rationalize business methods, and their efforts to win acceptance as professionals, to stabilize an industry caught in the web of economic change. California insurance men worked through their trade associations and state legislation to cope with alterations in their business environment, but they never completely succeeded. The insurance community included too many clashing interests to achieve harmony of purpose. Insurance agents fought insurance underwriters, mutual life battled assessment life companies, stock fire opposed mutual fire firms, and companies chartered in California contended with those incorporated elsewhere. The insurance business probably contained as many diverse, and often conflicting, elements as any other industry in California. Pressure from other business groups and bodies of policyholders also contributed to the instability of California's insurance industry. Like bankers, insurance men were at times troubled by other businessmen and state officials seeking to harness insurance funds for California's economic development, and, again as in the case of bankers, the goals of financial stability and economic growth sometimes conflicted. For these various reasons, the insurance business long remained one of the most difficult industries to regulate in California.

9

Big Business and Tax Reform

Like the campaign for railroad regulation, California's tax reform movement involved nearly all of the state's businessmen. Beginning in the
1890s, reformers sought to adjust California's system of taxation to
changes in their state's economic structure. Their plan, which finally won
approval in 1910, separated the sources of revenue for the state and local
governments. Under this scheme the state government derived its funds
almost entirely from taxes levied by a central state board of equalization
upon the gross earnings of the state's public service corporations. Counties
and cities relied upon an ad valorem tax on all forms of property other than
that of the public service corporations. This system replaced an arrangement in operation since 1879 by which all the revenues gathered in
California came from a general property tax collected by county boards of
assessment under the supervision of the state board of equalization. It was
expected that the new plan would both rationalize California's system of
tax collection and, by levying state taxes on public service corporations,
provide new funds to meet the growing expenses of the state government.[1]

Early Efforts at Tax Reform

In the 1890s, the California state government found itself chronically
short of money, and the growing gap between revenues and expenditures
turned the attention of Californians to tax reform. Government officials

often exhausted the state's general fund long before the next year's taxes were due. When this situation arose in 1897, Governor James Budd used the threat of his veto power to insure that all appropriations bills passed by the legislature included provisos that the funds allotted could not be spent until after taxes had been gathered ten months later. To avoid this condition in the future the governor called for a revamping of the state's tax system. In his messages to the legislature in 1897 and 1899 he declared that the burden fell too heavily on landed property and asked for the enactment of a corporate income tax.[2] Carl Plehn, a professor of economics and tax expert at the University of California, backed the governor's request for tax reform. In addresses before the California Bankers Association, the Convention of County Assessors, and the American Economics Association, Plehn claimed that the state's general property tax had grown obsolete, because it failed to reach forms of corporate property that had come into existence in the past twenty years. Too much of the tax weight fell on landed property, he thought, and thus on the state's farmers. Nor was even the tax on land equitable. Assessments and rates, Plehn amply demonstrated, varied widely from county to county, and the state board of equalization had failed in its attempts to make them uniform.[3]

The state legislature responded to these cries for reform during its 1899 session. Assemblyman A. Caminetti introduced a bill exempting all real estate from taxation for state purposes. The state should instead, Caminetti argued, receive its funds from a levy on railroad, express, telephone, and telegraph companies. Passed by the assembly, this measure died in the senate. Some senators disliked provisions in the bill exempting church and school property from taxation, and others feared that too strict a tax on public service corporations might retard California's economic development. Moreover, most advocates of tax reform, even many of those voting for Caminetti's proposal, felt that more time had to be given to a study of the problem. Accordingly, Senator F. S. Stratton secured passage for a measure, prepared by Carl Plehn, that set up a committee to investigate California's tax system.[4] After examining its operation in California and other states, the committee condemned the general property tax as "inequitable, unfair and positively unjust." Its report urged the legislature to make "a radical change" and concluded that "a large part of the burden should be shifted to business."[5]

California's new governor, Henry Gage, ignored the committee's recommendations. As a conservative Republican, he hoped to balance the budget by reducing state expenses rather than by altering the method of taxation. Upon taking office in 1901, Gage claimed that Californians had elected him to end "waste in the expenditure of state funds" and vowed to cut spending to the bone. The state legislature, probably believing that Gage's rhetoric would become reality, approved an unusually small tax levy for the next biennium. This action created a financial crisis, for not even Governor Gage could keep expenses down. Despite some efforts to reduce spending (Gage refused to pay the state bounty on coyote scalps, for instance), state expenditures rose 18 percent between 1901 and 1903.[6]

When George Pardee took over as governor in 1903, he found the state's general fund practically empty and immediately began looking for ways to increase the state's revenue. He revived the report of the senate committee and in his inaugural address spoke favorably of the efforts that New Jersey, Wisconsin, Pennsylvania, and New York were making to divide the sources of state and county revenues. He emphasized, however, the need to proceed slowly and carefully "so as to give the least shock to established industries and to vested interests." A successful jail break from the state prison at Folsom in July, 1903, upset his plans for gradual change. The escape heightened public awareness of the tax issue, for in widely publicized statements the prison's warden complained that the outbreak had been possible only because he lacked funds to buy cement to repair the institution's crumbling walls. He blamed the legislature's stinginess for the break and called for hikes in the tax rate.[7]

After this incident the tax problem never disappeared from sight. State expenditures continued to rise, 32 percent between 1903 and 1905 and another 14 percent in the next two years.[8] These increases pressed against state revenues and left the government strapped for funds. Economic rivalry between Los Angeles, Oakland, and San Francisco added more fuel to the fire, for the residents of each metropolis believed that they paid too large a share of the state's taxes and felt that the inhabitants of other cities gained at their expense. After the state board of equalization raised assessments in San Francisco in 1903, one of the city's largest newspapers condemned the board as "a pirate ship" and called for changes in the tax laws of the state.[9] When Oaklanders faced a similar prospect two years later, they accused San Franciscans of being "tax shirkers" and insinuated that they had bribed the board of equalization.[10] The continuing work of Carl Plehn also retained public interest in the matter. In 1902, he defended the separation of tax revenues at a meeting of university professors in Boston.[11] A year later he presented his ideas to the Commonwealth Club of California, and, in the spring of 1904, this group passed resolutions asking the legislature to abandon the attempt "to support both the state and local governments from taxes laid in the same sources of revenue" and instead to devise "a single and uniform system" of taxation.[12]

This agitation prodded Governor Pardee to accelerate the pace of reform. During his visit to the world exposition in St. Louis in the summer of 1904, Pardee surveyed the tax systems of eastern states, and he sent his secretary on a follow-up tour that fall to gather additional data. In his address opening the 1905 legislature the governor again acknowledged the necessity of increasing state revenues and called upon Californians to follow other states in revising their tax system. He specifically pointed to the efforts being made in New York, Pennsylvania, New Jersey, and Ohio to separate state and local revenues. Pardee reiterated the need for tax separation in California as a way to tap corporate income for state purposes and requested that the state legislature draft constitutional amendments embodying his desires.[13]

The legislature responded with a hodgepodge of legislation rather than the measures Pardee had hoped for. The issue of tax reform through the separation of revenues was still new in the United States and California. Consequently, many solons wanted further study of the matter before proceeding further. The opposition of some businessmen may also have influenced the decision to go slow. Although the Commonwealth Club backed Pardee's plan and lobbied for it in Sacramento, other business groups were dissatisfied with it. The San Francisco Merchants Exchange feared that any actions to change the state's tax system might "frighten capital away to other fields." Both the Los Angeles and San Francisco bank clearing houses, while accepting the principle of separation as a way to rationalize California's system of taxation, opposed specific bills designed to implement the governor's plan. Despite the appearance of Carl Plehn in the capital to argue for the governor's scheme and frequent conferences between Pardee and the senate and assembly committees on revenue and taxation, it soon became clear that the solons would not agree on any single program. Governor Pardee had to accept piecemeal changes: a state licensing fee for corporations, an inheritance tax, and an increase in the taxes levied on insurance companies.[14]

More importantly, the governor secured passage for a measure setting up a five-man commission to examine all aspects of the state's tax problems. As yet Californians actually knew little about how the separation of tax revenues would affect their state. The senate committee's report of 1901 was superficial, and the investigations of Carl Plehn and Governor Pardee, though adding to the store of knowledge, had been far from exhaustive. The legislature empowered the commission (composed of four senators and assemblymen under the chairmanship of Carl Plehn) to gather information and draft specific proposals for a new tax system in California.

Tax Reform Legislation

From the outset of their work members of the commission sought to design a comprehensive system of taxation rather than simply a set of unrelated laws and emphasized that tax reform would benefit businessmen.[15] For the first nine months of its existence the commissioners studied the tax plans of other states and collected data about California. By the end of this period they agreed that any future plan should separate the sources of county and state revenues and that the gross revenues of public service corporations should be taxed solely for state purposes. The commissioners stressed that taxation by the state government rather than by scattered county officials would aid those companies affected by their propositions. At the beginning of the commission's work Carl Plehn made a point of asserting that "this movement contains nothing that is hostile to or dangerous to capital or to the corporations."[16] He felt that his relations with company officials would be "entirely of an amiable nature" and doubted that he would have to use the powers given him by the legislature to command their cooperation. Senator Martin Ward, another member of the commission, claimed that although the public service corporations would have to render higher taxes than before, they would gain in other respects. "They will pay at the same rate on all their property," he noted, "and not at one rate in one county and at another in another." Furthermore, he continued, "they will pay all at one time, and not at a half a dozen or more different times, and at as many different places." Carl Plehn, speaking to the County Assessors Convention, also declared that "uniformity is the desire" most sought by the commission.[17]

Carl Plehn's predictions about the attitudes of businessmen proved correct, for most readily cooperated with the commission. In a series of hearings beginning in March, 1906, businessmen made it clear that they were willing to accept increased taxes in return for greater stability and predictability in their relations with government. Public service corporation spokesmen welcomed a way to escape perennial haggling with county officials, and some favored the plan as a means to escape the necessity of bribing local tax assessors. Most wanted a highly centralized method of taxation run along efficient, rational lines. At the end of the commission's studies Plehn reported that in only one instance had corporate officials attacked the principle or plan of taxation devised by the commission.[18]

Bankers were the first businessmen to appear before the commission. In laying the groundwork for this meeting the tax commission sent out questionnaires to all of the state's bankers asking for detailed information on their real estate holdings, solvent credits, holdings of stocks and bonds, and taxes paid in the past year.[19] The preparations of the bankers were equally elaborate. The executive council of the California Bankers Association circularized the organization's members for their ideas on taxation and set up a committee to study and compile the results.[20] The conference that followed revealed a high degree of harmony between business and government officials. The bankers readily endorsed the principle of tax separation as a move in the direction of uniformity and efficiency. Only a few points of friction arose. Whereas bankers wanted the taxes levied on the book value of a bank's capital stock, the commissioners hoped to see them based on the stock's market value. The commissioners were, however, simply using this issue as a bargaining counter and soon gave way on it. More importantly, the bankers complained that the proposed rate of taxation, 1 percent of a bank's capital and surplus, was too high. They found the commissioners "impossible to move" on this subject and finally agreed that the charge would be "partially offset by the advantages which would come from absolute uniformity and certainty in the taxation of all banks."[21]

Insurance men testified next and, like the bankers, praised the centralizing tendencies of the commission's plan. However, they too believed the commissioners desired too great a rate of taxation. They also feared that, if California imposed a state tax on companies incorporated in other states, these states would retaliate by taxing California firms. The discussion that followed uncovered a partial solution to these impasses. The insurance men explained that, if local licensing fees were abolished, they would be able to pay more to the state. The commissioners agreed, and their final report recommended ending all county and municipal charges.[22]

Railroad executives also came out in favor of tax reform. Some railroad men, most notably Southern Pacific officials, had initially opposed tax reform, because they feared that any alterations might increase their taxes. Meetings with the tax commission revealed that the railroad men had changed their attitudes by 1906. As early as November, 1905, officers of the Southern Pacific assured the commissioners that they were for tax reform, and in hearings on the matter a year and a half later representatives of other lines added their assent. As Carl Plehn described these sessions, the railroad men were reluctant to pay more taxes but did agree that the new system would be more equitable. Company officials particularly emphasized that they favored state taxation of their property as a way to eliminate the need to work with the many county officials.[23]

By their actions railroad officials had already shown that they desired state taxation of their companies. Unlike other public service corporations, railroads, under the terms of the state constitution of 1879, were taxed by both state and county governments. The state board of equalization taxed the operating property of all railroads providing service in more than one country, and the county assessors taxed the nonoperative property of the lines. (The division between operative and nonoperative property was fuzzy. In general, a railroad's roadbed, rails, and cars made up its operative property. Nonoperative property included land right-of-ways, buildings, and yards.) Despite the fact that the state board of equalization nearly doubled its assessments of railroad property between 1898 and 1906, railroad officers tried to place as much as possible of their roads' properties under state supervision. They hoped in this manner to decrease their total expenses by abolishing bribes to county officials, lowering bookkeeping costs, and ending other charges resulting from irregular practices concerning the taxation of nonoperative properties. In a ruling handed down in April, 1906, the Supreme Court of California thwarted these efforts of railroad men to secure greater uniformity in tax gathering. In a case pitting the city of Stockton against the San Francisco and San Joaquin Railroad, the court decided that the real property of the railroad—its real estate, terminal depots, passenger and freight sheds—could not be defined as operative property and, therefore, had to be taxed by the assessors of the various counties through which the line passed. This decision went against the wishes of the railroad's officials who argued that their line should be assessed as an entirety by the state board of equalization. Not surprisingly, railroad executives embraced the tax commission's plan for the separation of state and local tax revenues as a way to circumvent the court's ruling.[24]

Public utility officials also sought greater predictability in their tax arrangements. After attending the 1906 conference on the Pacific Coast Gas Association, John Britton, then manager of the Pacific Gas and Electric Company, wrote the commission, as Carl Plehn reported to Governor Pardee, that the light, heat, and power companies were overwhelmingly in favor of the commission's scheme.[25]

After a final meeting with representatives of the state's leading railroads and public utilities in October, 1906, the commission released its findings and recommendations. Its three-hundred-page report labeled the general property tax as hopelessly out of date. "The state has outgrown the simple conditions of economic life," it observed, "to which alone the system was adapted." With the expansion of industry and commerce new types of wealth had developed, but they remained virtually untouched by taxation. Corporate income, in particular, the commissioners thought, was taxed too lightly. The report demonstrated that, while farmers paid the equivalent of a 10 percent income tax, manufacturers paid only 2 percent. Personal property, money, and credits, the document revealed, "escape taxation almost entirely." The commissioners concluded by noting that the general property tax led to widespread tax evasion and condemned California's tax system as a "school for perjury" that "puts a penalty on honesty and pays high premiums for dishonesty." The solution, according to the commission, lay in the complete separation in the sources of revenue for the state and the counties. The state would still draw funds from a poll tax, the inheritance tax, a tax on insurance premiums modified to remove inequities, earnings from the sale of state lands, and a few other minor items. The state would now also receive revenue from gross-earnings taxes on railroads, street railroads, light, heat and power corporations, express firms, telephone and telegraph companies. Banks would pay 1 percent of the book value of their stock, and all corporations would yield 1 percent of the assessed valuations of their franchises. Counties and municipalities would continue to derive their income from the general property tax, but now the properties of public service corporations (except for those classed as nonoperative) would be exempted from city or county charges.[26]

The tax commission's report attracted immediate attention throughout the state and nation. Small-town newspapers and farm organizations found particular praise for the new tax scheme. The Watsonville *Register* lauded the commission's efforts as an "endeavor to bring order out of chaos and to devise a system in harmony with the scientific principles of taxation."[27] Papers in farming areas praised the proposed tax scheme for shifting the burden of taxation from agriculturalists to big businessmen. One journal, for instance, pictured Governor Pardee as following Robert LaFollette's footsteps in taxing corporate income in Wisconsin and predicted that any attempt "to make the corporations pay their just dues into the state treasury would assuredly be appreciated by the general public."[28] Not surprisingly, farm groups came out in favor of the tax commission's plan as a means to reduce taxes on farmers and fruit growers.[29] Reformers in other states hoped the California experiment would succeed and redound to their benefit. Speaking before the Commonwealth Club, E. R. A. Seligman, a professor at Columbia University and a tax reformer of national reknown, hailed the commission's report as the "clearest most logical, and best propounded document on taxation which has emanated from any of our states." Representatives of the Civic Federation of Chicago, appearing before the same body, added that the report "is regarded as one of the ablest of such documents."[30]

Senator J. B. Curtin, who had been a member of the tax commission, presented a measure to the 1907 session of the state legislature that incorporated the commission's recommendations. With some alterations his proposition passed the senate by the overwhelming vote of thirty-six to one, and the assembly quickly endorsed this action. As a constitutional amendment, Curtin's measure now had to win approval in a public referendum to be held in November, 1908.[31]

In the intervening months many public service corporation officials rallied to the support of the tax proposal. George Peltier in his presidential address to the California Bankers Association in 1908 extolled the measure because "it stands for an honest assessment return" and because under its terms "all public utilities, corporations, and quasi-public corporations are taxed alike in their respective classes."[32] Grayson Dutton of the Fireman's Fund Insurance Company also waxed enthusiastic. Speaking before the Commonwealth Club, he asserted that the "reason that we are willing to have this tax is that we are now beset by all kinds of difficulties in the way of payments." He pointed out that his firm paid so many different city and county license fees that "it makes a bookkeeper pretty nearly crazy" and concluded that "one flat rate" would be "a great relief." Dutton was even willing to risk the retaliation of other states, and thus a higher tax burden, in return for greater rationality in the payment of taxes.[33]

Farmers and agriculturalists also backed tax reform, though for a different reason. They hoped changes in California's tax system would shift some of the tax burden from themselves to big business. In late 1907, the California State Grange endorsed Curtin's proposal and urged passage for the measure in the upcoming election. Country newspapers also supported tax reform as aiding farmers. The *Rural Free Press* spoke for many similar journals when it defined the tax issue as one of "rural benefits" and observed that agriculturalists were "righteously inflamed by it."[34]

Yet, many Californians who had been ardent proponents of the separation of state and county taxation since the inception of the movement withheld their backing from the proposal, for they objected to changes made in the tax commission's original plans by the senate and assembly. They complained that in fixing the percentages to be charged against corporate earnings the legislature had in each case chosen the minimum levy suggested by the commission. They doubted that the revenues would be sufficient to run the state government and pointed out that, since the tax rates were to be embodied in a constitutional amendment, it would be difficult to raise them in the future. Some feared, in addition, that, because the proposal provided for the election of the board of equalization by district instead of at-large as the tax commission had recommended, the corporations might gain control of the agency set up to tax them. As one merchant complained, the new tax scheme, far from raising corporate taxes, would create in the public service corporations "a privileged class of tax payers."[35]

Yet another source of opposition came from city officials reluctant to relinquish their power to tax public service corporations. San Franciscans were especially stubborn in this respect. Following the 1906 earthquake and fire, they faced the massive task of rebuilding their city and proved loathe to yield any taxing authority to the state. Mayor James Phelan explained these issues at a meeting of the Commonwealth Club. Phelan claimed that under the proposed plan "we will lose valuable property on which the city might levy for municipal purposes" and feared that this situation would mean that the tax burden on "real estate, improvements, and the stocks of our merchants" would have to be raised, thus placing San Francisco at a competitive disadvantage in attracting business from other areas. Phelan concluded that the tax plan was "an ambush that has been prepared for an unsuspecting community." San Francisco businessmen (other than public service corporation executives) backed their mayor's stand. Like Phelan, they pointed to the need for additional corporate taxes in light of the "large bonded indebtedness" their city would have to incur in order to rebuild. The Commonwealth Club, after hearing such testimony, reversed its stance of a few years before. In 1905, the club's members had endorsed the separation of taxes as a way to rationalize California's system of taxation, but, in 1908, they withdrew their backing from the scheme because they were afraid that it might deprive San Francisco of badly needed tax revenues.[36]

Doubts and confusion about tax reform killed the constitutional amendment. Not even the frequent appearances of Carl Plehn in different areas of California could allay the fears of many. Nor were the issues clear. Despite the fact that the tax reform movement was now a decade old in California, many voters still failed to understand what tax reform was all about. Others, like the San Franciscans, voted against the proposal because they feared it might erode the tax bases of their local communities. As a result, the constitutional amendment lost at the polls by the margin of 87,977 to 114,104.

Faced with an 18 percent jump in state spending between 1907 and 1909 without a comparable boost in state revenues, the legislators tackled the tax problem anew in their regular 1909 session and in a special session a year later. Following Carl Plehn's advice, they remedied the objections that had helped defeat the constitutional amendment in 1908. To quiet fears that the state, by relying so heavily on public service corporations for its revenues, might be left without adequate funds the solons made it easier to raise the rates of taxation as the situation required. The legislature also returned to the tax commission's original plan of electing members of the state board of equalization at-large, and this move reassured those who were afraid that the public service corporations might capture control of the board. Passed by lopsided votes in the senate and assembly, the measure won Governor James Gillette's backing as "a movement in taxation along modern, progressive lines" and was again sent to the public for approval.[37]

As they had two years before, many corporate executives lifted their cudgels on behalf of the measure. The president of the Los Angeles Gas and Electric Company came out for the plan, because he felt it would "accomplish much in the way of a more equitable assessment of public service corporations" and because it would allow them "to avoid continual wrangling with equalization boards and expensive law suits." Members of the California State Realty Federation worked for the proposal for similar reasons. They hoped its passage would "insure a steady, adequate and non-political taxation of public service corporations and banks." San Francisco businessmen, with their city now almost completely rebuilt, were less anxious about tax revenues than in 1908, and the San Francisco Chamber of Commerce, the San Francisco Merchants Exchange, and the San Francisco Merchants Association all passed resolutions favoring the measure.[38]

Politicians, joined by the state grange and numerous business groups, carried on an extensive campaign to educate the voters about the merits of tax reform. Their arguments, combined with a growing public awareness of the tax problem, proved persuasive. In late 1910, the constitutional amendment separating the sources of state and local tax revenues won ratification by the vote of 141,312 to 96,493.

With the passage of this constitutional amendment California joined many other states that had already accepted similar types of tax reform. By 1908, nine states—New York, Pennsylvania, Connecticut, Ohio, New Jersey, Wisconsin, Massachusetts, Minnesota, and Missouri—had incorporated the principle of the separation of tax revenues into their fiscal systems. In many respects the movement for tax reform in California was like tax reform campaigns elsewhere. As the historian Clifton Yearly has shown, many other states were looking for new funds to meet the growing costs of government at the turn of the century. State officials, often backed by tax experts, farmers, and small businessmen, denounced the general property tax as antiquated and inadequate to supply their needs. Yet, however much the California experience resembled those of other states, it differed from them in one crucial regard. Whereas in many states big businessmen, fearing higher taxes on their companies, fought tax reform, in California they generally welcomed it and worked for it. California's nineteenth-century system of taxation was probably even more chaotic than the systems of other states. City and county officials competed with each other and state officials in their search for tax revenue. Public service corporation executives disliked the costly delays, uncertainties, and miscellaneous expenses (like bribes) involved in dealing with this swarm of tax collectors. They desired, instead, the establishment of a single state agency to levy taxes in a more efficient manner. In short, public service corporation officials backed tax reform because it promised to rationalize one of their major business expenses.[39]

Tax Reform in Practice

Public service corporation officials quickly demonstrated their approval of California's new tax system. Representatives of the Southern Pacific Railroad, the Pacific Gas and Electric Company, and the Pacific Telegraph and Telephone Company worked to obtain a broad definition of operative property in order to place as much as possible of their firms' properties under the taxing authority of the state rather than the many counties in which they did business. The Southern Pacific sought, for instance, to have all of its wharves, warehouses, fences, signal systems, ferryboats, steamboats, machine shops, tools, and rights-of-ways designated as operative property. When the line received only partial acceptance of its desires, its officers claimed that local governmental officials were discriminating against their company.[40] Other public service corporations went to court to press their claims. When the city of San Francisco tried to tax the Pacific Gas and Electric Company, the company brought suit against the city and received a favorable verdict that put nearly all of its property under state jurisdiction. In a similar case the Pacific Electric Railroad, an interurban line in Southern California, successfully sued the city of Los Angeles to allow state rather than municipal officials to tax its lines.[41]

Bankers, though they believed the tax rate on their institutions should be lowered, also endorsed the new tax system. In his 1911 presidential address before the California Bankers Association, William High, a San Francisco financier, praised the plan for making taxation simpler and more equitable. A short time later J. F. Sartori, a prominent Los Angeles banker, lauded the new system, because it "brought about uniformity of taxation" for corporations and banks. The editors of California's leading financial journal, the *Coast Banker,* summed up the thoughts of many, when they noted with approval that the new tax law set a rate of taxation that was "absolutely uniform on all banks." As a result, the journal concluded, bankers could now so closely estimate the amount owed the state "that a sum may be set aside monthly from the profits to care for it."[42]

Despite the success of the tax reformers, the tax question remained a central concern for Californians. Progressives, led by Hiram Johnson, won control of the statehouse and governorship in 1910, and under their rule the social and economic roles of the state government were significantly broadened. For instance, the number of pupils in state normal schools rose 30 percent between 1911 and 1913, and the number of insane in state hospitals increased by 15 percent in the same period. In addition, the Progressives set up new regulatory commissions and expanded the functions of old ones. This growth in state activity required more money, and, as a result, the Progressives, like their predecessors, found themselves strapped for funds. A special report issued by the state board of equalization in 1912 provided additional arguments for further tax reform. It showed that, although the public service corporations were paying more taxes than before, most still paid at a lower rate than the general public. For every one hundred dollars of taxable property, railroads paid an average of $0.91 in taxes, gas and electric corporations $0.75, telephone and telegraph companies $0.91, and express firms $1.54. The general public paid county and city levies amounting to $1.14 per hundred dollars worth of property. The findings also illustrated that some of the smaller companies were taxed more heavily than the larger ones.[43]

The state legislature tackled the tax problem again in 1913. Governor Johnson called for an immediate increase in the tax rates of public service corporations and an end to inequities between large and small concerns. The public service corporations quickly mobilized their forces to resist any such hikes. The California Bankers Association compiled statistics that purported to show that the tax rate on banks had increased 66 percent in the past three years, and insurance company and public utility officials also argued against proposed raises. J. H. Scott of the Southern Pacific Railroad offered the most spirited opposition. Presenting figures on his own, he challenged the accuracy of estimates of property valuation used by the state board of equalization. In a dramatic confrontation in the senate chambers Senator A. H. Breed of Alameda discredited Scott's testimony. He proved that Scott had falsified many of his calculations and revealed that in preparing his case Scott had employed, at the Southern Pacific's expense, county assessors to collect his data. When resistance collapsed following these disclosures, the legislators boosted taxes on all types of public service corporations except banks and express companies. They failed, however, to deal effectively with the more difficult problem of discrimination between large and small firms.[44]

The issues raised in 1913 recurred two years later. In his address opening the legislative session Governor Johnson again decried the existence of a deficit and accused the corporations of not paying their fair share of California's taxes. Most Progressives agreed with him, and the senate and assembly set up a joint committee to consider whether the tax rates should be raised. As they had in 1913, company executives fought the proposed increases. Warren Olney appeared before the committee on behalf of the Southern Pacific, Santa Fe, Western Pacific, and Northwestern Pacific railroads. He argued that time was too short during a single legislative session to arrive at any meaningful conclusions and urged the solons to leave the rates unchanged. Burke Corbett of the Pullman Company added that his firm already yielded enough revenue to the state. Disregarding these protests, the legislature boosted charges on express firms and railroads. Representatives of the state's major power companies also argued against increases, but the legislators ignored their pleas and raised their taxes. Nor did executives of the Pacific Telephone and Telegraph Company and the Home Telephone Company succeed in keeping their rates the same. Not even bankers could forestall a rate hike. John Drum, a lobbyist for the California Bankers Association, later explained to his organization's members that matters had already been discussed in Sacramento and that his presentations had no effect on the legislators.[45]

Despite the chronic complaints of Progressives that the public service corporations were evading their fair share of California's tax assessments, the new tax system did increase the tax burdens of the corporations. In 1910, tax experts estimated that, had the new system been in effect the previous year, corporate tax payments would have been $746,110 higher than they actually were. Once in effect, the revised tax system did boost corporate tax payments. During the first four years of its operation corporate levies rose from $10,454,215 to $13,609,663. The greatest percentage increases came from railroads, gas and electric companies, and insurance firms. Insurance companies, which had been paying about $110,000 annually to California before the new system went into effect, found themselves paying over seven times as much by 1914.[46]

The conflicts over taxation that enlivened politics during the Progressive Era continued into the 1920s. As the functions of the state government expanded (despite some temporary cutbacks), the legislature continued to raise the charges on public service corporations, and, as before, those corporations affected continued to protest that their tax rates were too high. In addition to seeking redress by having the legislature lower their tax rates, corporate executives sought to decrease their charges by pressing for a reduction in state spending and by having county and city governments assume some of the expenses of the state government. Yet, the public service corporation officers made no efforts to change the structure of California's tax system. They had become too devoted to the concepts of predictability and uniformity to tamper with the established arrangements. When a major overhaul of the state's financial system threatened to decentralize assessments and collections in 1929, many public service corporation executives joined those opposing revision.[47]

10

The Politics of Business

"Organization wins all the earth's victories," noted one of California's most prominent fruit growers in 1910, "whether of war or peace, of art, commerce, or religion." Organization, he continued, was "the wedding of strength to strength, of efficiency to efficiency, the abandonment of weakness, the enthronement of power."[1] These words well summed up the thoughts of most California businessmen, for they reacted to the disruptions in their economic environment by establishing a high degree of organization in their business world. Vertically and horizontally integrated firms replaced the single-level company, and trade associations, marketing bodies, and other organizations linked together single firms within most industries. In the legislative arena, as well, businessmen increasingly operated as self-conscious interest groups to obtain their goals.

The California experience suggests that on the local as well as on the national level it may be most valuable to understand the ways Americans lived and thought in the late nineteenth and early twentieth centuries in terms of what historians are calling the "organizational synthesis." That is, Americans, and especially businessmen, responded to the dislocations resulting from the modernization of their economy by trying to reorder their lives in ways that stressed the need for stability, efficiency, and professional expertise.[2] This was certainly the case in California. In both their private, nonlegislative actions and their public political activity

California businessmen labored to dampen competition, rationalize their business practices, and increase the efficiency of their operations. Finally, as they surmounted one crisis after another, they sought a professional identity for themselves and tried to gain acceptance as professional men from the general public.

Private Actions

Many California businessmen agreed with the assertion of one of their state's leading bankers that whatever could be "done by legislative activity can be more perfectly accomplished by association."[3] As the various sectors of their state's and nation's economy became increasingly complex and interdependent, Golden State businessmen hastened to reorganize the companies and industries along new lines. When the problems they faced became regional and national rather than simply local in scope, businessmen sought ways out of their difficulties by reshaping the nature of their individual firms and by banding together to undertake joint collective action.

The growing links between different regions within California and the connections between the state and the rest of the nation heightened competition among California businessmen and accentuated their vulnerability to market fluctuations. Those producing goods for statewide and national markets found it difficult to coordinate their actions and most urgently felt the need to limit competition. Faced with repeated gluts in their eastern markets, fruit growers formed cooperative marketing associations to reduce competition and raise prices. Lumbermen and oil men had to deal with the same problems, and both tried to insulate themselves from market dislocations by restructuring their firms along the lines of vertical integration. State and regional trade associations also aided them in cutting back production, fixing prices, and opening new markets. Competition and insecurity plagued the state's service industries as well. The intense rate wars that disrupted the insurance business in the 1890s led insurance men to set up organizations designed to combat rate-cutting, rebating on policies, and fraudulent advertising. Bankers faced a somewhat different problem. The rapid expansion of California's banking system, combined with its tightening connections with eastern financial centers, made bankers more susceptible to regional and national economic fluctuations. Bankers formed clearing houses and trade associations to aid them in reducing the chance of bank failures while at the same time providing credit and capital for California's growing industries.

Though helpful, none of these private efforts to lessen competition proved wholly successful; for at the same time that they wanted to stabilize their economic situation, businessmen were tempted to exploit the chaotic conditions to secure advantages over their competitors. Some fruit growers, desiring short-term rather than long-run profits, always remained outside of the ranks of the cooperative marketing and agricultural standardization bodies and, thus, limited the effectiveness of the organizations. Nor did the organizations of oil men and lumbermen operate smoothly. Because some companies refused to join, the bodies never achieved complete market control and most collapsed within a few years of their founding. In banking, investment banking, and insurance similar problems prevailed. Lacking the force of law, the trade associations that tried to organize these businesses could not compel adherence to their rules or guidelines; and, since some firms sought quick, speculative profits, none succeeded in eliminating instability or what they considered "unfair" competition.

Californians were better able to rationalize their business practices to meet the needs of the state's changing economy. Fruit growers and lumbermen standardized and specialized their production methods. For bankers, insurance men, and the like the movement took the form of a campaign for uniform business methods. All shared a growing concern for efficiency. Yet, as contests for the conservation of oil and timber demonstrated, businessmen adopted improved techniques only when these techniques promised to increase profits, and most businessmen were interested only in short-term gains.

Agriculturalists carried specialization farthest among California businessmen, but the tendency manifested itself in all lines of work. Production for national markets led fruit growers to specialize their output by region, function, and market. The state horticultural commissioner repeatedly urged each section of California to "select its especially adapted fruit and follow that up as far as possible," and the growers heeded his advice.[4] Different areas concentrated upon the crops they could raise most profitably: oranges in Southern California, grapes around Fresno, prunes in the Santa Clara Valley, and peaches, apricots, and cherries in various parts of the San Joaquin and Sacramento valleys. Fruit growers further specialized their operations by raising separate varieties of the same fruit to be sold fresh, dried or canned. Grapes destined for sale as raisins differed from those prepared for table use, and fresh peaches were unlike those grown for canning. Fruit and vegetable growers even adjusted the yearly cycles of their crops to coincide with market demands. Orange growers, in cooperation with state officials, developed two species, the Valencia and the Washington Navel, which matured at different seasons, to assure the nation's markets of a constant supply of the golden fruit. Lumbermen also felt the impact of market demands, and companies that had once produced only rough lumber expanded their offerings to include a wide variety of finished goods for different uses. In the financial world departmental banking became increasingly common, as bankers specialized their operations. Similarly, in the insurance and securities businesses the differences between the various types of agents and companies grew more pronounced.

The desire for predictability also led businessmen to regularize their business practices. Farmers and lumbermen, working through their trade associations, sought to establish standard grades for all products shipped out of state. City bankers set up clearing houses to speed transactions among themselves, and both city and country bankers tried to standardize their relations by setting up the California Bankers Association. Insurance men prepared uniform coinsurance and reinsurance clauses and, though never totally successful, attempted to work out standard rate risks for both the fire and life businesses.

As part of their program to rationalize their operations, businessmen placed a high value upon efficiency, a concern tempered, however, by their desire for short-term profits. In one line of work after another more advanced methods of production and providing services replaced the less efficient. Yet, unless the improvements promised to boost short-run profits, businessmen usually rejected them. New processes might be technologically more efficient than older ones, but, unless they were efficient in the economic sense as well, businessmen refused to institute them. The clash between economic and technologic efficiency was most apparent in the struggles over the conservation of petroleum and timber. In both cases businessmen wasted large quantities of California's natural resources by employing technologically inefficient methods of production. Yet, they made no improvements until convinced that innovations would pay handsome dividends. Only when water intrusion into their wells threatened their immediate profits did oil men form cooperative associations to shut it off; and timbermen supported scientific forestry only when increased prices during the First World War made it economically feasible to do so.

As the pace of change accelerated in the late nineteenth and early twentieth centuries, businessmen sought to define themselves as professional men. Bankers and insurance men carried this movement farthest, but it extended to those in almost every type of activity. By 1910, even fruit growers were calling themselves professionals. Businessmen likened themselves to clergymen and doctors and, through trade associations and professional organizations, tried to establish codes of ethics and "fair" business practices. In addition, they set up their own schools or helped start courses at the University of California and Stanford University to provide the growing body of knowledge needed for professional educations. Finally, businessmen tried to alter their relationships with the rest of society. They stressed their integration with the larger community around them and increased their involvement in public affairs. Although their rhetoric often exceeded reality, especially in the sphere of community relations, businessmen did win partial acceptance as experts capable of solving society's problems within their fields of specialization.

Business Legislation

Addressing the Commonwealth Club in late 1905, William Sproule, a high-ranking Southern Pacific officer, asserted that "the less political administration becomes fastened upon business the better." What was needed, he believed, was "more business administration in our political life, not more politics in our business."[5] Businessmen throughout California frequently expressed such sentiments. They particularly condemned what they viewed as the inefficiency of politics as a way to solve their difficulties and often tried to avoid politics, because they believed that politicians, lacking training in business specialties, could not properly understand the legitimate needs of businessmen. Some also feared that political contests would stimulate class hatred and accentuate divisions between clashing interest groups. Thus, Seth Mann, the San Franciscan who had been prominent in the drive for railroad regulation, decried the constant demand for new legislation and called instead for the return of public sentiment "such as existed in Old New England communities" so that "the laws will take care of themselves and you will have common honesty in truth."[6]

Historians and social scientists have recently been reexamining corporate political involvement in modern American history. Much of their work has centered upon the question of whether American politics have been elitist or pluralistic in nature and, especially, the extent to which businessmen have controlled politics for their own ends.[7] Historians, in particular, have been reevaluating the roles businessmen played in politics during the Progressive Era. Their studies in this field have focused upon how businessmen sought to use politics in dealing with the manifold problems resulting from the rapid industrialization and urbanization of the nation.[8] Although few of the findings are in complete agreement, many suggest that businessmen worked through politics to restrict competition and stabilize the general business environments.

In California, despite avowed reservations, businessmen were among the leading participants in the legislative process. Most of them quickly discovered that they could only partially control the forces of economic change through individual efforts or the work of trade associations and were soon traveling to Sacramento, as they sought political solutions for business problems. Though often influential in state politics, businessmen rarely, however, obtained all their desires. In California, at least, politics were pluralistic, and most pieces of business legislation were compromises resulting from the complex interplay of different interest groups. State officials, organized bodies of consumers, and conflicting groups of businessmen usually shared power in the legislative contests, and the degree of success that businessmen attained depended on more than their own efforts. Businessmen proved most effective when they were able to appeal beyond narrow group interests for the support of a broader public, sometimes through the use of symbolic issues.

Quite often businessmen resorted to legislation designed to limit competition when their trade associations had proven incapable of doing so. Oil men, for instance, sought measures limiting the output of crude only when their own attempts to set production quotas had failed; and insurance men pressed for legislation prohibiting rebating, twisting, and the stealing of agents only after the rate war of the 1890s demonstrated the inability of their trade associations to dampen competition. In like fashion, bankers and investment bankers sought state aid in stabilizing their industries, when their business organizations proved only partially successful. The rationalization of their industries was also of vital concern for businessmen, and in this realm, too, they turned to Sacramento for assistance. Fruit growers required legislation to give the agricultural standardization movement teeth, and the scientific forestry campaign that became, in its later stages at least, a drive to rationalize the lumber industry depended heavily upon state legislation. The attempts of businessmen to rationalize their businesses with state aid reached a climax in the tax-reform movement, in which public service corporation executives proved willing to trade an increase in their taxes for greater uniformity and regularity in the collection of them.

At times businessmen proved quite effective in politics. They were particularly successful when they could focus their attention upon specific issues directly affecting single industries or businesses. Upon occasion business groups were the only organized bodies on the scene, and, in the absence of opposition, legislators accepted businessmen's recommendations on business subjects. When businessmen could convince legislators that as professional men they were best capable of dealing with topics within their spheres of expertise, they could sometimes obtain their goals unimpeded by other groups. Thus, bankers drafted the Bank Act of 1909, and insurance men played major roles in drafting much of the legislation for state regulation of their industry.

Businessmen also often achieved success when able to enlist backing from beyond the business world; indeed, the support of groups outside the business community often proved essential for the passage of business legislation in Sacramento. Although many public service corporation executives favored tax reform as a way to rationalize their businesses, it is unlikely that the tax reform measures would have won approval without the backing of state officials seeking additional tax revenue and the support of farmers trying to shift California's tax load onto big business. The blue-sky law was passed not simply because investment bankers and stock brokers were hoping to stabilize their businesses, but also because progressive politicians wanted to protect small investors from fraud. The support of state officials, who were anxious to build up their bureaucratic empires, was frequently of special importance. The state forester and the larger lumber companies worked hand-in-hand to strengthen California's scientific forestry laws after 1915, and the labors of state mining officials were of great help to oil men trying to stem the flow of water in their oil fields. By the same token, Harris Weinstock, the state market director, greatly aided agriculturalists in their legislative contests in Sacramento.

Although definitely influential in the legislative arena, businessmen often faced opposition to their measures and usually had to accept compromises. Groups outside of the business world could seriously hinder or alter the political plans of businessmen. One of the characteristics of politics in California between 1890 and 1920 was the entrance of organized bodies of consumers into the legislative process. As was happening in Wisconsin and other parts of the nation in the same time period, consumers were forming their own groups to lobby in the state capital.[9] The conflict between consumer and business organizations was most apparent in the struggles surrounding the roles and power of the state market director. In these contests the businessmen-farmers emerged triumphant over the consumer bodies, but the opposition of the consumer groups prevented the agriculturalists from winning legislative sanction for all of their goals in Sacramento. Similar fights centered upon other pieces of business legislation. The pressure of organized groups of policyholders led to the passage of standard insurance policy legislation against the wishes of most insurance men, and consumers played significant roles in some of the oil and forestry legislation as well.

Divisions within business ranks still further eroded the power of businessmen to shape the course and nature of legislation. The goals of California's many business interests often collided, and the resulting conflicts could sometimes be resolved only by legislative action. There was no single, monolithic business community in California; rather, California possessed a wide variety of different, and often warring, business groups.

Business conflict took place between different industries. A major source of dissension was the struggle between those businessmen who wanted to stabilize the economic situation in California and those for whom rapid economic growth, even at the expense of stability, was the major goal. The tension between economic stability and economic expansion was most apparent in the debates on banking legislation, but it was evident in the consideration of other business measures as well. Contests over the blue-sky law, bills regulating the investments of insurance companies, and the tax-reform proposals revealed differing opinions among California businessmen on this subject. Many other issues also found businessmen from different industries on opposite sides of the fence in Sacramento. For a long time agriculturalists and lumbermen fought each other on timber conservation measures, and railroad officials opposed the efforts of other business interests to increase the power of the state government over their industry, at least until 1911.

Splits within industries also made business cooperation on legislative matters difficult. Cleavages opened on many lines, and only when businessmen healed these divisions were they effective in the state capital. Because of the different demands of their businesses the redwood and pine lumbermen found it hard to work in harmony on fire protection and reforestation measures. Not until the First World War united them did the lumbermen present a common front in Sacramento. Oil producers and refiners faced different problems and could only rarely agree upon legislation affecting their industry. Partly because of this situation, some of the initiative on oil-conservation and pipeline-control measures slipped from their hands into the hands of state officials. City and country bankers often clashed on key issues, and, as a result, banking legislation was usually some sort of compromise measure that failed to fully satisfy either group. Divisions were still more numerous within the insurance industry, with many different interests battling each other in the legislative arena.

Business participation in politics extended beyond the legislative battles, for businessmen tried to influence the policies of the state regulatory commissions set up to supervise their activities. Governor Hiram Johnson explained to another leading Progressive, Meyer Lissner, that it was "the desire of every business in the State to have state regulation for their profit."[10] As Johnson's statement suggests, businessmen in California would have liked to turn state regulation of their enterprises to their advantage.

Yet, in only a few cases did businessmen capture control of the commissions set up to supervise their activities, at least during the Progressive Era. Mutual life and stock fire insurance companies appear to have established hegemony over the state insurance commission and to have worked with the insurance commissioners to thwart the ambitions of their rivals. Many insurance commissioners, in turn, seem to have used their official position as a steppingstone for later employment with the insurance companies. Though not to the same extent, investment bankers exercised considerable power over the corporation commissioner who administered the blue-sky law, and bankers worked closely with the state superintendent of banks. Conflicts between the regulatory commissions and the businesses they supervised were, however, at least as numerous. The state forester, for instance, frequently found himself at odds with California's lumbermen particularly before the First World War. Moreover, the divisions between industries apparent in the struggles over legislation often reappeared in the form of contention before the commissions. The same interest groups that had fought over the establishment of a new railroad commission in 1911 continued to battle each other in later hearings before the commission, and these struggles helped insure that no single business interest would gain hegemony over the commission.

Nor should instances of cooperation between businessmen and regulatory agencies be accepted by themselves as proof that businessmen had taken over the commissions for their own ends. State officials could work with businessmen without betraying their public trust, for the goals of businessmen and the consuming public were not necessarily mutually exclusive. When the state superintendent of banks moved to end bank failures, he was both helping bankers stabilize their industry and protecting depositors from a loss of their savings. The efforts of the railroad commission to reduce competition between public service corporations was designed to aid both the utilities and the consuming public. As the railroad commissioners pointed out, rate wars often actually hurt the consumer, for at their conclusion the victorious company, now alone in the field, often boosted rates above previous levels.

State legislation was, then, an important means by which businessmen tried to resolve their difficulties, and the course of events in California indicates that there was a basic continuity in the approach of businessmen to public politics between the mid-1880s and the mid-1920s. As economic change continued throughout this period, so did the political responses of businessmen to it. In particular, the Progressive Era as a distinct epoch spanning the years between 1910 (when Hiram Johnson won election as governor) and 1915 or 1917 held little meaning for Californians, at least with regard to business legislation.

Most of the campaigns for business legislation were of long standing, and many of the most important measures won approval either before or after the progressive years in the Golden State. California's fundamental bank law, for example, was enacted in 1909, well before Progressives won control of the statehouse, and the most significant scientific forestry proposals became law only after the First World War, when progressivism was rapidly fading as a potent political force. Nor did the Progressive Era mark a sharp break or turning point in the types of business legislation considered or approved. Banking and insurance acts, passed before this time, were further extended and modified during it. Even the campaigns for railroad regulation and the blue-sky law, which were tagged as progressive reforms by Governor Johnson, were less creatures of the state's progressive movement than culminations of lengthy drives by interested business groups.

By the same token, few of the contests surrounding business legislation were fought out along strict party lines. Divisions usually opened on other lines instead. The campaign for the creation of a state market director was of utmost importance for both fruit growers and consumers but never became a bone of contention between the different political parties. Rather, battles on this subject exposed geographic divisions, with politicians from farm areas supporting the desires of agriculturalists and those from urban regions the requests of consumer bodies. Similarly, urban-rural distinctions proved more significant than party divisions on issues connected with state regulation of banking and forest resources. Only infrequently, as in the case of railroad regulation, did a piece of business legislation receive the progressive label; more often business measures were considered with little debate as to whether they were "progressive" or "reactionary" or whether they were inspired by Republicans or Democrats.

The California experience demonstrates that, like their counterparts throughout the nation, Golden State businessmen reacted to alterations in their business environment with a broad spectrum of private and public actions. By restructuring their individual firms, organizing their industries through trade associations, and entering the legislative arena, businessmen tried to control the modernization of their state's economy. They perceived, if usually only imperfectly, that the growing complexity of their economic situation required changes in their business methods. Yet, however much they sought to order events, California businessmen achieved only partial success. They failed to grasp the full meaning of the changes occurring around them and so were never totally effective in dealing with them. Then, too, divisions within business ranks and the frequent intercession of nonbusiness groups further limited the mastery businessmen sought. The result, in most cases, was compromise, for only rarely did California businessmen realize all their desires.

Appendix

Abbreviations used in the tables and notes

B.F.U.P.	Board of Fire Underwriters of the Pacific
C.B.A.	California Bankers Association
C.B.C.	California Bank Commission
C.B.F.	California Board of Forestry
C.D.C.	California Department of Corporations
C.F.G.A.	California Fruit Growers Association
C.F.G.E.	California Fruit Growers Exchange
C.H.C.	California Horticultural Commissioner
C.I.C.	California Insurance Commissioner
C.M.D.	California Market Director
C.R.C.	California Railroad Commission
C.S.B.	California Superintendent of Banks
C.S.M.B.	California State Mining Bureau
F.U.A.P.	Fire Underwriters Association of the Pacific
G.P.S.	George Pardee Scrapbook
H.W.S.	Harris Weinstock Scrapbook
P.C.G.A.	Pacific Coast Gas Association
P.W.L.	*Pioneer Western Lumberman*

TABLE 1

CALIFORNIA OIL PRODUCTION BY FIELD, 1900–1914

(Thousands of barrels)

Field	1900	1905	1910	1914
Ventura Co. and Newhall ..	443	476	652	968
Los Angeles and Salt Lake .	1,722	2,226	3,729	2,504
Coalinga	547	8,882	18,646	15,925
Whittier Fullerton	254	2,118	6,281	14,130
McKittrick	80	1,373	5,471	3,820
Kern River	826	15,253	14,776	7,030
Sunset	12	419	9,218	12,546
Midway	. . .	18	11,174	37,479
Santa Maria	. . .	3,402	7,607	4,303
Total*	4,319	34,298	77,697	103,623

SOURCE: F.T.C., *Pacific Coast Petroleum*, 1:227–29.
  *Minor fields not specified in this table are included in this total.

TABLE 2

PRODUCTION, CONSUMPTION, AND STOCKS OF OIL IN CALIFORNIA, 1910–1920

(Thousands of barrels)

	Production	Consumption	Price 18°B. oil at well[a]	Price 24°B. oil at well[a]
1910	77,697	66,543	$0.50	$0.65
1911	83,744	72,933	0.30	0.45
1912	90,074	86,075	0.30	0.48
1913	97,867	95,658	0.30	0.55
1914	103,623	92,967	0.39	0.55
1915	89,566	90,946	0.38	0.40
1916	91,822	104,933	0.48	0.55
1917	97,267	108,853	0.73	0.80
1918	101,637	102,045	0.98	1.05
1919	101,221	102,784	1.23	1.30
1920	105,721	113,961	1.27	1.55

SOURCE: F. T. C., *Pacific Coast Petroleum*, 1:68; 2:32.
  [a]End of first quarter of the year.

TABLE 3

COST OF PRODUCTION AND PRICE PER BARREL OF OIL PRODUCED, 1914–1918

YEAR	COST OF PRODUCTION PER BARREL				PRICE PER BARREL	
	Over 1,000,000	250,000– 1,000,000	50,000– 250,000	Under 50,000	Under 18°B.	24°B.
1914	$0.25	$0.29	$0.49	$0.72	$0.39	$0.48
1915	.28	.27	.43	.98	.36	.41
1916	.30	.33	.53	.96	.60	.67
1917	.34	.38	.62	1.09	.87	.94
1918	.38	.47	.69	1.19	1.15	1.22

SOURCE: F. T. C., *Pacific Coast Petroleum*, 1:134.

TABLE 4

CALIFORNIA LUMBER PRODUCTION AND PRICES

YEAR	REDWOOD Production[a]	REDWOOD Price[b]	WHITE PINE[c] Production[a]	WHITE PINE[c] Price[b]	SUGAR PINE Production[a]	SUGAR PINE Price[b]	TOTAL CALIFORNIA PRODUCTION
1899	360,167	$10.12	285,306	$10.87	52,108	n.a.	737,035
1904	519,267	12.83	388,623	12.75	n.a.	n.a.	1,077,499
1905	411,689	n.a.	363,932	n.a.	120,002	n.a.	1,061,608
1906	659,678	16.64	347,249	13.90	130,231	n.a.	1,348,599
1907	569,450	17.70	405,610	18.30	108,747	n.a.	1,345,943
1908	404,802	15.66	318,406	16.17	92,500	n.a.	996,115
1909	521,630	14.80	364,748	18.51	88,822	n.a.	1,143,507
1910	543,493	15.52	399,067	15.04	101,561	n.a.	1,254,826
1911	489,768	13.99	390,173	14.40	115,470	n.a.	1,207,561
1912	496,796	14.13	365,169	13.85	128,376	n.a.	1,203,059
1913	510,271	n.a.	317,053	n.a.	147,023	n.a.	1,183,380
1914	535,199	n.a.	409,953	n.a.	132,368	n.a.	1,303,183
1915	418,824	13.54	389,991[d]	14.89	114,494[d]	n.a.	1,119,458[d]
1916	490,828	13.93	494,973[d]	15.40	165,461[d]	n.a.	1,413,541[d]
1917	487,458	21.00	478,565[d]	22.50	127,951[d]	n.a.	1,417,068[d]
1918	443,231	24.30	357,351[d]	21.28	108,423[d]	n.a.	1,277,084[d]
1919	410,442	30.04	444,150	30.38	129,155	n.a.	1,259,363
1920	476,003	46.90	509,471[d]	37.50	141,134[d]	n.a.	1,482,102[d]

SOURCE: U.S. Department of Agriculture, *American Forests and Forest Products*, Statistical Bulletin 21 (Washington, 1921), pp. 130–31, 221–22, 260–61.

[a]Thousands of board feet.
[b]Per thousand board feet at the mill.
[c]Also called ponderosa or western yellow pine.
[d]Includes Nevada.

TABLE 5

CALIFORNIA BANKS

Year	State Savings	State Commercial	National	Private
1890	37	126	35	27
1894	60	166	35	17
1900	53	178	37	19
1906	122	302	108	33

SOURCE: C.B.C., *Annual Report*, 1890–1906.

TABLE 6

CALIFORNIA BANK ASSETS

Year	San Francisco Savings	Other Savings	San Francisco Commercial	Other Commercial
1895	$113,657,468	$31,333,260	$74,256,132	$56,258,492
1900	130,829,016	43,043,483	75,121,516	71,371,256
1905	171,010,363	95,197,846	124,864,921	113,870,387

SOURCE: C.B.C., *Annual Report*, 1890–1906.

TABLE 7

FIRE INSURANCE—CALIFORNIA BUSINESS

Year and Companies	Number	Premiums	Amount Written
1885:			
California ..	10	$1,355,798	$ 86,398,727
Out of state .	59	1,773,404	98,475,104
Foreign	38	2,056,569	123,647,668
1890:			
California ..	11	1,480,763	86,206,605
Out of state .	74	2,259,521	128,538,528
Foreign	37	2,563,038	153,866,232
1895:			
California ..	2	397,479	31,514,873
Out of state .	37	1,740,504	135,405,607
Foreign	33	2,566,600	191,818,679
1900:			
California ..	2	435,024	27,013,192
Out of state .	58	2,397,897	155,967,277
Foreign	37	2,962,585	206,197,099
1905:			
California ..	3	945,197	46,570,746
Out of state .	72	5,524,046	368,425,355
Foreign	31	3,884,564	260,691,211
1910:			
California ..	3	895,685	49,668,856
Out of state .	86	9,892,221	970,984,948
Foreign	23	5,112,617	314,574,194

SOURCE: C.I.C., *Report,* 1885, 1890, 1895, 1900, 1905, 1910.

TABLE 8

LIFE INSURANCE—CALIFORNIA BUSINESS

Year and Companies	Number	Premiums	Amount Written
1885:			
California ..	1	$ 224,469	$ 5,238,446
All other ...	19	1,365,874	41,484,162
1895:			
California ..	1	337,646	7,528,737
All other ...	22	21,456,586	106,222,353
1904:			
California ..	1	689,453	15,775,912
All other ...	33	9,549,725	258,928,374
1910:			
California ..	7	2,036,450	51,952,904
All other ...	36	12,749,970	353,547,336

SOURCE: C.I.C., *Report,* 1885, 1895, 1910; *Coast Review* 67 (March, 1905):119.

Notes

Preface

1. Samuel P. Hays, *The Response to Industrialism* (Chicago, 1957); Robert Wiebe, *The Search for Order* (New York, 1967).

2. One of the newest studies, a collection of essays edited by Jerry Israel, amply demonstrates that the desire to bring order out of chaos animated Americans in many walks of life, from the medical profession to the diplomatic corps. See Jerry Israel, ed., *Building the Organizational Society* (New York, 1972).

3. The term "organizational synthesis" was first used by Louis Galambos in "The Emerging Organizational Synthesis in Modern American History," *Business History Review* 44 (Autumn, 1970): 279–90. For an application of this approach to labor-management conflict, see K. Austin Kerr, "Labor-Management Cooperation: An 1897 Case," *Pennsylvania Magazine of History and Biography* 99 (January, 1975): 45–71.

4. Ralph Hidy, "Business History: Present Status and Future Needs," *Business History Review* 44 (Winter, 1970): 483–97.

5. Alfred Chandler, Jr., *Strategy and Structure* (Garden City, 1962).

6. For an attempt to do this, see Morrell Heald, *The Social Responsibilities of Business: Company and Community, 1900–1960* (Cleveland, 1970).

7. Gabriel Kolko, *The Triumph of Conservatism* (New York, 1963).

8. Robert Wiebe, "Business Disunity and the Progressive Movement, 1901–1914," *Mississippi Valley Historical Review* 44 (March, 1958): 664–85, and *Businessmen and Reform* (Cambridge, 1962).

9. Writings on this topic have been voluminous, but see: Peter Bachrach and Morton Baratz, "Two Faces of Power," *American Political Science Review* 56 (December, 1962): 947–52; Robert Dahl, *Who Governs?* (New Haven, 1961); Nelson Polsby, *Community Power and Political Theory* (New Haven, 1963); Michael Rogin, *The Intellectuals and*

McCarthy (Cambridge, Mass., 1967); E. E. Schattschneider, *The Semi-Sovereign People* (New York, 1960); David Truman, *The Governmental Process* (New York, 1955).

10. George Mowry, *The California Progressives* (Chicago, 1951); Spencer Olin, Jr., *California's Prodigal Sons* (Berkeley, 1968).

11. Gerald Nash, *State Government and Economic Development: A History of Administrative Policies in California, 1849–1933* (Berkeley, 1964).

Chapter 1: California's Changing Economy

1. *Coast Review* 65 (February, 1904): 73.

2. For an interpretation of California's economic development, see Gerald Nash, "Stages of California's Economic Growth, 1870–1970," *California Historical Quarterly* 51 (Winter, 1972): 315–30.

3. On the importance of the railroad in creating a national market, see Alfred Chandler, Jr., "The Coming of Big Business," in *The Comparative Approach to American History,* ed. C. Vann Woodward (New York, 1968), pp. 220–35.

4. Stuart Daggett, *Chapters on the History of the Southern Pacific* (New York, 1922), pp. 128–29; Robert Fogelson, *The Fragmented Metropolis* (Cambridge, Mass., 1967), chap. 4; Ward McAfee, *California's Railroad Era, 1850–1911* (San Marino, Ca. 1973), p. 3; Mel Scott, *The San Francisco Bay Area* (Berkeley, 1969), pp. 48–50, 139.

5. C.H.C., *Bulletin, July, 1916,* p. 265; California State Board of Trade, *Biennial Report, 1904–1905* (San Francisco, 1905), pp. 5, 19; Robert Cleland and Osgood Hardy, *March of Industry* (San Francisco, 1929), pp. 57–97; Osgood Hardy, "Agricultural Changes in California, 1860–1900," *Proceedings of the Pacific Coast Branch of the American Historical Association, 1929,* pp. 216–21; San Francisco Merchants Exchange, *Report, 1904–1905* (San Francisco, 1905), p. 9; Warren P. Tufts, "The Rich Pattern of California Crops," in *California Agriculture,* ed. Claude Hutchison (Berkeley, 1946), pp. 114–17.

6. United States Bureau of the Census, *Census Abstract for 1910, with a Supplement for California* (Washington, 1911), p., 631.

7. C.H.C., *Bulletin, July, 1916,* p. 265; *Census Abstract for 1910, with a Supplement for California,* pp. 676–77.

8. George Mowry, *The California Progressives* (Chicago, 1963), p. 4.

9. W. W. Cumberland, *Cooperative Marketing: Its Advantages as Exemplified in the California Fruit Growers Exchange* (London, 1917), pp. 15–41; Hardy, "Agricultural Changes," pp. 222–26; Gerald Nash, *State Government and Economic Development: A History of Administrative Policies in California, 1849–1933* (Berkeley, 1964), pp. 142–53.

10. *California Bankers Magazine, Commercial and Real Estate Review* 1 (May, 1891): 60–61; *Census Abstract for 1910 with a Supplement for California,* p. 661; Charles Coleman, *P. G. and E. of California: The Centennial Story of Pacific Gas and Electric Company, 1852–1952* (New York, 1952), pp. 201–2; S. Fortier, "Irrigated Agriculture, the Dominant Industry of California," in California State Board of Trade, *Biennial Report, 1904–1905,* pp. 50–51.

11. Rodman Paul, "The Wheat Trade Between California and the United Kingdom," *Mississippi Valley Historical Review* 45 (December, 1958): 391–412.

12. M. R. Benedict, "The Economic and Social Structure of California Agriculture," in *California Agriculture,* ed. Claude Hutchison (Berkeley, 1946), pp. 398–403; J. E. Boyd,

"Historical Import of the Orange Industry in Southern California" (Master's thesis, University of California at Berkeley, 1921), p. 82.

13. California State Board of Trade, *Annual Report, 1906,* p. 13.

14. *Western Banker and Financier* 6 (July, 1916): 15.

15. William Hutchison, *California Heritage: A History of Northern California Lumbering,* undated, unpaged pamphlet; Hyman Palais and Earl Roberts, "The History of the Lumber Industry in Humboldt County," *Pacific Historical Review* 19 (February, 1950): 1–16; Everett Stanford, "A Short History of California Lumbering" (Master's thesis, University of California at Berkeley, 1924), pp. 67–84; United States Department of Agriculture, *Lumber Cut of the United States, 1870–1920,* Bulletin 1119 (Washington, 1923), pp. 30–35; Ralph Wattenburger, "The Redwood Lumbering Industry in the Northern California Coast, 1850–1900" (Master's thesis, University of California at Berkeley, 1931), pp. 7–14, 25.

16. H. Brett Melendy, "One Hundred Years of the Redwood Lumber Industry, 1850–1950" (Ph.D. diss., Stanford University, 1952), p. 284; Stanford, "Lumbering in California," p. 82; Wattenburger, "Redwood Lumbering," p. 39.

17. *Census Abstract with Supplement for California, 1910,* pp. 698–99; William Hutchison, "The California Investment of the Diamond Match Company," typewritten copy (1957), pp. 31–43; D. T. Mason, "Forest Management in the Redwood Region of California," *Journal of Forestry* 20 (April, 1922): 396; United States Bureau of the Census, *The Lumber Industry,* Census Bulletin 203 (Washington, June 24, 1902), pp. 47; United States Department of Agriculture, *Lumber Cut of the United States, 1870–1920,* pp. 30–35; Wattenburger, "Redwood Lumbering," pp. 32–34.

18. Ralph Andreano, "The Structure of the California Petroleum Industry, 1895–1911," *Pacific Historical Review* 39 (May, 1970): 172–73; Arthur Johnson, "California and the National Oil Industry," Ibid., pp. 155, 164–69.

19. F. F. Latta, *Black Gold in the Joaquin* (Caldwell, Id., 1949), pp. 28–40; Lionel Redpath, *Petroleum in California* (Los Angeles, 1900), pp. 25–36; Earl M. Welty and Frank Taylor, *The Black Bonanza* (New York, 1956), pp. 19–51; Gerald T. White, *Formative Years in the Far West* (New York, 1962), pp. 1–58.

20. Kendall Beaton, *Enterprise in Oil: A History of Shell in the United States* (New York, 1957), pp. 84–94, 103; California Miners Association, *Proceedings of Annual Meeting 1900,* p. 32; *Census Abstract with Supplement for California, 1910,* p. 720; Latta, *Black Gold,* pp. 140–42; United States Federal Trade Commission, *Report on the Pacific Coast Petroleum Industry, Part I* (Washington, 1921), pp. 227–29; Welty and Taylor, *Black Bonanza,* pp. 54, 66; White, *Formative Years,* pp. 350–54.

21. C.B.A., *Proceedings of Annual Convention, 1894,* p. 18; Cleland and Osgood, *March of Industry,* pp. 71, 137; Ira Cross, *Financing an Empire,* 4 vols. (San Francisco, 1927), 1:363–443; William Fankhauser, "A Financial History of California, 1849–1910," *University of California Publications in Economics,* no. 3 (1913), pp. 228–73; Neil Wilson, *400 California Street: The Story of the Bank of California* (San Francisco, 1964), pp. 44–47.

22. John S. Hittell, *A History of San Francisco and Incidentally of the State of California* (San Francisco, 1878), p. 10.

23. William Wheeler (president of the San Francisco Traffic Bureau) to L. N. King (secretary of the San Francisco Merchants Association), June 7, 1910; reprinted in *Merchants Association Review* 14 (July, 1910): 3.

24. Daggett, *Chapters,* pp. 354–60; Neil Wilson and Frank Taylor, *The Southern*

Pacific (New York, 1952), p. 120. In 1911, of course, Edward Harriman of the Union Pacific had gained control of both the Central Pacific and Southern Pacific.

25. San Francisco Merchants Exchange, *Annual Report, 1908* (San Francisco, 1908), p. 9.

26. C.R.C., *Report, 1911–1912* (Sacramento, 1913), pp. 30–31; C.R.C., *Decisions* 1 (Sacramento, 1912): 95–97; *Merchants Association Review* 16 (February, 1911): 6; San Francisco *Chronicle,* Feb. 3, 1911.

27. Richard Barsness, "Railroads and Los Angeles: Quest for a Deep Water Port," *Southern California Quarterly* 47 (December, 1965): 379–94; Scott, *The San Francisco Bay Area,* pp. 86–87, 139–40; Robert Weinstein, "The Million-Dollar Mud Flat," *American West* 6 (January, 1969): 33–44.

28. California State Board of Harbor Commissioners, *Report* (Sacramento), *1910–1912,* p. 129; ibid., *1920–1922,* pp. 86–87; Fogelson, *Fragmented Metropolis,* p. 119; Scott, *San Francisco Bay Area,* p. 140.

29. Commonwealth Club of California, *Transactions* 7 (March, 1912): 1–68.

30. San Francisco *Chronicle,* Jan. 25, Feb. 3, 4, 22, 1911; Los Angeles *Herald,* Feb. 24, Mar. 1, 2, 1911.

31. San Francisco *Chronicle,* Mar. 7, 1911; Los Angeles *Herald,* Mar. 1, 3, 7, 10, 1911.

32. Fogelson, *Fragmented Metropolis,* p. 119; Harbor Commissioners, *Report, 1920–1922,* p. 87.

33. *Census Abstract with a Supplement for California, 1910,* pp. 700–704.

34. *Merchants Association Review* 14 (November, 1909): 3: ibid. 14 (July, 1910): 5; San Francisco Chamber of Commerce, *Annual Report, 1910* (San Francisco, 1910), p. 18; San Francisco *Bulletin,* Aug. 29, 1914; San Francisco *Call,* Mar. 2, 1912.

35. Cleland and Hardy, *March of Industry,* pp. 133–67; Fogelson, *Fragmented Metropolis,* p. 132; J. A. B. Scherer, "What Kind of Pittsburgh is L.A.?" *World's Work* 41 (February, 1921): 382–92.

36. Frank L. Beach, "The Transformation of California, 1900–1920: The Effects of the Western Movement on California's Growth and Development in the Progressive Period" (Ph.D. diss., University of California at Berkeley, 1963), pp. 1–27, 104; California State Board of Trade, *Report, 1903,* p. 5; *Census Abstract with a Supplement for California, 1910,* pp. 568–78.

37. Henry George, "What the Railroad Will Bring Us," *Overland Monthly* 1 (October, 1868): 298.

Chapter 2: Agriculture: Growers Against Consumers

1. Richard Hofstadter, *The Age of Reform* (New York, 1955), pp. 94–131; Theodore Saloutos and John D. Hicks, *Twentieth Century Populism* (Lincoln, Neb., 1951), pp. 56–87; Fred Shannon, *The Farmer's Last Frontier: Agriculture, 1860–1897* (New York, 1968), pp. 329–47.

2. C.F.G.A., *Proceedings, December, 1909,* p. 9.

3. Ibid., *November, 1920,* p. 619.

4. Ibid., p. 574.

5. W. W. Cumberland, *Cooperative Marketing: Its Advantages as Exemplified in the California Fruit Growers Exchange* (Princeton, 1917), pp. 43–45; H. Clark Powell, *The*

Organization of a Great Industry: The Success of the California Fruit-growers Exchange, Transvaal University College Bulletin Number 6 (Pretoria, 1925), pp. 4–5.

6. Cumberland, *Cooperative Marketing,* pp. 46–47, 55–57; H. E. Erdman, "The Development and Significance of California Cooperatives, 1900–1915," *Agricultural History* 32 (July, 1958): 181.

7. C.F.G.A., *Proceedings, December, 1911,* p. 40.

8. Cumberland, *Cooperative Marketing,* pp. 59–131; Powell, *Organization of a Great Industry,* pp. 6–16.

9. C.F.G.E., *Report, 1915,* unpaged; Cumberland, *Cooperative Marketing,* pp. 134, 169, 187.

10. C.F.G.A., *Proceedings, November, 1914,* p. 63; C.F.G.E., *Report, 1915,* unpaged; Cumberland, *Cooperative Marketing,* pp. 150, 153, 189–91.

11. Erich Kraemer and H. E. Erdman, *History of Cooperation in the Marketing of California Fresh Deciduous Fruits,* University of California, Agriculture Experiment Station, Bulletin 557 (Berkeley, September, 1933), p. 13.

12. Ibid., pp. 16, 19–23; A. J. Schoendorf, *Beginnings of Cooperation in the Marketing of California Fresh Deciduous Fruits and History of the California Fruit Exchange,* pamphlet (Sacramento, 1947), pp. 3–5.

13. Sacramento *Bee,* Feb. 19, 21, 27, March 9, 1895; San Francisco *Chronicle,* Feb. 19, 1895.

14. Kraemer and Erdman, *History of Cooperation,* pp. 38–41; Schoendorf, *Beginnings of Cooperation,* pp. 6–8.

15. Kraemer and Erdman, *History of Cooperation,* pp. 42–50; Schoendorf, *Beginnings of Cooperation,* pp. 8–18.

16. C.F.G.A., *Proceedings, May, 1919,* p. 350; Kraemer and Erdman, *History of Cooperation,* pp. 44, 53–54.

17. C.F.G.A., *Proceedings, December, 1909,* p. 12; *November, 1919,* p. 590; *November, 1920,* p. 613; Philip Webster, "An Analysis of the Development of Cooperative Marketing Policies in the California Prune and Apricot Growers Association" (Ph.D. diss., University of California at Berkeley, 1930).

18. C.F.G.A., *Proceedings, December, 1909,* p. 12; C.H.C., *Bulletin, November, 1916,* pp. 177–80; C.M.D. *Report, 1919* (Sacramento, 1919), pp. 12–15.

19. C.F.G.A., *Proceedings, December, 1909,* pp. 70–71, 79; *December, 1910,* pp. 63–66; *June, 1912,* pp. 299–300; *December, 1912,* pp. 474–75; *November, 1914,* pp. 231–33; *May, 1919,* pp. 356–57; *November, 1920,* p. 641; E. J. Wickson, *Rural California* (New York, 1923), p. 302.

20. C.F.G.A., *Proceedings, December, 1909,* p. 71.

21. Ibid., p. 79.

22. Ibid., *June, 1912,* p. 300; Carl Scholl, "An Economic Study of the California Almond Growers Exchange" (Ph.D. diss., University of California at Berkeley, 1927); Wickson, *Rural California,* p. 302.

23. Erdman, "California Cooperatives," p. 183.

24. C.F.G.A., *Proceedings, November, 1914,* p. 60.

25. Ibid., *November, 1917,* p. 47.

26. C.H.C., *Report, 1909–1910,* p. 9.

27. C.F.G.A., *Proceedings, March, 1911,* p. 113.

28. C.H.C., *Report, 1903–1904*, pp. 147–51.

29. C.F.G.A., *Proceedings, December, 1909*, p. 153; *December, 1910*, pp. 113–20; C.H.C., *Report, 1909–1910*, p. 10.

30. *California Cultivator* 36 (March 9, 1911): 294; *California Fruit Grower*, October 12, November 30, 1912, April 5, 1913; C.F.G.A., *Proceedings, November, 1911*, pp. 107–8, 186–90; C.H.C., *Report, 1911–1912*, p. 8.

31. *California Fruit Grower*, May 3, 10, 1913; C.F.G.A., *Proceedings, December, 1910*, pp. 59, 82; *March, 1911*, p. 118.

32. C.F.G.A., *Proceedings, December, 1912*, p. 162.

33. Ibid., *November, 1914*, p. 65; C.H.C., *Bulletin, September, 1913*, pp. 648–49; *October, 1914*, pp. 405–6; *Rural California* 35 (May, 1911): 129; ibid. (October, 1911): 304.

34. *Assembly Journal, 1913*, pp. 160, 2085, 2329, 2521; *California Fruit Grower*, May 3, 1913; Fresno *Republican*, March 6, May 3, 1913; *Senate Journal, 1913*, pp. 2467, 2565.

35. *California Fruit Grower*, December 13, 1913; C.H.C., *Bulletin, January, 1914*, p. 36.

36. C.F.G.A., *Proceedings, November, 1914*, pp. 64–65; C.H.C., *Bulletin, October, 1914*, pp. 424–25; *August, 1916*, pp. 295–99; *November, 1916*, pp. 415–17.

37. C.F.G.A., *Proceedings, November, 1915*, pp. 179–89; Fresno *Republican*, April 27, 1915.

38. C.F.G.A., *Proceedings, November, 1916*, pp. 132–33; C.H.C., *Bulletin, December, 1915*, pp. 534–35; C.H.C., *Report, 1915–1916*, p. 14; *Report, 1918*, p. 9.

39. C.F.G.A., *Proceedings, November, 1916*, p. 157; C.H.C., *Bulletin, August, 1915*, p. 295.

40. C.H.C., *Bulletin, November, 1919*, pp. 656–57.

41. Ibid., *November, 1915*, pp. 177–79; *November, 1919*, p. 699; *November, 1920*, p. 710.

42. C.F.G.E., *Report, 1914*, unpaged; *Report, 1915*, unpaged.

43. *Rural California* 35 (May, 1911): 135.

44. C.F.G.A., *Proceedings, March, 1911*, pp. 119, 123.

45. Sacramento *Bee*, Jan. 14, 1913; *California Fruit Grower*, January 4, 25, February 1, 1913; C.F.G.E., *Report, 1913*, p. 1; *Rural California* 37 (January, 1913): 6–7.

46. C.F.G.E., *Report, 1914*, p. 5.

47. C.F.G.A., *Proceedings, November, 1915*, p. 64; C. W. Towt, "Picking Oranges Under the New Government Regulations," *University of California Journal of Agriculture* 2 (March, 1915): 219–20; *Rural California* 37 (April, 1913): 129.

48. C.F.G.E., *Report, 1915*, unpaged; *Report, 1916*, pp. 10–11; *Report, 1917*, p. 8; *Report, 1919*, p. 9.

49. C.F.G.A., *Proceedings, November, 1914*, pp. 167–68; *November, 1915*, pp. 65, 68; C.H.C., *Bulletin, December, 1916*, p. 444.

50. C.F.G.E., *Report, 1916*, p. 6.

51. C.F.G.E., *Report, 1914*, p. 7.

52. Fresno *Republican*, May 4, 1915; San Francisco *Bulletin*, May 4, 1915.

53. C.F.G.E., *Report, 1916*, p. 6; *Report, 1917*, p. 5.

54. C.F.G.A., *Proceedings, November, 1914*, pp. 61, 269; *November, 1915*, p. 15; C.H.C., *Bulletin, March, 1912*, p. 142; *January, 1913*, p. 282; *July, 1914*, p. 283.

55. C.M.D., *Report, 1916,* p. 39.

56. C.H.C., *Report, 1917–1918,* p. 26.

57. Tom Hall, "Wilson and the Food Crisis: Agricultural Price Control During World War I," *Agricultural History* 47 (January, 1973): 25–46.

58. United States Bureau of Labor Statistics, *Consumer Price Index, 1953–1960* (Washington), series C-1, C-11, C-18.

59. See, for instance, Saloutos and Hicks, *Twentieth Century Populism,* pp. 56–87, 286–321, and Shannon, *Farmer's Last Frontier,* pp. 329–47. Grant McConnell, *The Decline of Agrarian Democracy* (Berkeley, 1959), takes a very different point of view toward farm organizations.

60. See, for example, Erdman, "Significance of California Cooperatives"; Grace Larsen, "Progressive in Agriculture: Harris Weinstock," *Agricultural History* 32 (July, 1958): 187–91; Grace Larsen and Henry Erdman, "Aaron Sapiro: Genius of Farm Cooperative Promotion," *Mississippi Valley Historical Review* 49 (September, 1962): 242–51.

61. *Rural California* 37 (June, 1913): 208.

62. S. B. Mosher, "Reestablishing the Municipal Market," *University of California Journal of Agriculture* 1 (October, 1913): 22; the markets were labeled as "free" because they charged no commission fees.

63. *Assembly Journal, 1915,* p. 2058; Sacramento *Bee,* May 3, 4, 1915; Commonwealth Club, *Transactions* 10 (May, 1915): 182–90; C.M.D., *Report, 1916,* pp. 100–102; *Senate Journal, 1915,* p. 2297.

64. C.F.G.A., *Proceedings, November, 1915,* p. 178; Larsen, "A Progressive in Agriculture," pp. 187–91; Harris Weinstock to Hiram Johnson, October 1, 1915, Hiram Johnson Papers.

65. C.M.D., *Report, 1916,* pp. 9–14, 23–26, 80–81; Monterey *Beacon,* Jan. 29, 1916, in Harris Weinstock, Scrapbooks, no. 16 (hereinafter cited as H.W.S. followed by the appropriate number); Harris Weinstock to Hiram Johnson, March 6, 9, 1916, Johnson Papers.

66. C.M.D., *Report, 1916,* pp. 9–56, 89–91; San Francisco *Chronicle,* Feb. 10, 1916, in H.W.S. 16; San Francisco *Bulletin,* Jan. 29, 1916, in H.W.S. 16; Woodland *Democrat,* Jan. 29, 1916, in H.W.S. 16.

67. C.F.G.A., *Proceedings, February, 1916,* pp. 63–75; *November, 1916,* pp. 166–75; C.M.D., *Report, 1916,* pp. 56–65.

68. Anaheim *Plaindealer,* Aug. 4, 1916, in H.W.S. 17; C.F.G.E., *Report, 1916,* pp. 15–16; Los Angeles *Examiner,* Mar. 14, 1916, in H.W.S. 16; Los Angeles *Tribune,* July 4, 1916, in H.W.S. 17; *Orange News,* July 6, 1916, in H.W.S. 17; San Francisco *Examiner,* Aug. 9, 1916, in H.W.S. 17.

69. San Francisco *Chronicle,* Aug. 8, 1916, in H.W.S. 17; C.F.G.A., *Proceedings, November, 1916,* pp. 168–71; Lodi *Sentinel,* Oct. 31, 1916, in H.W.S. 17.

70. C.M.D., *Report, 1916,* pp. 67–71.

71. C.M.D., *Report, 1916,* pp. 46–47; Oakland *Tribune,* May 5, 1915; Carl Plehn, "The State Market Commission in California: Its Beginnings, 1915–1917," *American Economic Review* 8 (March, 1918): 17–21; San Francisco *Bulletin,* May 4, 7, 1915.

72. C.M.D., *Report, 1917,* pp. 5–10.

73. San Francisco *Chronicle,* Feb. 12, 1917, Oakland *Tribune,* Feb. 27, 1917, San Francisco *Examiner,* Jan. 11, 1917, in H.W.S. 18.

74. Los Angeles *Examiner,* Feb. 22, 1917, Los Angeles *News,* March 3, 1917, Los Angeles *Record,* Jan. 1, 1917, in H.W.S. 18.

75. Los Angeles *Record,* Dec. 19, 1916, Los Angeles *Times,* Dec. 19, 1916, in H.W.S. 17.

76. Los Angeles *Express,* Feb. 27, 1917, in H.W.S. 18.

77. San Francisco *Chronicle,* Mar. 22, 1917, Oakland *Tribune,* Feb. 27, 1917, in H.W.S. 18.

78. Los Angeles *Examiner,* Feb. 25, 1917, Los Angeles *Tribune,* Jan. 27, 1917, in H.W.S. 18; Oakland *Enquirer,* Feb. 19, 1917, in H.W.S. 18.

79. San Francisco *Chronicle*, March 15, 1917, Dinuba *Sentinel*, Feb. 13, 1917, Eureka *Standard,* Feb. 2, 1917, Los Angeles *Examiner*, Mar. 22, 1917, Madera *Tribune*, Feb. 21, 1917, San Jose *News,* Feb. 7, 1917, in H.W.S. 18.

80. Los Angeles *Examiner,* Jan. 4, 1914, Los Angeles *Herald,* Jan. 4, 1917, in H.W.S. 18; see also San Francisco *Chronicle,* Jan. 10, 1917, San Francisco *Examiner,* Jan. 10, 1917, in H.W.S. 18.

81. Santa Cruz *Surf,* Jan. 16, 1917, Stockton *Record*, Jan. 17, 1917, Visalia *Delta,* Jan. 18, 1917, in H.W.S. 18.

82. Los Angeles *Express,* Apr. 3, 1917, Los Angeles *Herald,* Apr. 4, 1917, Los Angeles *Times,* Apr. 26, 1917, San Francisco *Bulletin,* Mar. 21, 1917, San Francisco *Call,* Mar. 27, 1917, San Francisco *Examiner,* Apr. 11, 1917, in H.W.S. 18.

83. Harris Weinstock to Los Angeles Housewives League, Feb. 23, 1917, Johnson Papers.

84. San Francisco *Bulletin,* Oct. 10, 29, 1918, in H.W.S. 21.

85. Oakland *Tribune,* Sept. 25, 1917, in H.W.S. 19; Oakland *Tribune,* Nov. 3, 1917, in H.W.S. 20; San Francisco *Bulletin,* Oct. 11, 1918, in H.W.S. 21.

86. Oakland *Enquirer,* Feb. 6, 28, 1918, Oakland *Tribune,* Feb. 6, 1918, in H.W.S. 20; Plehn, ''State Market Commission,'' pp. 21–24.

87. San Francisco *Bulletin,* Sept. 20, 1918, in H.W.S. 21.

88. Oakland *Tribune,* Feb. 2, 1918, in H.W.S. 20; see also Oakland *Post,* Feb. 8, 1918, in H.W.S. 20, and Oakland *Tribune,* Sept. 25, 1917, in H.W.S. 19.

89. Oakland *Enquirer,* Feb. 6, 1918, Oakland *Post,* May 24, 1918, Oakland *Tribune,* Feb. 6, 1918, in H.W.S. 20.

90. C.M.D., *Report, 1917,* p. 19; *Report, 1918,* p. 17; Los Angeles *Examiner,* Nov. 8, 9, 1917, Los Angeles *Times,* Nov. 8, 1917, Riverside *Press,* Nov. 9, 1917, Santa Rosa *Democrat,* Oct. 11, 1917, in H.W.S. 20.

91. San Francisco *Bulletin,* Feb. 4, 1919, Santa Rosa *Republican,* Feb. 5, 1919, in H.W.S. 21.

92. Sacramento *Bee,* Jan. 24, Feb. 8, 1919, in H.W.S. 21.

93. Fresno *Republican,* Jan. 21, Feb. 12, 13, 1919, Fullerton *Tribune,* Jan. 21, 1919, Napa *Register,* Mar. 10, 1919, Oakdale *Leader,* Mar. 12, 1919, San Francisco *Call,* Feb. 10, 1919, San Francisco *Examiner,* Feb. 7, 21, 27, 1919, in H.W.S. 21.

94. Oakland *Post,* Jan. 16, 1919, San Francisco *Call,* Jan. 16, 1919, in H.W.S. 21.

95. Los Angeles *Examiner,* Apr. 10, 1919, in H.W.S. 22.

96. Sacramento *Bee,* Apr. 15, 16, 1919, in H.W.S. 22.

97. Sacramento *Bee,* Mar. 20, 1919, Long Beach *Press,* Mar. 21, 1919, San Diego *Sun,* Mar. 20, 1919, San Francisco *Bulletin,* Apr. 3, 1919, San Francisco *Examiner,* Apr. 1, 1919, in H.W.S. 21.

98. San Diego *Union,* Apr. 6, 1919, in H.W.S. 22.

99. Sacramento *Bee,* Mar. 25, 1919, Los Angeles *Times,* Apr. 6, 1919, Sacramento *Star,* Mar. 19, 1919, San Francisco *Bulletin,* Apr. 8, May 31, 1919, San Francisco *Examiner,* Mar. 26, Apr. 17, 1919, in H.W.S. 21 and 22.

100. San Francisco *Bulletin,* May 29, 1919, in H.W.S. 22.

101. Oakland *Tribune,* Dec. 9, 1919, San Francisco *Bulletin,* May 30, Aug. 15, 1919, in H.W.S. 22 and 23.

102. Los Angeles *Examiner,* Sept. 4, Dec. 14, 1919, Los Angeles *Herald,* Jan. 22, 1920, Los Angeles *Times,* Dec. 16, 1919, in H.W.S. 23.

103. C.F.G.A., *Proceedings, November, 1919,* p. 634; Pasadena *Star-News,* Nov. 3, 1919, in H.W.S. 22.

104. C.F.G.A., *Proceedings, November, 1919,* p. 634; Oakland *Tribune,* Dec. 18, 1919, San Francisco *Bulletin,* Dec. 18, 1919, in H.W.S. 23.

105. Harris Weinstock to William Stephens, Jan. 13, 1920, in Chester Rowell Papers.

106. San Francisco *Chronicle,* Mar. 7, 1920, in H.W.S. 23.

107. United States Bureau of Labor Statistics, *Consumer Price Index, 1953–1960* (Washington), series C-1, C-11, C-18.

108. Walton Bean, "Ideas of Reform in California," *California Historical Quarterly* 51 (Fall, 1972): 213–26.

Chapter 3: The Oil Industry

1. Ralph Andreano, "The Structure of the California Petroleum Industry, 1895–1911," *Pacific Historical Review* 39 (May, 1970): 172–73; Arthur Johnson, "California and the National Oil Industry," Ibid., pp. 155, 164–69; Gerald White, "California's Other Mineral," Ibid., p. 137.

2. United States, Federal Trade Commission, *Report on the Pacific Coast Petroleum Industry, Part Two: Prices and Competitive Conditions* (Washington, 1921), p. 19.

3. The viscosity, or "stickiness" of petroleum is measured on a scale of degrees *Baume* (B.). Oil of around 12–15° *Baume* could be used for asphalt, oil of around 18°B. for fuel oil, and oil rating above 18–20° B. could be refined to obtain kerosene, gasoline, etc. Oil of 18°B. or less was usually not refined, but was sold as it came from the well.

4. F.T.C., *Pacific Coast Petroleum, Part One: Production, Ownership and Profits,* p. 55; Mark Requa, *Oil Resources of California,* p. 3, address to the American Mining Association, September, 1910, reprinted as a pamphlet.

5. White, "California's Other Mineral," pp. 139, 146–53.

6. F.T.C., *Pacific Coast Petroleum,* 1:227; see Appendix, table 1.

7. *Pacific Oil Review* 5 (August 24, 1904): 1; Harold Williamson, et al., *The American Petroleum Industry: The Age of Energy, 1899–1959* (Evanston, 1963), p. 39.

8. *Oil Fields and Furnaces* 1 (July, 1901): 11.

9. California Petroleum Miners Association, *Bulletin 2* (San Francisco, 1901), unpaged; *Pacific Oil Review* 3 (January 3, 1902): 3; 4 (January 31, 1903): 14; 5 (August 27, 1904): 1.

10. Ralph Arnold and V. R. Garfias, *Geology and Technology of the California Oil Fields,* American Institute of Mining Engineers, Bulletin 87 (New York, 1914), p. 391; William Hutchinson, *Oil, Land, and Politics,* 2 vols. (Norman, Okla., 1965), 2:12–13, 74–76; Lionel Redpath, *Petroleum in California: A Reliable History of the Oil Industry of the State,* pamphlet (Los Angeles, 1900), pp. 96–99; Gerald White, *Formative Years in the Far West* (New York, 1962), pp. 135, 148.

11. C.S.M.B., *Petroleum Industry of California* (Sacramento, 1914), p. 48.

12. *California Derrick* 2 (January, 1910): 1; 3 (June, 1910): 25; 3 (August, 1910): 20; 3 (December, 1910): 7; F.T.C. *Pacific Coast Petroleum,* 2:32, 38–39; *Oil Book* 3 (July 18, 1910): 1. See Appendix, table 2.

13. *Derrick* 5 (November, 1912): 8; 5 (December, 1912): 10; 5 (January, 1913): 2; United States Geological Survey, *Mineral Resources of the United States, 1912* (Washington, 1914), p. 1062.

14. *Derrick* 5 (January, 1913): 12; 5 (June, 1913): 4; 8 (December, 1914): 6; F.T.C., *Pacific Coast Petroleum,* 2:40; *Oil Age* 7 (June 27, 1913): 3.

15. See Appendix, table 3.

16. Andreano, "Structure of California Petroleum Industry," p. 187; California Miners Association, *Proceedings of Annual Meeting, 1901,* p. 127; F.T.C., *Pacific Coast Petroleum,* 1:101–3; *Pacific Oil Review* 4 (May 9, 1903): 11; 4 (May 16, 1903): 10; 4 (June 30, 1903): 4; White, *Formative Years,* p. 231.

17. *Pacific Oil Review* 3 (January 3, 1902): 4; 4 (May 23, 1903): 12; 4 (September 26, 1903): 4; 4 (December 12, 1903): 1.

18. Johnson, "California and the National Oil Industry," p. 160; San Francisco *Chronicle,* Jan. 7, 1905; *Pacific Oil Review* 5 (August 27, 1904): 12; White, *Formative Years,* pp. 261–62, 265.

19. San Francisco *Chronicle,* Jan. 7, 1905; F.T.C., *Pacific Coast Petroleum,* 2:19–20, 76–79.

20. F.T.C., *Pacific Coast Petroleum,* 1:101–4.

21. *Derrick* 2 (February, 1910): 1–2; 3 (June, 1910): 7; 3 (October, 1910): 10; 3 (November, 1910); 17; *Oil Book* 3 (July 18, 1910): 8.

22. *Derrick* 2 (October, 1909): 6; 7 (September, 1914): 10–11; United States Geological Survey, *Mineral Resources, 1911,* p. 426.

23. *Derrick* 2 (February, 1910): 1–2; 5 (January, 1913): 10; *Oil Book* 2 (February 1, 1910): 2; Welty and Taylor, *Black Bonanza,* pp. 106–7.

24. F.T.C., *Pacific Coast Petroleum,* 1: 106–7.

25. Ibid., p. 90; White, *Formative Years,* chaps. 8, 9, 13, 16.

26. Kendall Beaton, *Enterprise in Oil: A History of Shell in the United States* (New York, 1957), chap. 3; F.T.C., *Pacific Coast Petroleum,* 1:111–16.

27. Andreano, "Structure of the California Petroleum Industry," p. 189; Welty and Taylor, *Black Bonanza,* chaps. 6, 7.

28. F.T.C., *Pacific Coast Petroleum,* 2:45.

29. *Derrick* 5 (February, 1913): 8; F.T.C., *Pacific Coast Petroleum,* 2:7–12, 82–87, 106–26.

30. John Ise, *The United States Oil Policy* (New Haven, 1926), p. 133; Gerald Nash, *United States Oil Policy, 1890–1964* (Pittsburgh, 1968), pp. 1–22; Erich Zimmermann, *Conservation in the Production of the Petroleum* (London, 1957), pp. 136–39.

31. R. P. McLaughlin, "The Future of Oil Production in California," *Western Engineering* 1 (December, 1912): 705–9.

32. Commonwealth Club of California, *Transactions* 7 (June, 1912): 195–97.

33. California State Conservation Commission, *Report* (Sacramento, 1913), p. 81; *Derrick* 7 (December, 1914): 8.

34. C.S.M.B., *The Petroleum Industry of California*, Bulletin 69, p. 25; *Oil and Mining Bulletin* 1 (December, 1914): 17–18; 1 (March, 1915): 94; U. S. Geologic Survey, *Mineral Resources, 1914*, pp. 13–14, 19.

35. Mark Requa, "Present Conditions in the California Oil Fields," *Transactions of the American Institute of Mining and Metallurgical Engineers* 42 (1912): 837–47.

36. California Oil and Gas Supervisor, *Biennial Report, 1916–1917*, p. 81.

37. Commonwealth Club, *Transactions* 7 (June, 1912): 54.

38. *Derrick* 7 (December, 1914): 8.

39. *Derrick* 7 (April, 1915): 7; *Senate Journal, 1915*, p. 1345.

40. Fresno *Republican*, Apr. 30, 1915.

41. *Derrick* 7 (January, 1915): 5; 7 (April, 1915): 7; Fresno *Republican*, Apr. 22, 23, 1915; *Oil and Mining Bulletin* 1 (March, 1915): 96; Sacramento *Bee*, Apr. 23, 1915.

42. *Senate Journal, 1915*, pp. 1695, 1918.

43. Frank Latta, *Black Gold in the Joaquin* (Caldwell, Id., 1949), pp. 95–101.

44. *Assembly Journal, 1905*, p. 207; *Derrick* 1 (November, 1908): 8.

45. F.T.C., *Pacific Coast Petroleum*, 1:152.

46. Ibid., pp. 153–55; Hutchinson, *Oil, Land, and Politics*, 2:11, 25–26, 61.

47. F.T.C., *Pacific Coast Petroleum*, 1:162–63, 261.

48. White, *Formative Years*, p. 239.

49. *Derrick* 6 (August, 1913): 4–5; F.T.C., *Pacific Coast Petroleum*, 1: 153–54.

50. Arthur Johnson, *Pipelines and Public Policy, 1906–1959* (Cambridge, Mass., 1967), pp. 20–33.

51. San Francisco *Chronicle*, Jan. 12, Feb. 19, 1905; San Francisco *Examiner*, Jan. 17, 1905.

52. Sacramento *Bee*, Jan. 24, 1905; San Francisco *Chronicle*, Feb. 17, 25, 1905.

53. *Assembly Journal, 1905*, p. 1107; *Senate Journal, 1905*, pp. 891, 949.

54. *Derrick* 5 (November, 1912): 10; 5 (December, 1912): 11; 5 (June, 1913): 7.

55. *Derrick* 5 (January, 1913): 12; 5 (February, 1913): 11; White, *Formative Years*, p. 399.

56. *Derrick* 5 (April, 1913): 1–2; 6 (August, 1913): 3–7; Fresno *Republican*, Mar. 25, 1913; Franklin Hichborn, *Story of the Session of the California Legislature of 1913* (San Francisco, 1913), pp. 277–82; *Oil Age* 7 (February 21, 1913): 1, 8.

57. *Derrick* 5 (April, 1913): 1–2; Hichborn, *Legislature of 1913*, p. 282; *Oil Age* 7 (March 28, 1913): 5; White, *Formative Years*, p. 399.

58. Johnson, *Pipelines*, pp. 37, 73, 100–125; *Oil Age* 5 (May, 1913): 11; *Senate Journal, 1913*, p. 2607.

59. *Derrick* 5 (June, 1913): 6; 6 (August, 1913): 6, 7.

60. C.R.C., *Decisions* 5 (Sacramento, 1914): 1009–11.

61. Johnson, "California and the National Oil Industry," pp. 162–63; White, *Formative Years*, p. 400.

62. Welty and Taylor, *Black Bonanza*, p. 86; Williamson, *Petroleum Industry*, p. 44.

63. California Oil and Gas Supervisor, *Biennial Report, 1916–1917* (Sacramento, 1917), pp. 9–11; White, "California's Other Minerals," pp. 145, 149.

64. For a list of publications prior to 1918, see C.S.M.B., *Catalogue of Publications,* Bulletin 77 (Sacramento, 1918).

65. Welty and Taylor, *Black Bonanza,* p. 66.

66. C.S.M.B., *Production and Use of Petroleum in California,* Bulletin 32 (Sacramento, 1904), p. 220.

67. Latta, *Black Gold,* pp. 140–42; Welty and Taylor, *Black Bonanza,* p. 54; White, "California's Other Mineral," p. 139.

68. Beaton, *Enterprise in Oil,* pp. 84–94; Williamson, *Petroleum Industry,* pp. 128–32.

69. California Miners Association, *Proceedings, 1900,* pp. 113–14; C.S.M.B. *Notes on Damage by Water in California Oil Fields,* Preliminary Report (Sacramento, 1914), p. 3; United States Department of the Interior, Bureau of Mines, *The Cementing Process of Excluding Water from Oil Wells, As Practiced in California,* Technical Paper 32, (Washington, January, 1913), p. 5.

70. *Pacific Oil Review* 5 (April 30, 1904): 1; Welty and Taylor, *Black Bonanza,* pp. 95–96; White, *Formative Years,* p. 355.

71. San Francisco *Chronicle,* Apr. 1, 1903; *Pacific Oil Review* 4 (Aug. 8, 1903): 9; San Francisco *Examiner,* Mar. 24, 1903.

72. C.S.M.B., *Mineral Production, 1913,* Bulletin 68 (Sacramento, 1914), p. 123; *Derrick* 1 (November, 1908): 8; 1 (February, 1909): 9.

73. C.S.M.B., *Notes on Damage,* Preliminary Reports 1, 2; *Derrick* 4 (March, 1912): 10; 5 (July, 1912): 12–13; 6 (March, 1914): 9; 7 (October, 1914): 13; *Oil Age* 7 (August 15, 1913): 6–7; 8 (October 10, 1913): 8; 8 (January 16, 1914): 6.

74. Mark Requa, *Oil Resources of California,* p. 23.

75. Commonwealth Club, *Transactions* 7 (June, 1912): 19.

76. California Conservation Commission, *Report,* p. 80; W. H. Storms and P. W. Prutzman, "The Menace of Water in Oil Fields," *Western Engineering* 1 (May, 1912): 107, 113–14.

77. Sacramento *Bee,* Apr. 9, 1913; C.S.M.B., *Notes on Damage,* Preliminary Report 2, p. 2; *Derrick* 5 (April, 1913): 9; Fresno *Republican,* Mar. 24, Apr. 19, 1913; *Oil Age* 7 (April 4, 1913): 1; *Senate Journal, 1913,* p. 1496.

78. C.S.M.B., *The Petroleum Industry of California,* Bulletin 69, p. 3.

79. *Derrick* 7 (January, 1915): 13; 7 (March 13, 1915): 13; *Oil and Mining Bulletin* 1 (February, 1915): 63.

80. *Assembly Journal, 1915,* p. 2300; *Senate Journal, 1915,* p. 1940.

81. *Derrick* 7 (August, 1915): 9; Oil and Gas Supervisor, *Report, 1915–1916,* pp. 1, 5.

82. *Oil and Mining Bulletin* 1 (June, 1915): 177.

83. Oil and Gas Supervisor, *Report, 1915–1916,* p. 30.

84. Chun Chan, "An Investigation of the Effects of Water Incursion in the Coalinga Oil Field of California" (Ph.D. diss., University of California at Berkeley, 1922), pp. 9, 15.

Chapter 4: The Lumber Industry and Scientific Forestry

1. Everett Stanford, "A Short History of California Lumbering" (Master's thesis, University of California at Berkeley, 1924), pp. 81–83; United States Department of Agriculture, *Forest Products Statistics of the Pacific Coast States,* Statistical Bulletin 65 (Washington, 1938), p. 15.

2. See Appendix, table 4.

3. Swift Berry, "Lumbering in the Sugar and Yellow Pine Region of California," typewritten pamphlet (April, 1915), pp. 226a, 226f; William Hutchinson, *California Heritage: A History of Northern California Lumbering,* unpaged and undated pamphlet; H. Brett Melendy, "One Hundred Years of the Redwood Lumber Industry, 1850–1950" (Ph.D. diss., Stanford University, 1952), p. 289; United States Bureau of the Census, *The Lumber Industry,* Census Bulletin 203 (Washington, 1902), p. 21; Ralph Wattenburger, "The Redwood Lumbering Industry in the Northern California Coast, 1850–1900" (Master's thesis, University of California at Berkeley, 1931), pp. 50–51.

4. John Cox, "Organizations of the Lumber Industry in the Pacific Northwest, 1889–1914" (Ph.D. diss., University of California, Berkeley, 1937). chaps. 3, 4, 10; Richard Current, *Pine Logs and Politics: A Life of Philetus Sawyer, 1816–1900* (Madison, Wis., 1950), chaps. 2, 3; Robert Fries, *Empire in Pine: The Story of Lumbering in Wisconsin, 1830–1900* (Madison, Wis., 1951), pp. 122–40; Ralph Ridy, Frank Hill, and Allan Nevins, *Timber and Men: The Weyerhaeuser Story* (New York, 1963), chaps. 10–15; Agnes Larson, *History of the White Pine Industry in Minnesota* (Minneapolis, 1949), chaps. 8, 18; Arthur Reynolds, *The Daniel Shaw Lumber Company: A Case Study of the Wisconsin Lumbering Frontier* (New York, 1957), chaps. 5, 6, 7; United States Federal Trade Commission, *Report on Lumber Manufacturers Trade Associations* (Washington, 1921–22).

5. *P.W.L.* 67 (March, 1917): 23; 67 (September 15, 1917): 19–20; United States Bureau of the Census, *The Lumber Industry,* Bulletin 203 (Washington, 1902), p. 26; United States Department of Agriculture, *Lumber Cut of the United States, 1870–1920,* Bulletin 1119 (Washington, 1923), p. 27.

6. Hutchinson, *California Heritage;* William Hutchinson, "The California Investment of the Diamond Match Company," typewritten copy (1957), pp. 31–43.

7. *Wood and Iron* 20 (November, 1893): 194; 20 (December, 1893): 234–35; 21 (February, 1894): 60; 22 (December, 1894): 220; 23 (January, 1895): 20; 23 (February, 1895): 57; 24 (October, 1895): 140; 25 (January, 1896): 20; 25 (April, 1896): 140; 25 (June, 1896): 222; 27 (January, 1897): 20.

8. Melendy, "One Hundred Years," pp. 293–96; *P.W.L.* 58 (October 1, 1912): 26; *Wood and Iron* 40 (October, 1903): 17; 41 (January, 1904): 10–12; 41 (June, 1904): 11; 42 (July, 1904): 19; 43 (January, 1905): 18.

9. California Redwood Association, *Standard Grade Specifications,* unpaged pamphlet (San Francisco, 1921); Melendy, "One Hundred Years," pp. 311–12; *P.W.L.* 65 (January 15, 1916): 10; 65 (March 1, 1916): 7; 66 (September 1, 1916): 11; 66 (September 15, 1916): 11; 66 (October 1, 1916): 19; 67 (January 1, 1917): 11; 67 (January 15, 1917): 7; 67 (February 15, 1917): 3; 67 (March 1, 1917): 3, 23; *Timberman* 18 (February, 1971): 30, 35.

10. *Wood and Iron* 23 (January, 1895): 20; 25 (April, 1896): 140; 26 (June, 1896): 12; 26 (November, 1896): 170–71; 27 (January, 1897): 20.

11. *P.W.L.* 54 (August 15, 1910): 5; 54 (October 1, 1910): 11.

12. California White and Sugar Pine Manufacturerers Association, *Association Standard Rules,* pamphlet (San Francisco, 1916), pp. 7–35; *P.W.L.* 65 (June 1, 1916): 7–8; 66 (July 1, 1916): 10; 66 (September 1, 1916): 17; 66 (October 15, 1916): 7; 66 (November 15, 1916): 1; 66 (December 1, 1916): 8; 67 (June 1, 1917): 12; 68 (July 15, 1917): 15; *Timberman* 18 (May, 1917): 48D–48E; 20 (February, 1919): 4.

13. Wattenburger, "Redwood Lumbering," pp. 40–41.

14. See, for instance, *P.W.L.* 66 (November 15, 1916): 11; 66 (December 1, 1916): 8; *Timberman* 20 (February, 1919): 4.

15. *P.W.L.* 66 (July 1, 1916): 3.

16. *Daily Humboldt Standard,* Jan. 22, Feb. 9, 1909; *P.W.L.* 58 (January 1, 1912): 6; 66 (November 1, 1916): 11; 66 (December 1, 1916): 11; 67 (April 1, 1917): 3; Stanford, "California Lumbering," pp. 81–83; *Timberman* 18 (May, 1917): 48D–48E; *Wood and Iron* 26 (November, 1896): 171; 51 (February 15, 1909): 12.

17. This section of Chapter Four was delivered as a paper, "The Lumber Industry and the Movement for Scientific Forestry in California, 1885–1926," at the Business History Conference, Northwestern University, February 28, 1975, and was published under the same title in *Business and Economic History*, 2d ser., vol. 4, ed. Paul Uselding (Urbana, 1975). Reprinted by permission.

18. *P.W.L.* 59 (March 15, 1913):11.

19. Gerald Nash, *State Government and Economic Development: A History of Administrative Policies in California, 1849–1933* (Berkeley, 1964), pp. 195–198; M. B. Pratt, "The California State Forest Service: Its Growth and Its Objectives," *Journal of Forestry* 29 (April, 1931): 497–99.

20. Wallace Everett, "The Practical in Forestry," *The Forester* 5 (December, 1899): 276–78; E. A. Sterling, "The Attitude of Lumbermen Toward Forest Fires," *United States Department of Agriculture Yearbook, 1904* (Washington, 1905), pp. 133–40; *Water and Forest* 4 (July, 1904): 8; 4 (January, 1905): 6.

21. C. Raymond Clar, *California Government and Forestry from Spanish Days until the Creation of the Department of Natural Resources in 1927* (Sacramento, 1959), pp. 161–76, 195–210; Nash, *State Government and Economic Development*, p. 309.

22. San Francisco *Chronicle,* Feb. 13, 1905; E. A. Sterling, "Forest Legislation in California," *Forestry Quarterly* 3 (August, 1905): 271; *Water and Forest* 4 (May, 1904): 12; 4 (January, 1905): 2–3, 13–15.

23. *Water and Forest* 4 (October, 1904): 6.

24. *Mining and Engineering Review,* January 14, 1905, unpaged, in George Pardee, Scrapbooks, no. 12 (hereinafter G.P.S. followed by the appropriate number); *Santa Barbara Press,* Jan. 7, 1905, in G.P.S. 14; *Water and Forest* 4 (July 4, 1904):4.

25. *Water and Forest* 4 (January, 1905):12.

26. *California Weekly* 1 (February 19, 1909):194; Edward Stanford, "Governor in the Middle: George Pardee, 1903–1907" (Ph.D. diss., University of California at Berkeley, 1953), p. 305; Sterling, "Forest Legislation," p. 270; *Water and Forest* 4 (October, 1904):8.

27. San Francisco *Chronicle,* Jan. 4, 1905; W. C. Hodge, "A Report on the Forest Policy for the State of California," quoted at length in Clar, *Government and Forestry,* p. 224; G. B. Lull, "The Forest Laws of California," *Forestry Quarterly* 5 (September, 1907): 279; Sacramento *Bee,* Feb. 25, 1905; Sterling, "Forest Legislation," 272.

28. Henry Clepper, *Professional Forestry in the United States* (Baltimore, 1971), p. 87; Fries, *Empire in Pine,* pp. 122–40; Samuel P. Hays, *Conservation and the Gospel of Efficiency* (New York, 1969), pp. 22–48; Hidy, *Timber and Men,* chap. 20; James Hurst, *Law and Economic Growth: The Legal History of the Lumber Industry in Wisconsin, 1836–1915* (Cambridge, 1964), pp. 442–61; Larson, *History of the White Pine,* p. 342.

29. Sacramento *Bee,* Feb. 25, 1905; *Wood and Iron* 43 (April, 1905): 23.

30. *Water and Forest* 5 (July, 1905): 9.

31. Sterling, "Forest Legislation," p. 269; *Water and Forest* 5 (April, 1905): 8.

32. E. T. Allen to A. B. Nye, May 18, 1906, George Pardee Papers; Berkeley *Gazette,* Jan. 5, 1906, in G.P.S. 12; C.B.F., *Report, 1905–1906,* pp. 23–24, 28–30; *1908,* pp.

5–10, 63–83; *1912*, pp. 11–16; Eureka *Herald*, Mar. 3, 1906, in G.P.S. 12; Sacramento *Union*, July 13, 1905.

33. C.B.F. *Report, 1905–1906*, p. 31; *1908*, p. 12; *1910*, pp. 54–55, 79, 91–94; *1912*, pp. 14–15; *1914*, pp. 66–67, 159–60; *1916*, pp. 13–16, 19–20; *1918*, pp. 43–44; Commonwealth Club of California, *Transactions* 4 (April, 1909): 31–117; California Forest Protective Association, *Bulletin 3* (1913), pp. 3, 6–7; D. T. Mason, "A Forest Policy for California," *Journal of Forestry* 15 (April, 1917): 427; *P.W.L.* 54 (Dec. 15, 1910): 19; San Francisco *Call*, Mar. 20, 1906.

34. E. T. Allen to A. B. Nye, May 18, 1906, Pardee Papers.

35. Commonwealth Club, *Transactions* 4 (April, 1909): 48; Clar, *Government and Forestry*, pp. 271–74; G. B. Lull, "Forest Laws," pp. 280–82.

36. C.B.F., *Report, 1908*, pp. 5–10, 26–27; *1910*, pp. 84–88; Commonwealth Club, *Transactions* 4 (April, 1909): 97–98, 105–6; *California Weekly* 1 (Feb. 19, 1909): 203–4; Clar, *Government and Forestry*, pp. 290–91, 314–17.

37. Louis Glavis to George Pardee, March 8, 1912, Pardee Papers.

38. California Conservation Commission, *Discussion of Forestry Problems*, pamphlet (Sacramento, 1913), pp. 4–19, 22–23, 31, 34–35; California Conservation Commission, *Report to the Governor, 1913* (Sacramento, 1913), p. 46.

39. C.B.F., *Report, 1914*, pp. 13–17, 45, 152, 193–96; *1916*, p. 51; California Fire Protective Association, *Bulletin 3*, pp. 4–5, 9–10; Clar, *Government and Forestry*, pp. 350–59, 384–92, 406–9; *Assembly Journal, 1917* (Sacramento), pp. 113, 1846, 2211, 2294; *Senate Journal, 1917* (Sacramento), pp. 226, 1530, 1550–52, 1790; *Timberman* 18 (February, 1917): 48J; 18 (June, 1917):48G, 71.

40. C.B.F., *Report, 1918*, pp. 14–38; *1920*, pp. 14–16; Clar, *Government and Forestry*, pp. 414, 416–23; *P.W.L.* 71 (January 15, 1919): 22; *Timberman* 20 (May, 1919): 32.

41. *Assembly Journal, 1919*, pp. 1945, 1954; C.B.F., *Report, 1920*, p. 8; Clar, *Government and Forestry*, pp. 427–35; *Senate Journal, 1919*, pp. 822, 831, 841, 887, 921, 928–29; *Timberman* 20 (January, 1919): 103; 20 (February, 1919): 4, 91, 93.

42. C.B.F., *Report, 1920*, pp. 12–33; Clepper, *Professional Forestry*, pp. 138–41.

43. Hays, *Conservation*, pp. 27–47; John Ise, *United States Forest Policy* (New Haven, 1924), pp. 62–119; Larson, *White Pine Industry*, chap. 17; Stanford, "Lumbering in California," pp. 70–72; Wattenberger, "Redwood Lumbering," pp. 63–80. Of course, California did possess some national forests, and by the 1920s they were being managed along the lines of scientific forestry, including reforestation. On this topic, see R. W. Ayres, *History of Timber Management in the California National Forests, 1850 to 1937* (Forest Service, U. S. Department of Agriculture, 1958), pp. 42–52; Hays, *Conservation*, p. 24; Stanford, "Lumbering in California," p. 69.

44. *Water and Forest* 4 (July, 1904): 6.

45. Commonwealth Club, *Transactions* 4 (April, 1909): 66–74.

46. C.B.F., *Report, 1912*, pp. 72–73, 84–85; Conservation Commission, *Forestry Problems*, pp. 52, 57–60, 76–77, 82–87.

47. Clar, *Government and Forestry*, pp. 393–94.

48. *Timberman* 18 (January, 1917): 28–29; 18 (February, 1917): 481.

49. C.B.F., *Report, 1920*, pp. 12–33; Clar, *Government and Forestry*, pp. 472–73; *Timberman* 22 (February, 1921): 55; 22 (April, 1921): 55.

50. C.B.F., *Report, 1920–1922*, pp. 8–26; Clar, *Government and Forestry*, pp. 574–75.

Chapter 5: Railroad and Public Utility Regulation

1. Part of this chapter was presented as a paper, "Businessmen and the Regulation of Railroads and Public Utilities in California During the Progressive Era," at the 1970 Business History Conference and was later published under the same title in the *Business History Review* 44 (Autumn, 1970): 307–19. Reprinted by permission.

2. Sacramento *Bee,* Feb. 14, 18, 19, 20, 1895; San Francisco *Chronicle,* Jan. 24, Feb. 14, 19, 20, 21, 1895.

3. W. W. Cumberland, *Cooperative Marketing: Its Advantages as Exemplified in the California Fruit Growers Exchange* (Princeton, 1917), pp. 203–6; C.F.G.C., *Proceedings, May, 1908,* p. 72; *Pacific Rural Press* 81 (April 15, 1911): 290–91; *Rural Californian* 33 (February, 1910):45.

4. United States Bureau of Corporations, *Report on the Transportation of Petroleum* (Washington, 1906), pp. 19, 404–6.

5. Commonwealth Club of California, *Transactions* 3 (September, 1908): 347–49; *Oil Fields and Furnaces* 1 (December, 1901): 95–96.

6. *Assembly Journal, 1905,* pp. 207, 1107.

7. Richard Barsness, "Railroads and Los Angeles: Quest for a Deep Water Port," *Southern California Quarterly* 47 (December, 1965): 379–94; Robert Weinstein, "The Million-Dollar Mud Flat," *American West* 6 (January, 1969): 33–34.

8. C.R.C., *Decisions* 1 (Sacramento, 1912): 45–51; San Francisco *Chronicle,* Jan. 14, 1911.

9. Stuart Daggett, *Chapters on the History of the Southern Pacific* (New York, 1922), pp. 271–74, 281–83, 288.

10. Ibid., pp. 238–39.

11. Ward McAfee, "A Constitutional History of Railroad Regulation in California, 1879–1911," *Pacific Historical Review* 37 (August, 1968):265–79; Ward McAfee, *California's Railroad Era, 1850–1911* (San Marino, Ca., 1974), p. 5; Ward M. McAfee, "Local Interests and Railroad Regulation in California During the Granger Decade," *Pacific Historical Review* 37 (Feb. 1, 1968):51–66; Samuel Moffett, "The Railroad Commission of California: A Study in Irresponsible Government," *Annals of American Academy of Political and Social Science* 6 (1895): 469–77; Gerald Nash, "The California Railroad Commission, 1876–1911," *Southern California Quarterly* 44 (December, 1962): 287–305.

12. John Blum, *The Republican Roosevelt* (New York, 1964), chap. 6; Stanley Caine, *The Myth of a Progressive Reform: Railroad Regulation in Wisconsin, 1903–1910* (Madison, 1970), chap. 5; K. Austin Kerr, *American Railroad Politics, 1914–1920* (Pittsburgh, 1968); Albro Martin, *Enterprise Denied, Origins of the Decline of American Railroads, 1897–1917* (New York, 1971).

13. Bureau of Corporations, *Report on Transportation of Petroleum,* p. 19.

14. Sacramento *Bee,* Oct. 3, 4, 5, 1907, Feb. 17, 1908; Commonwealth Club, *Transactions* 3 (September, 1908): 364–65, 379.

15. Sacramento *Bee,* Nov. 13, 1907; C.R.C., *Report, 1908* (Sacramento, 1908), pp. 50–51.

16. California State Attorney General, *Report, 1906–1908* (Sacramento, 1909), p. 13.

17. Sacramento *Bee,* Dec. 30, 31, 1908; San Francisco *Chronicle,* Dec. 5, 6, 29, 31, 1908.

18. Arthur Pillsbury, "The Wright Law and Webb Bill Compared," *California Weekly* 3 (Mar. 4, 1910): 235–36.

19. Sacramento *Bee*, Feb. 16, 26, 1909.

20. Ibid., Feb. 16, 1909; San Francisco *Chronicle*, Feb. 16, 1909.

21. Sacramento *Bee*, Feb. 10, 1909; Franklin Hichborn, *Story of the Session of the California Legislature of 1909* (San Francisco, 1909), p. 133.

22. Sacramento *Bee*, Jan. 11, 14, Feb. 3, Mar. 6, 1909; *Derrick* 1 (November, 1908): 8.

23. Sacramento *Bee*, March 13, 15, 1909; *Senate Journal, 1910*, p. 59.

24. *California Fruit News*, Jan. 22, Dec. 17, 1910; C.F.G.A., *Proceedings, Dec. 1909*, pp. 109, 211; *Dec. 1910*, pp. 71–78, 194; *P.W.L.* 55 (Feb. 1, 1911): 5; 55 (March 15, 1911): 13–14; San Francisco Chamber of Commerce, *Annual Report, 1910* (San Francisco, 1910), p. 52.

25. George Mowry, *The California Progressives* (Chicago, 1951), chap. 5; Spencer Olin, Jr., *California's Prodigal Sons* (Berkeley, 1968), chap. 2.

26. *Pacific Outlook* 13 (March 19, 1910): 7.

27. Sacramento *Bee*, Jan. 4, 1911.

28. Sacramento *Bee*, Jan. 26, 1911; San Francisco *Chronicle*, Jan. 12, 14, 1911. Seth Mann was on the committee. The other members were: Senator Stetson, State Attorney General Webb, state railroad commissioners John Eshleman, H. D. Loveland, Alexander Gordon, and F. M. Gregson, manager of the Los Angeles Traffic Association.

29. San Francisco *Chronicle*, Jan. 14, 1911.

30. Ibid.

31. Commonwealth Club, *Transactions* 6 (August, 1911): 251–52.

32. Sacramento *Bee*, Feb. 9, 1911.

33. Max Thelen, *Report on Leading Railroad and Public Service Commissions*, pamphlet (Sacramento, 1911), pp. 2–88.

34. *Coast Banker* 2 (April, 1909): 189; Charles Coleman, *P. G. and E.: The Centennial Story of the Pacific Gas and Electric Company, 1852–1952* (New York, 1952), pp. 218, 227–48; Aloysius F. O'Donnell, "The Financial Plan of Certain Hydro-Electric Corporations in California" (Master's thesis, University of California at Berkeley, 1922), pp. 16, 25–26, 33, 36.

35. *Coast Banker* 5 (Dec., 1910): 454.

36. Walton Bean, *Boss Ruef's San Francisco* (Berkeley, 1968), pp. 97–107, 117.

37. John McCarty, *Municipal Government and Public Utilities: The California Experience* (Berkeley, 1956), pp. 1, 4.

38. *Coast Banker* 2 (April, 1909): 153–54.

39. P.C.G.A., *Proceedings of Annual Meeting, 1909*, p. 23.

40. *Pacific Gas and Electric Magazine* 2 (February, 1910): 339.

41. P.C.G.A., *Proceedings, 1910*, p. 506.

42. Ibid.

43. C.R.C., *Report, 1911–1912*, p. 91; Franklin Hichborn, *Story of the Session of the California Legislature of 1911* (San Francisco, 1911), p. 155; Thelen, "Report on Leading Railroad and Public Service Corporations," pp. 97–98.

44. Sacramento *Bee,* Dec. 7, 8, 9, 12, 1911; San Francisco *Chronicle,* Dec. 7, 1911; San Francisco *Examiner,* Dec. 8, 1911.

45. San Francisco *Chronicle,* Dec. 17, 1911.

46. *Pacific Telephone Magazine* 2 (May, 1912): 5–6.

47. P.C.G.A.,*Proceedings, 1911,* p. 30; *Pacific Gas and Electric Magazine* 4 (March, 1912): 392.

48. P.C.G.A., *Proceedings, 1912,* p. 247.

49. *Pacific Gas and Electric Magazine* 4 (March, 1912): 392–93.

50. Ibid., 5 (August, 1913): 100; 5 (October, 1913): 175.

51. Sacramento *Bee,* Mar. 12, 1915.

52. C.R.C., *Reports, 1909,* p. 9; *1911–1912,* p. 10; *1913–1914,* p. 5.

53. C.R.C., *Decisions,* 5:19–20; John Eshleman, "Control of Public Utilities in California," *California Law Review* 2 (January, 1914): 104–23; Max Thelen, "A Just and Scientific Basis for the Establishment of Public Utility Rates with Particular Attention to Land Values," *California Law Review* 2 (November, 1913): 3–24.

54. C.R.C., *Decisions,* 2:300–319.

55. Ibid., 1: 298–303.

56. John Eshleman, Speech before the San Francisco Chamber of Commerce, *San Francisco Chamber of Commerce Activities* 1 (Aug. 6, 1914): 3.

57. C.R.C., *Decisions,* 1:45–51.

58. Ibid., pp. 95–97.

59. Ibid., 2:584–88.

60. Ibid., pp. 83–84.

61. *Coast Banker* 14 (February, 1915): 100.

62. "Transcript of Public Hearing Before Railroad Commission on Application 844," p. 6, in California Public Utility Commission Archives, Sacramento, California.

63. C.R.C., *Decisisons,* 2: 748–74.

64. *Bulletin* 2 (Feb. 1, 1914): 1 (house organ of the Southern Pacific Railroad); *Coast Banker* 14 (February, 1915): 100; *San Francisco Chamber of Commerce Activities* 1 (April 2, 1914): 3; Max Thelen, *Southern Pacific-Central Pacific Dissolution Case,* pamphlet, undated, no place of publication.

65. *Coast Banker* 10 (January, 1913): 81; 10 (February, 1913): 180; 14 (February, 1915): 100–101.

66. C.R.C., *Reports, 1911–1912,* pp. 8–15; *Derrick* 5 (July, 1912): 10; *Merchants Association Review* 15 (March, 1911): 4; *San Francisco Bulletin,* March 28, 1912.

67. *California Outlook* 3 (January 13, 1914): 14.

68. *Coast Banker* 9 (July, 1912): 51.

69. William Herrin, "Government Regulation of Railroads," *California Law Review* 2 (January, 1914): 89.

Chapter 6: Banking and Bank Legislation

1. This chapter appeared as "Banking and Bank Legislation in California, 1890–1915," *Business History Review* 47 (Winter, 1973): 482–507. Reprinted by permission.

2. C.B.C., *Annual Reports, 1890–1908.* See also Appendix, tables 5, 6.

3. *California Banker* 2 (May, 1909), unpaged.

4. On the development of correspondent banking, see Gerald Fischer, *American Banking Structure* (New York, 1968), pp. 110–21.

5. C.B.A., *Proceedings of Annual Convention* (San Francisco), *1909*, p. 102; *1912*, p. 231.

6. For the structure of banking on the national level, see Margaret Myers, *A Financial History of the United States* (New York, 1970), p. 248; Fritz Redlich, *The Molding of American Banking*, 2 vols. (New York, 1968), 2:175–80; Richard Sylla, "American Banking and Growth in the Nineteenth Century: A Partial View of the Terrain," *Explorations in Economic History* 9 (Winter, 1971–72): 197–227.

7. Leroy Armstrong and J. O. Denny, eds., *Financial California: An Historical Review of the Beginnings and Progress of Banking in the State* (San Francisco, 1916), p. 26; *California Bankers Magazine* 1 (June, 1890): 81; "Constitution of the San Francisco Clearing House of 1876 as Amended February 9, 1886" (San Francisco, 1886), p. 1; J. A. Graves, *My Seventy Years in California, 1857–1927* (Los Angeles, 1929), p. 320.

8. C.B.C., *Report, 1896*, p. 4; *California Bankers* 2 (January, 1891): 483–84; John Finlay, "Banks and Banking in California," *Overland Monthly* 27 (January, 1896), p. 94; Graves, *My Seventy Years*, p. 320; San Francisco Clearing House, *Minutes of the Board of Directors Meetings, 1884–1900*.

9. James Cannon, *Clearing-houses* (New York, 1905), chaps. 3, 10; Redlich, *Molding*, 2:45–59, 158–66.

10. C.B.A., *Proceedings, 1909*, p. 44; Graves, *Seventy Years*, pp. 323–24; Benjamin Wright, *Banking in California, 1849–1910* (San Francisco, 1910), pp. 53–55.

11. Carl Plehn, "The San Francisco Clearing House Certificates of 1907–1908," *Academy of Pacific Coast History* 1 (January, 1909): 3–14.

12. Sacramento *Bee*, Nov. 1, 13, 1907; Ira Cross, *Financing an Empire*, 4 vols. (San Francisco, 1927), 2:895; O. M. Souden, "Los Angeles Bank Scrip," in Armstrong and Denny, *Financial California*, p. 141.

13. C.B.C., *Report, 1908*, p. 16; "Constitution of the San Francisco Clearing House Association, 1909" (San Francisco, 1909), pp. 10–12.

14. Bank of California, *Minutes of the Board of Directors Meeting, June 23, 1908* (contains contract between San Francisco Clearing House and its first examiner).

15. C.B.A., *Proceedings, 1912*, p. 224.

16. Ibid., p. 228; Robert Cleland and Frank Putnam, *Isaias Hellman and the Farmers and Merchants Bank* (San Marino, Ca., 1965), p. 82; Graves, *My Seventy Years*, p. 326.

17. *Coast Banker* 3 (November, 1909): 213; *Merchants Association Review* 13 (September, 1908): 4.

18. *Insurance and Investment News* 10 (September 12, 1912): 191.

19. *Coast Banker* 2 (May, 1909), unpaged.

20. Aloysius F. O'Donnell, "The Financial Plan of Certain Hydro-Electric Corporations in California" (Master's thesis, University of California at Berkeley, 1922), pp. 16, 25–26, 33, 36.

21. William Hutchinson, "The California Investment of the Diamond Match Company," typewritten copy (1957).

22. Redlich, *Molding*, 2: 276–82, 301.

23. C.B.A., *Proceedings, 1891*, p. 78; *1894*, pp. 30, 45–48; *1895*, pp. 51–55; *1898*, pp. 63–68; *1900*, pp. 32–47; *1901*, pp. 16–19; *1902*, p. 36; *1914*, pp. 55–57.

24. C.B.A., *Bulletin,* September 28, 1912, February 10, 1914; C.B.A. *Proceedings, 1912,* p. 90; *1913,* pp. 55, 113–22; *1914,* pp. 61–64, 129; *Coast Banker* 9 (December, 1912): 436–37; *Western Banker and Financier* 6 (November, 1916): 113; 9 (December, 1918): 294; 12 (December, 1920): 129. This system should not be confused with chain-banking or bank-holding companies. Each bank in California groups maintained its individuality of ownership.

25. C.B.A., *Proceedings, 1897,* p. 18; *1908,* pp. 265, 304; *1909,* pp. 136–40, 164; *1912,* pp. 54–56; *Coast Banker* 1 (October, 1908); 32.

26. Gerald Nash, *State Government and Economic Development: A History of Administrative Policies in California, 1849–1933* (Berkeley, 1964), p. 281.

27. *California Bankers* 4 (April, 1894): 844–54; 5 (January, 1895): 636–39; Cross, *Financing an Empire,* 2: 617.

28. C.B.A., *Proceedings, 1894,* pp. 83–85, 89, 94–113.

29. Ibid., *1895,* p. 25; Lovell White (president of C.B.A.) to all members, February 8, 1895, in C.B.A. Scrapbook 3.

30. Sacramento *Bee,* Jan. 17, Feb. 15, 1895; Cross, *Financing an Empire,* 2:628–29; Joseph Crumb, "Banking Regulation in California" (Ph.D. diss., University of California at Berkeley, 1935), pp. 60–61; San Francisco *Chronicle,* Jan. 17, Feb. 19, March 14, 1895.

31. C.B.A., *Proceedings, 1895,* pp. 38–58; C.B.C. *Report, 1895,* p. 3.

32. Sacramento *Bee,* Jan. 23, 31, Feb. 17, 1905; San Francisco *Chronicle,* Feb. 17, 18, 1905.

33. Milton Friedman and Anna Schwartz, *A Monetary History of the United States, 1867–1960* (Princeton, 1963), pp. 156–73; Myers, *A Financial History,* pp. 245–56, 258–63.

34. Crumb, "Banking Regulation," pp. 71–72, Wright, *Banking in California,* pp. 54–55.

35. C.B.A., *Proceedings, 1908,* p. 44.

36. Sacramento *Bee,* Nov. 7, 8, 15, 19, 1907; C.B.A., *Proceedings, 1908,* pp. 187–90; San Francisco *Chronicle,* Oct. 31, Nov. 8, 12, 15, 16, 20, 21, 23, 1907.

37. C.B.A., *Proceedings, 1908,* pp. 181, 217–29.

38. Ibid., pp. 237–57.

39. Ibid., pp. 232–36.

40. Ibid.

41. Commonwealth Club of California, *Transactions* 3 (June, 1908): 222–23, 234–35.

42. C.B.A., *Proceedings, 1908,* pp. 259–60; *1909,* pp. 81–83.

43. Ibid., *1909,* pp. 102, 114; *1912,* p. 231; *Coast Banker* 7 (December, 1911): 37; "Draft of an Act Prepared at the Request of the Joint Legislative Committee on Reform of the State Banking Laws by the Legislative Committee of the California Bankers Association, October, 1908," in C.B.A. Scrapbook 1.

44. "Proposed Laws Defining and Regulating the Business of Banking in the State of California by Special Joint Legislative Committee on Banking Laws, November, 1908," in C.B.A. Scrapbook 1.

45. Sacramento *Bee,* Jan. 22, 1909; San Francisco *Chronicle,* Jan. 22, 1909.

46. Friedman and Schwartz, *A Monetary History,* pp. 171–72.

47. Sacramento *Bee,* Feb. 2, 1909; C.B.A., *Proceedings, 1911,* p. 39; *Coast Review* 2 (October, 1908): 4.

48. C.B.A., *Proceedings, 1909,* p. 44.

49. John Drum to C.B.A. members, Sept. 17, 1910, in C.B.A. Scrapbook 1.

50. C.B.A., *Proceedings, 1910,* p. 77.

51. Ibid., *1909,* p. 132; *Coast Banker* 3 (September, 1909): 129; 4 (February, 1910): 63; 4 (April, 1910): 172.

52. C.B.A., *Proceedings, 1911,* pp. 56–64; *Coast Banker* 6 (May, 1911): 294.

53. C.S.B., *Annual Report, 1911* (Sacramento, 1911), pp. 4–11.

54. Ibid.

55. C.B.A., *Proceedings, 1912,* pp. 13–18; *1913,* pp. 45, 94–96; *1914,* pp. 50–51; C.S.B., *Report, 1911,* p. 4; *1913,* p. 45.

56. C.S.B., *Reports, 1909–1919.*

57. Nash, *State Government and Economic Development,* p. 279.

58. Marquis and Bessie James, *Biography of a Bank: The Story of the Bank of America N.T. and S.A.* (New York, 1945); Nash, *State Government and Economic Development,* pp. 290–91.

59. C.B.A., *Proceedings, 1905,* p. 38.

60. On the professionalization of American business in this period, see Morrell Heald, *The Social Responsibilities of Business: Company and Community, 1900–1960* (Cleveland, 1970), chaps. 2, 3.

61. C.B.A., *Proceedings, 1907,* pp. 80–88; Heald, *Social Responsibilities,* p. 71.

62. C.B.A., *Proceedings, 1909,* pp. 227–28; *Coast Banker* 1 (October, 1908): 15; 3 (November, 1909): 223; 4 (March, 1910): 132–37; 8 (June, 1912): 487; *Western Banker* 8 (February, 1917): 31; 11 (February, 1920): 185; 11 (April, 1920): 229.

63. *Coast Banker* 2 (April, 1909): 170; 3 (November, 1909): 223; *Western Banker* 11 (September, 1919): 53; 11 (April, 1920): 229.

64. *Coast Banker* 9 (December, 1912): 436.

65. Ibid., 1 (October, 1908): 15; 2 (April, 1909): 190; 3 (November, 1909): 254; 10 (June, 1913): 521; 13 (September, 1914): 230; 13 (December, 1914): 487; *Western Banker* 6 (January, 1916): 15; 6 (June, 1916): 141.

66. C.B.A., *Proceedings, 1895,* p. 37; *1901,* pp. 77–81; *Coast Banker* 13 (November, 1914), 388; *Western Banker* 11 (January, 1920): 147.

67. C.B.A., *Proceedings, 1907,* p. 112; Commonwealth Club, *Transactions* 3 (June, 1908): 222–23, 260.

Chapter 7: Investment Banking and the Blue-sky Law

1. Joseph L. King, *History of the San Francisco Stock and Exchange Board* (San Francisco, 1910), p. 4.

2. Armstrong and Denny, eds., *Financial California, An Historical Review of the Beginnings and Progress of Banking in the State* (San Francisco, 1916), pp. 153–58; King, *History,* p. 3–5, 90; San Francisco Stock and Exchange Board, *Constitution and By-Laws* (San Francisco, 1870), p. 17.

3. Los Angeles Stock Exchange, *Annual Report* (Los Angeles), *1916,* pp. 14–16; *1917,* pp. 9–10; *1918,* pp. 32–33.

4. In early San Francisco the names of stocks and bonds offered for sale were read verbally from lists by the heads of the different exchanges. Only securities on these lists could be traded on the floors of the exchanges.

5. San Francisco Stock and Exchange Board, *Constitution and By-Laws, 1867,* p. 9; *1874,* p. 5; *1880,* p. 37; *1899,* p. 39; *1907,* p. 3.

6. Armstrong and Denny, *Financial California,* p. 154; *San Francisco Stock Exchange,* pamphlet (San Francisco, 1930), unpaged; *San Francisco Stock Exchange History, Organization, Operation,* pamphlet (San Francisco, 1938), pp. 5–10.

7. Los Angeles Stock Exchange, *Annual Report, 1916,* p. 3; idem, *Constitution and By-Laws* (Los Angeles, 1917), p. 12.

8. John P. Young, *San Francisco, A History of the Pacific Coast Metropolis* (San Francisco, 1912), 2:495.

9. King, *History,* pp. 5, 73.

10. Armstrong and Denny, *Financial California,* pp. 154–55.

11. Los Angeles Stock Exchange, *Annual Report, 1918,* p. 33.

12. Vincent P. Carosso, *Investment Banking in America* (Cambridge, Mass., 1970), p. 168.

13. Ibid., p. 170; *Coast Banker* 9 (August, 1912): 115; 9 (December, 1912):432; 15 (November, 1915): 370.

14. *Coast Banker* 14 (May 27, 1915): 49.

15. Los Angeles Stock Exchange, *Annual Report, 1916,* p. 11.

16. C.S.M.B., *Annual Report* (Sacramento), *1902,* p. 16; *1903–1904,* p. 11; on the role of the state mineralogist in working for securities regulation, see also Gerald Nash, "Government and Business: A Case Study of State Regulation of Corporate Securities, 1850–1933," *Business History Review* 38 (Summer, 1964): 155.

17. *Mining and Engineering Review* 17 (November 21, 1903), 17 (Nov. 28, 1903), in G.P.S. 42.

18. C.S.M.B., *Annual Report, 1903–1904,* p. 11.

19. Ibid., *1906,* pp. 11–12; Gerald Nash, *State Government and Economic Development: A History of Administrative Policies in California, 1849–1933* (Berkeley, 1964), p. 270.

20. C.S.M.B., *Annual Report, 1906,* p. 12.

21. California Miners Association, *Proceedings of Annual Convention, 1912* (San Francisco, 1912), p. 210.

22. Carosso, *Investment Banking,* chap. 7; Nash, "Government and Business," pp. 151, 155–56.

23. C.B.A., *Proceedings, 1903,* p. 38; *1912,* pp. 70–74; *Coast Banker* 9 (December, 1912): 438; 10 (February, 1913): 164.

24. *California Outlook* 18 (March 1, 1913): 10.

25. Sacramento *Bee,* Jan. 17, 1913.

26. *Insurance and Investment News* 10 (September 26, 1912): 298; 11 (December 12, 1912): 17.

27. *Coast Banker* 10 (February, 1913): 104; Fresno *Republican,* Jan. 9, 10, Mar. 6, 1913; *Insurance and Investment News* 11 (December 26, 1912): 59; *Los Angeles Investment Company Protective Association Report to Stockholders, Jan., 1915,* Hiram Johnson Papers.

28. "The Investment Securities Act," reprinted in *Bank Laws* (San Francisco, 1913), pp. 111–21.

29. C.S.B., *Report, 1914* (Sacramento, 1914), p. 5.

30. *Coast Banker* 10 (May, 1913): 410.

31. Commonwealth Club of California, *Transactions* 9 (October, 1914): 596–98.

32. *Coast Banker* 11 (July, 1913): 87; 13 (October, 1914): 362–63; *Insurance and Investment News* 12 (June 12, 1913): 5; 13 (July, 1913): 12.

33. Virginia Clopton to Hiram Johnson, May 15, June 24, 1915, Johnson Papers; Hiram Johnson to Frank Flint, May 25, 1915, Johnson Papers; *Insurance and Investment News* 13 (December 11, 1913): 22; 9 (January 8, 1914): 2; J. H. McCarthy to Hiram Johnson, May 10, 1915, Johnson Papers; R. C. Rofhoal to Hiram Johnson, September 10, 1914, Johnson Papers; "Stockholders Proxy Committee Petition to Hiram Johnson, May 13, 1915," Johnson Papers.

34. Los Angeles Investment Company's Protective Association to stockholders, early November, 1914, Johnson Papers.

35. C.D.C., *Biennial Report, 1917–1918*, pp. 6–7.

36. C.D.C., *Report, 1915–1916*, pp. 6–7, 10, 13–14, 17; *1917–1918*, pp. 5–9; *1919–1920*, pp. 4, 7.

37. C.D.C., *Report, 1915–1916*, pp. 11–12, 19; *1917–1918*, p. 8; *1919–1920*, p. 10; *Oil and Mining Bulletin* 2 (March, 1915): 55.

38. *Western Banker* 8 (October, 1917): 237.

39. Ibid., 6 (January, 1916): 164; 6 (May, 1916): 124; 6 (October, 1916): 88; 6 (December, 1916): 124; 8 (April, 1917): 82; 8 (September, 1917): 197; C.D.C., *Report, 1917–1918*, p. 13; *1919–1920*, p. 14; Los Angeles Stock Exchange, *Report, 1916*, p. 16; *1918*, p. 13.

40. C.D.C., *Report, 1919–1920*, p. 12–13.

Chapter 8: The Insurance Industry

1. For the beginnings of fire insurance in California, see William Bronson, *Still Flying and Nailed to the Mast: The First Hundred Years of the Fireman's Fund Insurance Company* (Garden City, N.Y., 1963); Herbert Kirschner, *Fire Insurance Development on the Pacific Coast* (San Francisco, 1922); Clarence McIntosh, "Insurance History Project Report, October 18, 1954, Industrial Indemnity Company, San Francisco," typewritten manuscript; Archibald MacPhail, *Of Men and Fire, A Story of Fire Insurance in the Far West* (San Francisco, 1948); Frank Todd, *A Romance of Insurance—A History of the Fireman's Fund Insurance Company* (San Francisco, 1929). See also Appendix, table 7.

2. R. C. Buley, *The American Life Convention*, 2 vols. (New York, 1953), 1: 105–26, 147–53; Morton Keller, *The Life Insurance Enterprise, 1885–1910* (Cambridge, Mass., 1963), chaps. 2, 5; C. I. D. Moore, *The Pacific Mutual Insurance Company of California* (Los Angeles, 1928); Douglas North, "Large Life Insurance Companies Before 1906" (Ph.D. diss., University of California at Berkeley, 1952), chaps. 1, 9. See also Appendix, table 8.

3. *Coast Review* 50 (September, 1896): 398; F.U.A.P., *Proceedings, 1892*, pp. 12, 197.

4. C.I.C., *Report, 1890*, p. 4–5; *1895*, p. 111; San Francisco *Chronicle*, Jan. 9, 11, 16, Feb. 1, 1895; F.U.A.P., *Proceedings, 1892*, pp. 198–200; *1894*, p. 72.

5. San Francisco *Chronicle*, Jan. 16, Feb. 17, 21, 24, Mar. 10, 1895; *Coast Review* 49 (February, 1895): 69, 78; 49 (April, 1895): 160a; 50 (February, 1896): 69–70.

6. C.I.C., *Report, 1895,* pp. 7, 111; *Coast Review* 50 (January, 1896): 12; 50 (September, 1896): 415; 51 (January, 1897): 1; F.U.A.P., *Proceedings, 1896,* p. 8.

7. B.F.U.P., *Constitution and General Rules* (San Francisco, 1897).

8. *Coast Review* 54 (May, 1901): 272; 88 (July, 1915): 277; F.U.A.P., *Proceedings, 1901,* p. 155; *1906,* p. 63; *Insurance Sun* 13 (January, 1902): 169–70; *Western Insurance News* 5 (February 25, 1910): 10.

9. R. Carlyle Buley, *The Equitable Life Assurance Society of the United States,* 2 vols. (New York, 1967), 1:396; *Coast Review* 49 (December, 1895): 485–86; 51 (January, 1897): 7; 53 (November, 1899): 517; 55 (May, 1902): 273–75; 57 (May, 1904): 330–32.

10. C.I.C., *Report, 1895,* p. 11; *Coast Review* 49 (April, 1895): 156; 71 (April, 1907): 65, 186; *Insurance and Investment News* 15 (January 28, 1915): 10; *Western Insurance News* 5 (February 25, 1910): 9.

11. Sacramento *Bee,* Feb. 27, 1913; *Coast Review* 84 (February, 1913): 92; *Insurance and Investment News* 11 (July 10, 1913): 90; *Western Insurance News* 10 (May 23, 1912): 10.

12. *Coast Review* 88 (March, 1915): 122, 127; Fresno *Republican,* April 23, 1915; *Insurance and Investment News* 14 (January 28, 1915): 12; 14 (April 25, 1915): 281; 14 (May 27, 1915): 361.

13. Hiram Johnson to H. Stanley Benedict, June 12, 1915, Hiram Johnson Papers.

14. Sacramento *Bee,* Feb. 26, 1913; *Coast Review* 70 (July, 1906): 235; 73 (May, 1908): 517–18; F.U.A.P., *Proceedings, 1907,* p. 79; *Insurance and Investment News* 10 (September 26, 1912): 1; *Western Insurance News* 6 (November 10, 1910): 7.

15. Sacramento *Bee,* Mar. 10, 1913; *Coast Review* 83 (December, 1912): 570; 84 (March, 1913): 117; *Insurance and Investment News* 10 (September 26, 1912): 1; 10 (November 14, 1912): 319; F.U.A.P., *Proceedings, 1915,* pp. 170–71.

16. Sacramento *Bee,* Apr. 9, 10, 1913.

17. Ibid., Apr. 23, 25, 1913.

18. *Coast Review* 88 (March, 1915): 127; 88 (April, 1915): 173; F.U.A.P., *Proceedings, 1915,* pp. 170–71; Fresno *Republican,* Apr. 7, 1915.

19. C.I.C., *Report, 1890,* p. 6; *1894,* p. 7; *1895,* p. 8.

20. Sacramento *Bee,* Feb. 24, 1909, Feb. 8, 1911; C.I.C., *Report, 1902,* p. 14; *1909,* p. 27; San Francisco *Chronicle,* Feb. 7, 1895, Feb. 8, 1911; *Coast Review* 49 (April, 1895): 148, 156–57; 51 (February, 1897): 103; 51 (April, 1897): 221–22; 63 (March, 1903): 160; 71 (February, 1907): 88; 71 (April, 1907): 181.

21. C.I.C., *Report, 1888,* p. 8; *1903,* p. 141; *Coast Review* 52 (September, 1897): 457–62; 53 (May, 1898); 266–69; Keller, *Life Insurance Enterprise,* p. 208; North, "Large Life Insurance Companies," pp. 186–87.

22. *Coast Review* 50 (January, 1896): 20–21; 55 (January, 1899): 10; 59 (January, 1901): 30; 61 (May, 1902): 276; 87 (July, 1914): 334; *Western Insurance News* 5 (June 25, 1910): 7.

23. *Coast Review* 61 (March, 1902): 200–201.

24. B.F.U.P., *Book of Rates for San Francisco* (San Francisco, 1912); Pacific Insurance Union, *Book of Rates, San Francisco* (San Francisco 1887); San Francisco Board of Underwriters, *Book of Rates* (San Francisco, 1869).

25. F.U.A.P., *Proceedings, 1879,* p. 14; *1888,* pp. 99–100; *1896,* pp. 28, 48; *1897,* pp. 43–44; *1902,* p. 34; *1914,* p. 202.

26. Ibid, *1899,* pp. 122–23; *1904,* p. 64; *1908,* pp. 140–41; *1909,* p. 118.

27. Ibid., *1878,* p. 30; *1879,* pp. 36–41; *1914,* p. 34.

28. *Coast Review* 63 (July, 1903): 354; F.U.A.P., *Proceedings, 1902,* pp. 68–69; *1903,* pp. 108–9.

29. *Coast Review* 63 (July, 1903): 378; 70 (December, 1906): 458–60; 71 (January, 1907): 42.

30. F.U.A.P., *Proceedings, 1910,* pp. 120–21; MacPhail, *Of Men and Fire,* pp. 74–75.

31. *Coast Review* 70 (August, 1906): 295; 71 (January, 1907): 27; 71 (March, 1907): 138–40; F.U.A.P. *Proceedings, 1910,* pp. 122–29.

32. *Coast Review* 75 (May, 1909): 216; F.U.A.P., *Proceedings, 1910,* pp. 129–30.

33. Association of Life Insurance Presidents, *Proceedings of Annual Meeting, 1924,* p. 147; *Coast Review* 51 (February, 1897): 90; 81 (October, 1911): 1032; 84 (March, 1913): 143; Keller, *Life Insurance Enterprise,* pp. 135, 148.

34. Association of Life Insurance Presidents, *Proceedings of Annual Meeting, 1921,* p. 118; *Coast Review* 52 (July, 1897): 350–51; 79 (September, 1910): 932; 81 (July, 1911): 743; Lance Davis, "The Investment Market, 1870–1914: The Evolution of a National Market," *Journal of Economic History* 25 (September, 1965): 354–93.

35. C.I.C., *Report, 1904,* pp. 17–20; *1912,* pp. 37–38; *Coast Review* 67 (February, 1905): 75.

36. Sacramento *Bee,* Feb. 14, Mar. 12, 1895; C.I.C., *Report, 1894,* pp. 4–5; San Francisco *Chronicle,* Feb. 15, Mar. 14, 1895; *Coast Review* 71 (January, 1907): 19; 71 (April, 1907): 179; Myron Wolf to George Pardee, December 31, 1906, George Pardee Papers.

37. F.U.A.P., *Proceedings, 1879,* p. 28; *1910,* p. 11.

38. Ibid., *1894,* p. 63.

39. *Coast Review* 86 (May, 1914): 227; F.U.A.P., *Proceedings, 1904,* pp. 151–52; *1906,* pp. 79–85; *1914,* pp. 13–14.

40. *Coast Review* 73 (February, 1908): 236; F.U.A.P., *Proceedings, 1877,* p. 4; *1881,* p. 5; *1897,* 141; *1910,* p. 12; *Pacific Underwriter* 25 (November 25, 1911): 394; *Western Insurance News* 4 (December, 1909): 9; 5 (January 25, 1910): 6.

Chapter 9: Big Business and Tax Reform

1. For a description of the evolution of California's tax system from 1850 to 1890, see William Fankhauser, *"A Financial History of California, Public Revenues, Debts, and Expenditures,"* University of California Publications in Economics no. 3 (Nov. 13, 1913): 106–366. As defined by those desiring tax reform, public service corporations included: railroads, street railroads, power companies, insurance firms, banks, express corporations, telephone and telegraph companies.

2. James H. Budd, "First Biennial Message," *Appendices to the Journals of the Senate and Assembly, 1897* (Sacramento), 1: 9, 13; Budd, "Second Biennial Message," *Appendices, 1899,* 1: 5–6, 12.

3. C.B.A., *Proceedings of Annual Meeting, 1898* (San Francisco), pp. 50–52; Oakland *Examiner,* Aug. 19, 1896, Apr. 6, 1898, in Carl Plehn Scrapbook 4; Carl Plehn, "The General Property Tax in California," *Economic Studies* 2 (February, 1897): 145–50; 2 (June, 1897): 111–98; Sacramento *Record-Union,* Nov. 26, 1896, Plehn Scrapbook 4.

4. *Assembly Journal, 1899* (Sacramento), p. 1324; Sacramento *Bee,* Feb. 18, 21, Mar. 8, 1899; San Francisco *Chronicle,* Feb. 17, 22, 23, Mar. 9, 1899.

5. "Report of the Special Committee on Taxation and Revenue," *Senate Journal, 1901* (Sacramento), pp. 259–62.

6. San Francisco *Chronicle,* Jan. 5, 1899, Jan. 25, 1901; Henry Gage, "First Biennial Message," *Appendices, 1901,* 1:4; San Francisco *Examiner,* Jan. 25, 1901.

7. San Francisco *Chronicle,* Feb. 1, 1903; Los Angeles *Times,* Feb. 2, 1903; George Pardee, "Inaugural Address," *Appendices, 1903,* 1:18–21; San Francisco *Post,* Jul. 31, 1903.

8. Franklin Hichborn, *The Story of the Session of the California State Legislature of 1913* (San Francisco, 1913), p. 77.

9. San Francisco *Examiner,* Sept. 11, 1903, G.P.S. 43.

10. Oakland *Tribune,* Aug. 7, 1905, G.P.S. 56.

11. Boston *Herald,* Dec. 9, 1902, in Carl Plehn Papers.

12. Commonwealth Club of California, *Transactions* 1 (January 20, 1905): 7.

13. Sacramento *Bee,* Jan. 3, 1905; San Francisco *Chronicle,* Jan. 4, 1905.

14. Sacramento *Bee,* Jan. 23, 30, Mar. 6, 1905; San Francisco *Chronicle,* Jan. 8, 20, Feb. 8, Mar. 2, 8, 1905; San Francisco *Bulletin,* Mar. 7, 1905.

15. Carl Plehn to George Pardee, April 7, 1905, George Pardee Papers.

16. C.B.A., *Proceedings, 1905,* p. 51.

17. Sacramento *Union,* May 28, 1905; San Diego *Union,* Oct., date unclear, 1905; Santa Rosa *Republican,* Dec. 13, 1905; all in G.P.S. 56.

18. State of California, *Report of the Commission on Revenue and Taxation, 1906* (Sacramento, 1906), p. 6.

19. "Blanks of the Commission on Revenue and Taxation," Plehn Papers.

20. Joseph Radford to C.B.A. members, February 1, 1906, in C.B.A. Scrapbook 1.

21. "Minutes of the Meetings of the Commission on Revenue and Taxation," March 4, 5, 6, 1906, Pardee Papers; Carl Plehn to George Pardee, February 19, 1906, Pardee Papers; San Francisco *Call,* Mar. 11, 1906, G.P.S. 56; R. M. Welch to all C.B.A. members, August 8, 1906, C.B.A. Scrapbook 1.

22. "Minutes of the Commission on Revenue and Taxation," March 4, 5, 6, 1906, Pardee Papers; *Report of the Commission on Revenue and Taxation, 1906,* p. 255; San Francisco *Call,* Mar. 11, 1906, G.P.S. 56.

23. San Francisco *Chronicle,* July 3, 1906; Carl Plehn to George Pardee, July 19, 1906, Pardee Papers; Martin Ward to George Pardee, November 20, 1905, Pardee Papers; Edward Staniford, "Governor in the Middle: George Pardee, 1903–1907" (Ph.D. diss., University of California at Berkeley, 1953), pp. 136, 141.

24. California State Board of Equalization, *Biennial Report, 1905–1906* (Sacramento), p. 8; San Francisco *Call,* Apr. 10, 1906, G.P.S. 56.

25. Carl Plehn to George Pardee, July 17, 1906, Pardee Papers.

26. *Report of the Commission on Revenue and Taxation, 1906,* pp. 9–12, 54–55.

27. Watsonville *Register,* Nov. 7, 1906, G.P.S. 56.

28. Ocean Park *Journal,* Dec. 23, 1905, G.P.S. 56.

29. *California Cultivator,* Dec. 13, 1906; Stockton *Independent,* Dec. 7, 1906; Ventura *Democrat,* Dec. 7, 1906; all in G.P.S. 56.

30. Commonwealth Club, *Transactions* 3 (May, 1908): 104.

31. *Senate Journal, 1907,* pp. 85, 869–73, 1348.

32. C.B.A., *Proceedings, 1908,* p. 42.

33. Commonwealth Club, *Transactions* 3 (May, 1908): 190–91.

34. State of California, *Report of Commission on Revenue and Taxation* (Sacramento, 1911), p. 49–50.

35. Commonwealth Club, *Transactions* 3 (May, 1908): 118–19, 136.

36. Ibid., pp. 121–25, 131–32, 164.

37. *Assembly Journal, 1909,* pp. 1403, 1415, 1480; *Special Session, 1910,* pp. 66–67; Commonwealth Club, *Transactions* 5 (September, 1910): 361–66; San Francisco *Chronicle,* Feb. 5, 1909; *Senate Journal, 1909,* pp. 52, 988, 1219–29, 1228, 1382, 1435, *Special Session, 1910,* pp. 54–55, 61–66.

38. P.C.G.A., *Proceedings, 1910,* pp. 288–89; *Western Insurance News* 6 (Oct. 25, 1910): 16.

39. For an analysis of tax reform in the northeast states, see C. K. Yearly, *The Money Machines: The Breakdown and Reform of Governmental and Party Finance in the North, 1860–1920* (Albany, 1970). Businessmen did sometimes back tax reform in other states, for much the same reasons that California public service corporation officers did, but the extent of business support for tax reform was much greater in California than elsewhere.

40. Sacramento *Bee,* Jan. 19, 25, Feb. 7, 1911; Fresno *Republican,* Jan. 19, 1911.

41. California State Board of Equalization, *Biennial Report, 1910–1912* (Sacramento), pp. 13–14; *Special Report, 1911,* p. 8.

42. C.B.A., *Proceedings, 1911,* p. 35; California State Board of Equalization, *Biennial Report, 1911–1912,* p. 111; *Coast Banker* 6 (January, 1911): 8.

43. California State Board of Equalization, *The Relative Burden of State and Local Taxes in 1912* (Sacramento, 1913), pp. 5, 19; Hichborn, *Story of Legislature of 1913,* pp. 77–78.

44. Sacramento *Bee,* Jan. 23, 1913; C.B.A., *Proceedings, 1913,* pp. 43, 97–98; Fresno *Republican,* Jan. 14, 23, 25, 1913; Hichborn, *Story of Legislature of 1913,* pp. 89–106.

45. Sacramento *Bee,* Jan. 6, 13, 1915; John Drum to C.B.A. members, January 6, 1915, C.B.A. Scrapbook 3; Fresno *Republican,* Jan. 13, 15, 16, 1915; Franklin Hichborn, *Story of the Session of the California Legislature of 1915* (San Francisco, 1915), pp. 28–37.

46. California State Board of Equalization, *Biennial Report, 1913–1914,* p. 27; Commonwealth Club, *Transactions* 5 (September, 1910), p. 386; Fresno *Republican,* Jan. 16, 1915.

47. Franklin Hichborn, *Story of the Session of the California Legislature of 1921* (San Francisco, 1921), pp. 18–122; Jackson Putnam, "The Persistence of Progressivism in the 1920's: the Case of California," *Pacific Historical Review* 35 (November, 1966): 395–411; Marvel M. Stockwell, *Studies in California State Taxation* (Berkeley, 1939), pp. 16–41.

Chapter 10: The Politics of Business

1. C.F.G.A., *Proceedings, December, 1910,* p. 82.

2. Louis Galambos, "The Emerging Organizational Synthesis in Modern American History," *Business History Review* 44 (Autumn, 1970): 279–90; Robert Wiebe, *The Search for Order* (New York, 1967).

3. C.B.A., *Proceedings,* 1892, p. 42.

4. C.F.G.A., *Proceedings, December, 1910,* pp. 142–44.

5. Commonwealth Club of California, *Transactions* 1 (November, 1905): 15.

6. Ibid., 3 (June, 1908): 225.

7. Writings on this topic have been voluminous, but see Peter Bachrach and Morton Baratz, ''Two Faces of Power,'' *American Political Science Review* 56 (December, 1962): 947–52; Robert Dahl, *Who Governs?* (New Haven, 1961); Nelson Polsby, *Community Power and Political Theory* (New Haven, 1963); Michael Rogin, *The Intellectuals and McCarthy* (Cambridge, 1967); E. E. Schattschneider, *The Semi-Sovereign People* (New York, 1960); David Truman, *The Governmental Process* (New York, 1955).

8. See, especially Gabriel Kolko, *The Triumph of Conservatism* (New York, 1963) and Wiebe, *Search for Order.*

9. On the Wisconsin experience, see David Thelen, *The New Citizenship* (Columbia, Mo., 1972).

10. Hiram Johnson to Meyer Lissner, June 17, 1915, Hiram Johnson Papers.

Bibliography

Manuscripts and Scrapbooks

Bank of California. *Minutes of Board of Directors Meetings, 1893*. Bank of California Archives, San Francisco.

——. Scrapbook, 1912–1920. Bank of California Archives, San Francisco.

California Bankers Association. Scrapbooks. California Bankers Association, San Francisco.

Hiram Johnson Papers. Bancroft Library, University of California at Berkeley.

George Pardee Papers. Bancroft Library, University of California at Berkeley.

George Pardee. Scrapbooks. Bancroft Library, University of California at Berkeley.

Carl Plehn Papers. Bancroft Library, University of California at Berkeley.

Carl Plehn. Scrapbooks. Bancroft Library, University of California at Berkeley.

Chester Rowell Papers. Bancroft Library, University of California at Berkeley.

San Francisco Clearing House. *Minutes of Board of Directors Meetings, 1884–1900*. Bank of California Archives, San Francisco.

Harris Weinstock. Scrapbooks. Bancroft Library, University of California at Berkeley.

Newspapers

Daily Humboldt Standard, 1909

Fresno *Republican*, 1909–15

Los Angeles *Examiner*, 1913

Los Angeles *Herald*, 1911

Sacramento *Bee*, 1895, 1899, 1905–15

San Francisco *Bulletin,* 1905
San Francisco *Chronicle,* 1895, 1899, 1905–15
San Francisco *Examiner,* 1905, 1907, 1909

Periodicals

Bulletin, 1913–15
California Bankers Magazine, Commercial and Real Estate Review, 1890–95
California Cultivator, 1911
California Derrick, 1908–17
California Fruit Grower, 1911–15
California Fruit News, 1909–10
California Oil Bulletin, 1909–1912
California Orchard and Farm, 1911, 1913
California Outlook, 1912–15
California Weekly, 1909–10
Coast Banker, 1908–15
Coast Review, 1895–1915
Great Western Power, 1912
Insurance and Investment News, 1913–15
Insurance Sun, 1902–4
Los Angeles Mining Review, 1900–1902, 1904–13
Merchants Association Review, 1906–11
Oil Age, 1910–14
Oil and Mining Bulletin, 1914–15
Oil Book, 1909–11
Oil Fields and Furnaces, 1901
Pacific Coast Wood and Iron, 1894–96, 1904–5
Pacific Gas and Electric Magazine, 1909–15
Pacific Mining and Oil Reporter, 1902–4
Pacific Mutual News, 1914, 1916
Pacific Outlook, 1909–12
Pacific Rural Press, 1911
Pacific Underwriter, 1909–15
Pacific Telephone Magazine, 1909–15
Pioneer Western Lumbermen, 1910–20
Rural Californian, 1911, 1913
San Francisco Chamber of Commerce Activities, 1914–15
San Francisco Chamber of Commerce Journal, 1911–13
Standard Oil Bulletin, 1913–15
Timberman, 1917, 1919
University of California Journal of Agriculture, 1913–16

Water and Forest, 1901–7
Western Banker and Financier, 1915–21
Western Insurance News, 1909–12

Business Reports and Other Business Publications

Association of Life Insurance Presidents. *Proceedings of Annual Meeting.* New York, 1921, 1924.

Board of Fire Underwriters of the Pacific. *Book of Rates for San Francisco.* San Francisco, 1912.

———. *Constitution and General Rules.* San Francisco,˙1897.

———. *Constitution and General Rules.* San Francisco, 1908.

California Bankers Association. *Proceedings of Annual Meeting.* San Francisco, 1891–1920.

California Forest Protective Association. *Bulletin 3.* San Francisco, 1913.

California Fruit Growers. *Memorial on Transportation.* San Francisco, 1901–15.

California Fruit Growers Association. *Proceedings of Convention.* Sacramento, 1909–17.

California Fruit Growers Exchange. *Annual Report.* Los Angeles, 1912–20.

California Miners Association. *Proceedings of Annual Meeting.* San Francisco, 1894–1906, 1912.

California Petroleum Miners Association. *Bulletin.* San Francisco, 1901–4.

California Redwood Association. *Standard Grade Specifications Adopted June 1, 1921.* San Francisco, 1921.

California White and Sugar Pine Manufacturers Association. *Rules for Grading Adopted 1916.* San Francisco, 1916.

Commonwealth Club of California. *Transactions.* San Francisco, 1905–15.

Fire Underwriters Association of the Pacific. *Proceedings of Annual Meeting.* San Francisco, 1877–82, 1888, 1890, 1892–1915.

Los Angeles Stock Exchange. *Annual Report.* Los Angeles, 1916–22.

———. *Constitution and By-Laws Adopted 1917.* Los Angeles, 1917.

Pacific Coast Gas Association. *Proceedings of Annual Meeting.* San Francisco, 1909–15.

Pacific Insurance Union. *Book of Rates for San Francisco.* San Francisco, 1887.

San Francisco Chamber of Commerce. *Annual Report.* San Francisco, 1907–10, 1912, 1915.

San Francisco Clearing House. *Constitution, 1876.* San Francisco, 1876.

———. *Constitution, 1909.* San Francisco, 1909.

San Francisco Merchants Association. *Annual Report.* San Francisco, 1905–11.

San Francisco Merchants Exchange. *Annual Report.* San Francisco, 1906–11.

San Francisco Stock and Exchange Board. *Constitution and By-Laws, 1867.* San Francisco, 1867.

———. *Constitution and By-Laws, 1874.* San Francisco, 1874.

———. *Constitution and By-Laws, 1880.* San Francisco, 1880.

———. *Constitution and By-Laws, 1899.* San Francisco, 1899.

———. *Constitution and By-Laws, 1907.* San Francisco, 1907.

Government Documents

State

California State. *Appendix to the Journals of the Senate and Assembly*. Sacramento, 1897, 1899, 1901, 1903.

California State, *Assembly Journal*. Sacramento, 1895–1920.

California Conservation Commission. *Discussion of Forestry Problems*. Pamphlet. Sacramento, 1912.

———. *Report to the Governor*. Sacramento, 1912.

California Commission on Revenue and Taxation. *Final Report*. Sacramento, 1906.

California State Attorney General. *Biennial Report*. Sacramento, 1906–8.

California State Banking Commission. *Annual Report*. Sacramento, 1886–88, 1891–96, 1898–1900, 1905–6.

California State Board of Equalization. *Biennial Report*. Sacramento, 1905–15.

———. *Special Report on Taxation Showing First Effects of Separation on State, County, and Municipal Revenues and Tax Rates*. Sacramento, 1911.

———. *The Relative Burden of State and Local Taxes in 1912*. Sacramento, 1913.

California State Board of Forestry. *Biennial Report*. Sacramento, 1906–20.

California State Board of Harbor Commissioners. *Biennial Report*. Sacramento, 1910–12, 1920–22.

California State Board of Trade. *Annual Report*. Sacramento, 1896–1909.

California State Commissioner of Horticulture. *Annual Report*. Sacramento, 1909–21.

———. *Monthly Bulletin*. Sacramento, 1911–18.

California State Department of Corporations. *Biennial Report*. Sacramento, 1915–20.

California State Insurance Commissioner. *Annual Report*. Sacramento, 1884–95, 1899–1900, 1902–15.

California Market Director. *Biennial Report*. Sacramento, 1916–19.

California State Mineralogist. *Annual Report*. Sacramento, 1905–8, 1913–15.

California State Mining Bureau. *Notes on Damage By Water in California Oil Fields*. Preliminary Report. Sacramento, 1914.

———. *Petroleum in Southern California*. Bulletin 63. Sacramento, 1913.

———. *Petroleum Industry of California*. Bulletin 69. Sacramento, 1914.

———. *Production and Use of Petroleum in California*. Bulletin 32. Sacramento, 1904.

California State Oil and Gas Supervisor. *Biennial Report*. Sacramento, 1915–19.

California State Public Utilities Commission. "Transcript of Hearing Before Railroad Commission on Application 844."

California State Railroad Commission. *Annual Report*. Sacramento, 1911–15.

———. *Decisions*. Sacramento, 1911–15.

———. *Report on Leading Railroad and Public Utility Commissions*. Sacramento, 1911.

California State Superintendent of Banks. *Annual Report,* Sacramento, 1909–15.

California State, *Senate Journal*. Sacramento, 1895–1920.

Federal

United States Bureau of the Census. *The Lumber Industry*. Bulletin 203. Washington, 1902.

————. *Thirteenth Census of the United States, 1910: Abstract of the Census with a Supplement for California.* Washington, 1913.

United States Bureau of Corporations. *The Transportation of Petroleum.* Washington, 1906.

————. *Investigation Into the Lumber Industry, 1913–1914.* Washington, 1914.

United States Bureau of Mines. *The Cementing Process of Excluding Water from Oil Wells as Practiced in California.* Technical Paper 32. Washington, 1913.

United States Department of Agriculture. *American Forests and Forest Products.* Bulletin 21. Washington, 1928.

————. *Forest Products Statistics of the Pacific Coast States.* Statistical Bulletin 65. Washington, 1938.

————. *Lumber Cut in the United States, 1870–1920.* Bulletin 1119. Washington, 1923.

United States Federal Trade Commission. *Report on Lumber Manufacturers Trade Associations,* Washington, 1921.

————. *Report on the Pacific Coast Petroleum Industry.* Washington, 1922.

United States Geologic Survey. *The Mineral Resources of the United States: Annual Report.* Washington, 1907–15.

Books

Armstrong, Leroy, and Denny, J. O., eds. *Financial California: An Historical Review of the Beginnings and Progress of Banking in the State.* San Francisco, 1916.

Bain, J. S. *Economics of the Pacific Coast Petroleum Industry.* Berkeley, 1945.

Bean, Walton. *Boss Ruef's San Francisco.* Berkeley, 1968.

————. *California.* Berkeley, 1968.

Beaton, Kendall. *Enterprise in Oil: A History of Shell in the United States.* New York, 1957.

Blum, John M. *The Republican Roosevelt.* New York, 1964.

Bronson, William. *Still Flying and Nailed to the Mast: The First Hundred Years of the Fireman's Fund Insurance Company.* New York, 1963.

Brooks, George. *The Spirit of 1906: The California Insurance Company of San Francisco.* San Francisco, 1921.

Buley, R. Carlyle. *The American Life Convention, 1906–1912.* 2 vols. New York, 1953.

————. *The Equitable Life Assurance Society of the United States, 1859–1964.* New York, 1967.

Caine, Stanley. *The Myth of a Progressive Reform.* Madison, 1970.

Cannon, James. *Clearing Houses.* New York, 1905.

Carosso, Vincent. *Investment Banking in America.* Cambridge, Mass., 1970.

Chandler, Alfred, Jr. *Strategy and Structure.* New York, 1966.

Clar, C. Raymond. *California Government and Forestry From Spanish Days Until the Creation of the Department of Natural Resources in 1927.* Sacramento, 1959.

Cleland, Robert, and Hardy, Osgood. *The March of Industry.* Los Angeles, 1929.

Cleland, Robert, and Putnam, Frank. *Isaias Hellman and the Farmers and Merchants Bank.* San Marino, 1965.

Clepper, Henry. *Professional Forestry in the United States.* Baltimore, 1971.

Coleman, Charles. *P. G. and E. of California.* New York, 1952.

Cross, Ira. *Financing an Empire.* 4 vols. San Francisco, 1927.

Cumberland, William. *Cooperative Marketing: Its Advantages as Exemplified in the California Fruit Growers Exchange.* London, 1917.

Current, Richard. *Pine Logs and Politics: A Life of Philetus Sawyer, 1816–1900.* Madison, 1950.

Daggett, Stuart. *Chapters on the History of the Southern Pacific.* New York, 1922.

Dahl, Robert. *Who Governs?* New Haven, 1961.

Fischer, Gerald. *American Banking Structure.* New York, 1968.

Fogelson, Robert. *The Fragmented Metropolis.* Cambridge, Mass. 1967.

Fries, Robert. *Empire in Pine: The Story of Lumbering in Wisconsin, 1830–1900.* Madison, 1951.

Graves, Jackson. *My Seventy Years in California.* Los Angeles, 1929.

Hays, Samuel P. *Conservation and the Gospel of Efficiency.* New York, 1969.

––––––. *The Response to Industrialism.* Chicago, 1957.

Heald, Morrell. *The Social Responsibilities of Business: Company and Community, 1900–1960.* Cleveland, 1970.

Hichborn, Franklin. *Story of the Session of the California Legislature of 1909.* San Francisco, 1909.

––––––. *Story of the Session of the California Legislature of 1911.* San Francisco, 1911.

––––––. *Story of the Session of the California Legislature of 1913.* San Francisco, 1913.

––––––. *Story of the Session of the California Legislature of 1915.* San Francisco, 1915.

––––––. *Story of the Session of the California Legislature of 1921.* San Francisco, 1921.

Hidy, Ralph; Hill, Frank; and Nevins, Allan. *Timber and Men: The Weyerhaeuser Story.* New York, 1963.

Hittell, John S. *A History of San Francisco and Incidentally of the State of California.* San Francisco, 1878.

Hofstadter, Richard. *The Age of Reform.* New York, 1955.

Hurst, James. *Law and Economic Growth: The Legal History of the Lumber Industry in Wisconsin, 1836–1915.* Cambridge, Mass., 1964.

Hutchison, Claude, ed. *California Agriculture.* Berkeley, 1946.

Hutchinson, W. M. *Oil, Land, and Politics.* 2 vols. Norman, Okla., 1965.

Ise, John. *United States Forest Policy.* New Haven, 1924.

––––––. *United States Oil Policy.* New Haven, 1926.

Israel, Jerry, ed. *Building the Organizational Society.* New York, 1973.

Johnson, Arthur. *Pipelines and Public Policy, 1906–1959.* Cambridge, Mass., 1967.

Keller, Morton. *The Life Insurance Enterprise, 1885–1910.* Cambridge, Mass., 1963.

Kerr, K. Austin. *American Railroad Politics, 1914–1920.* Pittsburgh, 1968.

King, Joseph L. *History of the San Francisco Stock and Exchange Board.* San Francisco, 1910.

Kirschner, Herbert. *Fire Insurance Development on the Pacific Coast.* San Francisco, 1922.

Kolko, Gabriel. *Railroads and Regulation, 1877–1916.* Princeton, 1965.

––––––. *The Triumph of Conservatism.* Chicago, 1963.

Larson, Agnes. *The White Pine Industry in Minnesota.* Minneapolis, 1949.

Latta, Frank. *Black Gold in the Joaquin,* Caldwell, Id., 1949.

MacCurdy, Rahno. *History of the California Fruit Growers Exchange.* Los Angeles, 1925.

Martin, Albro. *Enterprise Denied: Origins of the Decline of American Railroads, 1897–1917.* New York, 1971.

McAfee, Ward. *California's Railroad Era, 1850–1911.* San Marino, 1973.

McConnell, Grant. *The Decline of Agrarian Democracy.* Berkeley, 1959.

McPhail, Archibald. *Of Men and Fire: A History of Fire Insurance in the Far West.* San Francisco, 1948.

Moore, C. I. C. *Pacific Mutual Life Insurance Company of California.* Los Angeles, 1928.

Mowry, George. *The California Progressives.* Chicago, 1951.

Myers, Margaret. *A Financial History of the United States.* New York, 1970.

Nash, Gerald. *State Government and Economic Development: A History of Administrative Policies in California, 1849–1933.* Berkeley, 1964.

———. *United States Oil Policy, 1890–1964.* Pittsburgh, 1968.

Olin, Spencer, Jr. *California's Prodigal Sons: Hiram Johnson and the Progressives, 1911–1917.* Berkeley, 1968.

Polsby, Nelson. *Community Power and Political Theory.* New Haven, 1963.

Pomeroy, Earl. *The Pacific Slope.* Seattle, 1965.

Redlich, Fritz. *The Molding of American Banking.* 2 vols. New York, 1968.

Reynolds, Arthur. *The Daniel Shaw Lumber Company: A Case Study of the Wisconsin Lumbering Frontier.* New York, 1957.

Rogin, Michael. *The Intellectuals and McCarthy.* Cambridge, Mass., 1967.

Saloutos, Theodore, and Hicks, John D. *Twentieth Century Populism: Agricultural Discontent in the Middle West, 1900–1939.* Lincoln, Neb., 1951.

Schattschneider, E. E. *The Semi-Sovereign People.* New York, 1960.

Scott, Mel. *The San Francisco Bay Area.* Berkeley, 1969.

Shannon, Fred A. *The Farmers Last Frontier: Agriculture, 1860–1897.* New York, 1945.

Stockwell, Marvel. *Studies in California State Taxation, 1910–1935.* Berkeley, 1939.

Thelen, David. *The New Citizenship: Origins of Progressivism in Wisconsin, 1885–1900.* Columbia, Mo., 1972.

Todd, Frank M. *A Romance of Insurance: A History of the Fireman's Fund Insurance Company of San Francisco.* San Francisco, 1929.

Truman, David. *The Governmental Process.* New York, 1955.

Welty, Earl, and Taylor, Frank. *The Black Bonanza.* New York, 1956.

Wickson, E. J. *Rural California.* New York, 1923.

Wiebe, Robert. *Businessmen and Reform.* Cambridge, Mass. 1962.

———. *The Search For Order.* New York, 1967.

White, Gerald. *Formative Years in the Far West: A History of Standard Oil Company of California and Its Predecessors Through 1910.* New York, 1962.

Williamson, Harold, and Daum, Arnold. *The American Petroleum Industry: The Age of Energy, 1899–1959.* Evanston, Ill., 1963.

Wilson, Neil. *400 California Street: The Story of the Bank of California.* San Francisco, 1964.

———. and Taylor, Frank. *Southern Pacific*. New York, 1952.

Woodward, C. Vann. *The Comparative Approach to American History*. New York, 1968.

Wright, Benjamin. *Banking in California, 1849–1910*. San Francisco, 1910.

Yearly, Cifton. *The Money Machines*. Albany, N.Y., 1970.

Young, John P. *San Francisco: A History of the Pacific Coast Metropolis*. San Francisco, 1912.

Zimmermenn, Erich. *Conservation in the Production of Petroleum*. London, 1957.

Dissertations and Theses

Beach, Frank. "The Transformation of California, 1900–1920: The Effects of the Westward Movement on California's Growth and Development in the Progressive Period." Ph.D. dissertation, University of California at Berkeley, 1963.

Blackford, Mansel. "The Politics of Business in California, 1890–1920." Ph.D. dissertation, University of California at Berkeley, 1972.

Boyd, J. E. "The Historical Import of the Orange Industry in Southern California." Master's thesis, University of California at Berkeley, 1931.

Chan, Chun. "A Study of the Effects of Water Intrusion in the Coalinga Oil Field of California." Ph.D. dissertation, University of California at Berkeley, 1922.

Cox, John. "Organizations of the Lumber Industry in the Pacific Northwest, 1889–1914." Ph.D. dissertation, University of California at Berkeley, 1937.

Crumb, Joseph. "Banking Regulation in California." Ph.D. dissertation, University of California at Berkeley, 1935.

Hoflich, Harold. "The Investments of American Life Insurance Companies Since 1906." Ph.D. dissertation, University of California at Berkeley, 1933.

Melendy, H. Brett. "One Hundred Years of the Redwood Lumber Industry, 1850–1950." Ph.D. dissertation, Stanford University, 1952.

North, D. C. "Large Life Insurance Companies Before 1906." Ph.D. dissertation, University of California at Berkeley, 1952.

O'Donnell, Aloysius F. "The Financial Plan of Certain Hydro-Electric Corporations in California." Master's thesis, University of California at Berkeley, 1922.

Pegrum, Dudley. "Public Utility Rate Theories and the California Railroad Commission." Ph.D. dissertation, University of California at Berkeley, 1927.

Riegal, Robert. "Fire Underwriters Associations in the United States." Ph.D. dissertation, University of Pennsylvania, 1916.

Scholl, Carl A. "An Economic Study of the California Almond Growers Exchange." Ph.D. dissertation, University of California at Berkeley, 1927.

Shaw, John. "Commercialization in an Agricultural Economy: Fresno County, California, 1856–1900." Ph.D. dissertation, Purdue University, 1969.

Stanford, Everett, "A Short History of California Lumbering." Master's thesis, University of California at Berkeley, 1924.

Staniford, Edward. "Governor in the Middle: George Pardee, 1903–1907." Ph.D. dissertation, University of California at Berkeley, 1953.

Wattenburger, Ralph. "The Redwood Lumbering Industry in the Northern California Coast, 1850–1900." Master's thesis, University of California at Berkeley, 1931.

Webster, Philip. "An Analysis of the Development of Cooperative Marketing Policies in the California Prune and Apricot Growers Association." Ph.D. dissertation, University of California at Berkeley, 1930.

Articles, Pamphlets, and Other Materials

Andreano, Ralph. "The Structure of the California Petroleum Industry, 1895–1911." *Pacific Historical Review* 39 (May, 1970): 171–92.

Arnold, Ralph, and Garfias, V. R. "Geology and Technology of the California Oil Fields." *American Institute of Mining Engineers, Bulletin 87* (March, 1914).

Ayres, P. W. *History of Timber Management in California National Forests, 1850 to 1937.* Pamphlet. Washington, D.C., 1958.

Bachrach, Peter, and Baratz, Morton. "Two Faces of Power." *American Political Science Review* 56 (December, 1962): 947–52.

Barsness, Richard. "Railroads and Los Angeles: Quest for a Deep Water Port." *Southern California Quarterly* 48 (December, 1965): 379–94.

Bean, Walton. "Ideas of Reform in California." *California Historical Quarterly* 51 (Fall, 1972): 213–26.

———. "James Warren and the Beginnings of Agricultural Institutions in California." *Pacific Historical Review* 13 (December, 1944): 361–75.

Benas, Lionel. "The Corporate Securities Act: Recent Cases and Amendments." *California Law Review* 14 (January, 1926): 101–25.

Berry, Swift. *Lumbering in the Sugar and Yellow Pine Region of California.* Pamphlet. Washington, D.C., April, 1915.

Blackford, Mansel G. "Banking and Bank Legislation in California, 1890–1915." *Business History Review* 47 (Winter, 1973): 482–507.

———. "Businessmen and the Regulation of Railroads and Public Utilities in California During the Progressive Era." *Business History Review* 44 (Autumn, 1970): 307–19.

Boerker, R. H. "Light Burning Versus Forest Management in California." *Forestry Quarterly* 10 (June, 1912): 184–94.

Dalton, John. "The California Corporate Securities Act." *California Law Review* 18 (January, 1930): 115–36; 18 (March, 1930): 254–66; 18 (May, 1930): 373–99.

Davis, Lance. "The Investment Market, 1870–1914: The Evolution of a National Market." *Journal of Economic History* 25 (September, 1965): 355–99.

Eilebacher, Albert. "The Wisconsin Life Insurance Reform of 1907." *Wisconsin Magazine of History* 55 (Spring, 1972): 213–30.

Erdman, H. E. "The Development and Significance of California Cooperatives, 1900–1915." *Agricultural History* 32 (July, 1958): 179–84.

Eshleman, John. "Control of Public Utilities in California." *California Law Review* 2 (January, 1914): 103–24.

Everett, Wallace. "The Practical in Forestry." *Forester* 5 (December, 1899): 275–78.

Fankhauser, William C. *A Financial History of California, 1849–1910.* University of California Publications in Economics, no. 3 (1913), pp. 106–366.

Finlay, James. "Banks and Banking in California." *Overland Monthly* 27 (January, 1896): 81–108.

Galambos, Louis. "The Emerging Organizational Synthesis in Modern American History." *Business History Review* 44 (Autumn, 1970): 279–90.

George, Henry. "What the Railroad Will Bring Us." *Overland Monthly* 1 (October, 1868): 297–306.

Hall, Tom. "Wilson and the Food Crisis: Agricultural Price Control During World War I." *Agricultural History* 47 (January, 1973): 25–46.

Hardy, Osgood. "Agricultural Change in California, 1860–1890." *Proceedings of the Pacific Coast Branch of the American Historical Association, 1929,* pp. 216–30.

Herrin, William. "Government Regulation of Railroads." *California Law Review* 2 (January, 1914): 87–91.

Hidy, Ralph. "Business History: Present Status and Future Needs." *Business History Review* 44 (Winter, 1970): 483–97.

Hutchinson, W. H. *California Heritage: A History of Northern California Lumbering.* Undated pamphlet.

——. *The California Investment of the Diamond Match Company.* Pamphlet. 1957.

——. "Prologue to Reform: California's Anti-Railroad Republicans, 1899–1905." *Southern California Quarterly* 44 (September, 1962): 175–219.

Johnson, Arthur. "California and the National Oil Industry." *Pacific Historical Review* 39 (May, 1970): 155–69.

Kerr, K. Austin. "Labor-Management Cooperation: An 1897 Case." *Pennsylvania Magazine of History and Biography* 99 (January, 1975): 45–71.

Kraemer, Erich, and Erdman, H. E. *History of Cooperation in the Marketing of California Fresh Deciduous Fruits.* University of California Experiment Station Bulletin 557. 1933.

Larsen, Grace. "A Progressive in Agriculture: Harris Weinstock." *Agricultural History* 30 (July, 1958): 187–91.

Lull, G. B. "The Forest Laws of California." *Forestry Quarterly* 5 (September, 1907): 278–82.

Mason, D. T. "A Forest Policy for California." *Journal of Forestry* 15 (April, 1917): 424–30.

——. "The Management of Redwoods in California." *Journal of Forestry* 20 (April, 1922): 396–97.

McAfee, Ward. "Constitutional History of Railroad Rate Regulation in California, 1879–1911." *Pacific Historical Review* 37 (August, 1968): 265–79.

——. "Local Interests and Railroad Regulation in California During the Granger Decade." *Pacific Historical Review* 37 (February, 1968): 51–66.

McCarty, John. *Municipal Government and Public Utilities: the California Experience.* Pamphlet. Berkeley, 1956.

McIntosh, Clarence. *Insurance History Project Report, October 18, 1954, Industrial Indemnity Company, San Francisco.* Pamphlet. 1954.

McLaughlin, R. P. "The Future of Oil Production in California." *Western Engineering* 1 (December, 1912): 705–9.

——. "Water in Oil Fields." *Mining and Scientific Press* 12 (February 25, 1911): 295.

Moffett, Samuel. "The Railroad Commission of California: A Study in Irresponsible Government." *Annals of the American Academy of Political and Social Science* 6 (1895): 469–77.

Nash, Gerald. "The California Railroad Commission, 1876–1911." *Southern California Quarterly* 44 (December, 1962): 287–305.

————. "Government and Business: A Case Study of State Regulation of Corporate Securities, 1850–1933." *Business History Review* 38 (Summer, 1964): 144–62.

————. "Oil in the West: Reflections on the Historiography of an Unexplored Field." *Pacific Historical Review* 39 (May, 1970): 193–204.

————. "Stages of California's Economic Growth, 1870–1970: An Interpretation." *California Historical Quarterly* 51 (Winter, 1972): 315–30.

Nordhauser, Norman. "Origins of Federal Oil Regulation in the 1920's." *Business History Review* 47 (Spring, 1973): 53–71.

North, D. C. "Life Insurance and Investment Banking at the Time of the Armstrong Investigation, 1905–1906." *Journal of Economic History* 14 (Summer, 1954): 209–29.

O'Callaghan, John. "Senator Mitchell and the Oregon Land Frauds." *Pacific Historical Review* 21 (August, 1952): 255–61.

Palais, Hyman, and Roberts, Early. "The History of the Lumber Industry in Humboldt County." *Pacific Historical Review* 19 (February, 1950): 1–16.

Palmer Union Oil Company. *California's Greatest Industry*. Pamphlet. San Francisco, 1912.

Paul, Rodman. "The Wheat Trade Between California and the United Kingdom." *Mississippi Valley Historical Reivew* 45 (December, 1958): 391–412.

Pillsbury, Arthur. "Wright Law and Webb Bill Compared." *California Weekly* 3 (March 4, 1910): 235–36.

Plehn, Carl. "The General Property Tax in California." *Economic Studies* 2 (February, 1897): 145–50; 2 (June, 1897): 111–98.

————. "The San Francisco Clearing House Certificates of 1907–1908." *Academy of Pacific Coast History* 1 (January, 1909): 3–14.

————. "The State Market Commission of California, Its Beginnings, 1915–1917." *American Economic Review* 8 (March, 1918): 1–27.

Powell, H. Clark. *The Organization of a Great Industry: The Success of the California Fruit Growers Exchange*. Transvaal University College Bulletin 6. Pretoria, 1925.

Pratt, M. B. "The California State Forest Service: Its Growth and Its Objectives." *Journal of Forestry* 29 (April, 1931): 497–504.

Putnam, Jackson K. "The Persistence of Progressivism in the 1920's: The Case of California." *Pacific Historical Review* 35 (November, 1966): 395–411.

Redlich, Fritz. "American Banking and Growth in the Nineteenth Century: Epistemological Considerations." *Explorations in Economic History* 10 (Spring, 1973): 305–14.

Redpath, Lionel. *Petroleum in California: A Concise and Reliable History of the Oil Industry of the State*. Pamphlet. Los Angeles, 1900.

Requa, Mark. "Oil Resources of California." Address to the American Mining Association, September, 1910. Reprinted as a pamphlet. 1910.

————. "Present Conditions in California Oil Fields." *Transactions of the American Institute of Mining and Metallurgical Engineers* 42 (1912): 837–47.

San Francisco Stock Exchange. Pamphlet. San Francisco, 1930.

San Francisco Stock Exchange, History, Organization, Operation. Pamphlet. San Francisco, 1938.

Shaw, John. "Railroads, Irrigation, and Economic Growth in the San Joaquin Valley of California." *Explorations in Economic History* 10 (Winter, 1973): 211–27.

Scherer, J. A. B. ''What Kind of Pittsburgh is Los Angeles?'' *World's Work* 41 (February, 1921): 382–92.

Schoendorf, A. J. *Beginnings of Cooperation in the Marketing of California Fresh Deciduous Fruits and History of the California Fruit Exchange.* Pamphlet. Sacramento, 1947.

Sterling, E. A. ''The Attitude of Lumbermen Toward Forest Fires.'' In *United States Department of Agriculture Yearbook, 1904*, pp. 133–40. Washington, 1905.

———. ''Forestry Legislation in California.'' *Forestry Quarterly* 3 (August, 1905): 269–74.

———. ''Striking Features of the Forest and Water Situation in California.'' *Proceedings of the Society of American Foresters* 2 (1907): 20–28.

Storms, W. H., and Prutzman, P. W. ''The Menace of Water in Oil Fields.'' *Western Engineering* 1 (May, 1912): 106–14.

Sylla, Richard. ''American Banking and Growth in the Nineteenth Century: A Partial View of the Terrain.'' *Explorations in Economic History* 9 (Winter, 1971–72): 195–227.

Thelen, Max. ''A Just and Scientific Basis for the Establishment of Public Utility Rates With Particular Attention to Land Values.'' *California Law Review* 2 (November, 1913): 3–24.

———. *Southern Pacific-Central Pacific Dissolution Case.* Undated pamphlet.

Weinstein, Robert. ''The Million-Dollar Mud Flat.'' *American West* 6 (January, 1969): 33–44.

White, Gerald. ''California's Other Mineral.'' *Pacific Historical Review* 39 (May, 1970): 135–54.

Index

Adair, Noah, 134

Agricultural standardization movement: for citrus fruit, 26–29; for deciduous fruit, 21–26; state legislation for, 25–26, 28–29; for vegetables, 28–29

Agriculture, 13–39; and consumers, 29–39; cooperative marketing in, 13–21; development of, 4–5, 9, 12–14, 79, 84, 93; standardization of, 21–29; and tax reform, 153–54. *See also* Agricultural standardization movement; Cooperative marketing

Aldrich-Vreeland Act, 104, 107

Allen, E. T., 71

American Institute of Banking, 113–14, 120

Ancient and Honorable Order of the Blue Goose, 144

Anderson, Alden, 110–11

Associated Oil Company: formation of, 43; and pipeline common-carrier legislation, 53; involved in price-fixing, 45

Atchison, Topeka and Santa Fe Railroad, 4, 79–86, 159

Athearn, F. G., 86

Ballard, J. W., 34

Bank of California, 8

Bank of Italy, 112

Banking, 96–116; and work of California Bankers Association, 103–16; clearing houses in, 98–102; development of, 8, 96–98; professionalization of, 112–15; state regulation of, 104–12, 115–16; and tax reform, 151, 154, 159–60. *See also* Investment banking

Baurhyte, William, 90

Blue-sky law, 120–23

Board of Fire Underwriters of the Pacific: and competition, 130–31, 145; and fire rating schedules, 137–38; involvement in state regulation, 132–35, 140; and reinsurance, 138–39

Breed, A. H., 159

Britton, John, 87, 89, 94, 152

Brown, William, 30, 34–37

Budd, James, 147

Butler, H. E., 25

California Association of Investment Corporations, 123–24

California Bankers Association: favors blue-sky law, 122–23; formation of, 103; sets up group banking, 104; involvement in legislation on banking, 104–12, 115–16; and professionalization of banking, 112–14; involved in tax reform, 151, 159–60

California Building and Loan League, 122

California Cured Fruit Exchange, 24

California Deciduous Fruit Protective League, 24

California Fire Protective Association, 70–72

California Fruit Exchange, 19–20, 32

California Fruit Growers' and Shippers' Association, 18–19

California Fruit Growers Association, 23, 25–26, 31

California Fruit Growers Exchange: involved in agricultural standardization movement, 27–28; and commission market act, 32, 34; formation of, 16–17; resists railroad rate hikes, 79

California Fruit Union, 18

California Railroad Commission, 90–95

California Redwood Association, 64, 66

California Safe Deposit and Trust Company, 107–8

California Shippers Executive Committee, 82–83

California State Association of Local Fire Insurance Agents, 132, 134, 136

California State Realty Federation, 122, 156

California Water and Forest Association, 68, 70–71, 75

California White and Sugar Pine Manufacturers Association, 64–66, 72

Caminetti, A., 147

Carr, William J., 47–48

Carroll, B. C., 50

Cartwright Anti-Trust Act, 66

Cary, L. B., 25

Casper Lumber Company, 64

Central Lumber Company of California, 64

Central Pacific Railroad, 3, 92–93

Chandler, Alfred, Jr., x, 178 n.3

Clunie, Andrew, 136, 141

Clunie, Thomas, 136

Coalinga Oil Producers Agency, 43–44

Coalinga Water Arbitration Association, 56

Commission market act, 30–39

Commonwealth Club of California: on banking legislation, 109; calls for production controls on oil, 46; involvement in tax reform, 154

Conservation, 163–64; of food, 30–31; of oil, 46–48; and scientific forestry, 60–61, 66–77

Consumers, 166–68, 170; and food buyers, 29–30; and the insurance industry, 132–33, 140; and oil industry, 53; and public utilities, 91, 95

Cooperative marketing: for citrus fruits, 15–17; for deciduous fruits, 17–20; goals of, 13–15, 18; for vegetables, 20–21

Corbett, Bert, 159

Cummins, Albert, 64–65

Curtin, J. B., 154

Daniels, Gilbert, 38

Delaney, Marion, 35

Depression: of 1870s, 8; of 1890s, 8, 105, 128–29; panic of 1907, 8, 100–102, 104, 107; impact of, on banking, 96–100, 104–7

Diamond Match Company, 62–63, 70, 102

Dorsey, J. R., 50

Drum, John, 110, 160

Dunn, P. F., 84

Dutton, William, 140, 154

Economic growth, in California: and development of internal commerce, 9–10; and foreign trade, 10–11; impact of banking upon, 96–99, 102, 106, 108, 112; impact of insurance industry upon, 8, 129, 140–43; impact of investment banking upon, 117, 119, 122, 125–26; and manufacturing, 11; and politics, 168; impact of railroad upon, 3–9; regional shifts in, 9–11, 79–81; and tax reform, 147. *See also* Depression

Elder, Charles, 123–24

Elliot, J. M., 114

Emmons, E. J., 50

Equitable Life Insurance Company, 128, 131, 136

Eshleman, John, 88–89, 122, 193 n.28

Farming. *See* Agriculture

Federal Reserve Act, 98, 104, 107, 112

Fire Underwriters Association of the Pacific, 138–40, 143–44

Ford, Tirey, 89

Forest Industries Committee of California, 73

Fruit growing. *See* Agriculture

Gage, Henry, 147–48

Galambos, Louis, 177 n.3

Gates, Lee, 122

General Petroleum Company, 44–45

Gillette, James: and banking regulation, 110; and insurance regulation, 140; and railroad regulation, 83; and tax reform, 156

Graves, James, 108, 120

Hamilton, Fletcher, 58
Hays, Samuel P., ix
Heney, Francis, 51
Hepburn Act, 50, 81
Herrin, William, 94
Hewitt, L. R., 51–52
Higgins, M. R., 135–36
Homans, George, 73
Home Savings Bank, 105
Home Telephone Company, 87, 90, 92, 160
Hoxie, George, 72

Independent Oil Producers Agency, 43–45, 48, 51–52
Independent Petroleum Marketers Association, 45
Insurance industry, 128–45; competition within, 129–35, 139–40; development of, 8, 128–29; professionalization of, 143–44; rationalization of, 137–40, 164; state regulation of, 132–36, 139–43; and tax reform, 151, 154, 159–60
Insurance Institute of America, 144
Interstate Commerce Commission: regulates oil pipelines, 50–51; regulates railroads, 81–82; role in Southern Pacific–Central Pacific dissolution case, 92–93
Investment Bankers Association of America, 117, 119–20, 126
Investment banking: development of, 117–20, 125–26, 197 n.4; and economic growth, 117, 119, 122; state regulation of, 120–27. *See also* Blue-sky law

Jeffrey, J. A., 23–24, 27
Johnson, Hiram, 169–70; and state regulation of banking, 111; works for blue-sky law, 121–23; and commission market act, 31, 33, 38; and state regulation of insurance, 132–33, 136; and oil industry, 46, 57–58; and railroad regulation, 84–86, 95; and scientific forestry, 71, 75–76; works for tax reform, 158–59

Kehoe, William, 134
Kern County Oil Protective Association, 56–57
Kolko, Gabriel, x–xi

La Follette, Robert, 81, 153
Lane, Franklin, 82

Lissner, Meyer, 169
Los Angeles: harbor development of, 10–11, 80; and intercity rivalry, 9–11, 80–83, 91–93; development of manufacturing in, 11
Los Angeles Clearing House, 98–102, 149
Los Angeles Fire Underwriters Association, 132
Los Angeles Gas and Electric Company, 88, 90, 156
Los Angeles Investment Company, 123–24
Los Angeles Life Underwriters Association, 132–33
Los Angeles Realty Board, 122
Los Angeles Stock Exchange, 118–20, 126
Luce, E. A., 32–34
Lumber industry, 60–77; and antitrust laws, 66; development of, 5–7, 61–63, 102; faces problem of overproduction, 60–66; and scientific forestry, 66–77; favors tariffs, 65
Lynch, James, 114–15

McCloud River Lumber Company, 70
McKevitt, F. B., 25
McLaughlin, R. P., 57–58
McPherson, H. E., 30
McReynolds, James, 92
Mann, Seth, 83, 165, 193 n.28
Mann-Elkins Act, 52
Miller, E. O., 84
Mills, C. B., 26
Mowry, George, xi
Murphy, Daniel, 35
Mutual Life Insurance Company of New York, 128, 131, 136, 141

Nash, Gerald, xi, 105, 178 n.2, 198 n.16
National Monetary Commission, 107
New York Life Insurance Company, 128, 131, 136, 141
Neylan, John, 34
Northern California Fish Exchange, 32–33
Northern Electric Railroad, 94

Oakland, Calif., 9–11
Oil Conservation Association, 47
Oil industry, 40–59; and conservation, 46–48, 55–59; development of, 7–8, 41–42; and overproduction, 40–48; pipeline development for, 7, 40–44, 48–54; technological problems in, 7, 41, 54–58

Oil Producers and Consumers League, 53

Olin, Spencer, Jr., xi

Olney, Warren, 159

Orange Growers Protective Union, 15

Organizational synthesis, in American history, ix–xi, 161–62, 165–66, 170–71, 177 n.3

Oro Electric Company, 92

Pacific Bank, 105

Pacific Coast Gas Association, 88, 90

Pacific Coast Oil Company, 43–44, 50, 55

Pacific Gas and Electric Company, 87–90, 94, 152, 158

Pacific Insurance Union, 129, 137

Pacific Lighting Company, 88

Pacific Stock Exchange, 118

Pacific Telephone and Telegraph Company, 87, 89–90, 92, 157, 159

Pardee, George: supports scientific forestry, 69; works for tax reform, 148–49, 152–53

Peltier, George, 154

Petroleum. *See* Oil industry

Phelan, James, 155

Phelps, J. E., 136

Pierce, Cyrus, 119

Pinchot, Gifford, 70

Pipelines. *See* Oil industry

Plehn, Carl, 147–50, 152, 154

Politics: business attitudes toward, 165; business involvement in, ix–xi, 166–69; role of consumers in, 166–69; and state regulation of business, 169–70. *See also* Progressive Movement; and names of specific industries and companies

Population, shifts in California, 11–12

Progressive Movement: nature of, in California, 38, 170; and political parties, 171. *See also* Johnson, Hiram; and names of specific industries

Public utilities: experience difficulty raising capital, 102; state regulation of, 86–90; involvement in tax reform, 152, 156–60

Pullman Company, 159

Railroads: development of, 3–4; impact on economy, 3–13, 48–49, 60–63, 78–81, 85; role of, in intercity rivalry, 9–10, 80–81, 83, 85–86, 91–92; state regulation of, 78–86, 94–95; and tax reform, 151–52, 157–60. *See also* names of specific railroads

Redwood Manufacturers Association, 63

Redwood Manufacturers Company, 63

Requa, Mark, 47, 57

Rhorer, M. M., 136

Rolph, James, 133–34

Ruef, Abe, 51

San Francisco: harbor development of, 10–11; and intercity rivalry, 9–11, 80, 83, 91–93; development of manufacturing in, 11

San Francisco Board of Fire Underwriters, 137

San Francisco Clearing House Association, 98–102, 149

San Francisco Life Underwriters Association, 132, 136

San Francisco Stock and Bond Exchange, 118–19

San Francisco Stock and Exchange Board, 118–19

Sartori, J. F., 158

Saxton, William, 137

Scharrenburg, Paul, 35

Scientific forestry, 66–76

Scott, J. H., 159

Scott, William, 35–36

Seligman, E. R. A., 154

Shaw, Lucien, 85

Shell Company of California, 44–45, 48

Sherman Anti-Trust Act, 66

Sierra and San Francisco Light and Power Company, 89

Southern California Edison Company, 90

Southern California Fruit Exchange, 16

Southern Pacific Railroad: and agricultural cooperatives, 17; development of, 3–4; dissolution suit with Central Pacific Railroad, 92–93; impact of, on intercity rivalry, 9–10, 80–81, 91–92; involvement of, with oil industry, 41, 43, 48, 54, 79, 81, 84, 93; and railroad regulation, 78–86, 91–92, 95; and scientific forestry, 69, 72; favors tax reform, 151–52, 157–59

Spellacy, Timothy, 51, 53

Spreckles, Rudolph, 34

Sproule, William, 165

Standard Oil Company, 42–45, 49–53, 55

Stark, E. A., 55

Stephens, William, 37

Sterling, E. A., 68–70

Stetson, John, 83–86, 193 n.28

Stevens, A. F., 76

Stoddard, Jesse, 114

Stratton, F. S., 147

Sugar and White Pine Manufacturers Association of California and Adjacent States, 64

Sullivan, Matthew, 133–34

Tax reform, 146–60; and big business, 150–54, 156, 158–60, 166–67; early movement for, 146–50; and intercity rivalry, 148; legislation for, 150–59; and scientific forestry, 75–76

Thelen, Max, 88–90

Timber. *See* Lumber industry

Trade associations, 162–65; in agriculture, 13–29; in banking, 98–104; in the insurance industry, 129–32, 137–40, 143; in investment banking, 119–20; in the lumber industry, 63–65, 70–72; in the oil industry, 45–46, 56–57; of public utilities, 88, 90

Traffic Association of California, 82–83

Traffic Bureau of San Francisco, 10, 82–83

Union Oil Company, 44–45, 48, 51, 54–55

Union Pacific Railroad, 3

United Railroads of San Francisco, 87, 93

Wadsworth, J. L., 136

Walker, T. B., 67, 72

Ward, Martin, 150

Ward, Russella, 35

Webb, U.S., 82–83, 193 n.28

Webb-Pomerene Act, 66

Weinstock, Harris, 31–38, 167

Western Pacific Railroad, 4, 159

Western States Gas and Electric Company, 92

Wiebe, Robert, ix–x

Williams, W. R., 111–12

Wilson, Woodrow, 37

Wilson-Gorman Act, 65

Wolf, Myron, 135–36, 143

Wright, Leroy, 83–84

Yearly, Clifton, 157